STACEY: MY STORY SO FAR

Stacey Solomon caught the nation's attention on *The X Factor* 2009 when she was one of the finalists. In November 2010 she entered the Australian jungle to take part in *I'm a Celebrity . . . Get Me Out of Here!* She began her presenting career on ITV's *Sing if You Can* and now lives in Dagenham, Essex, with her son, Zachary, and her boyfriend, Aaron.

Stacey

My Story So Far

STACEY SOLOMON

PENGUIN BOOKS

PENGUIN BOOKS

Published by the Penguin Group
Penguin Books Ltd, 80 Strand, London WC2R 0RL, England
Penguin Group (USA) Inc., 375 Hudson Street, New York, New York 10014, USA
Penguin Group (Canada), 90 Eglinton Avenue East, Suite 700, Toronto, Ontario, Canada M4P 2Y3
(a division of Pearson Penguin Canada Inc.)
Penguin Ireland, 25 St Stephen's Green, Dublin 2, Ireland (a division of Penguin Books Ltd)
Penguin Group (Australia), 250 Camberwell Road, Camberwell, Victoria 3124, Australia
(a division of Pearson Australia Group Pty Ltd)
Penguin Books India Pvt Ltd, 11 Community Centre, Panchsheel Park, New Delhi – 110 017, India
Penguin Group (NZ), 67 Apollo Drive, Rosedale, Auckland 0632, New Zealand
(a division of Pearson New Zealand Ltd)
Penguin Books (South Africa) (Pty) Ltd, 24 Sturdee Avenue, Rosebank,
Johannesburg 2196, South Africa

Penguin Books Ltd, Registered Offices: 80 Strand, London WC2R 0RL, England

www.penguin.com

First published by Michael Joseph 2011
Published in Penguin Books 2011

1

See page 289 for a list of photo credits

Typeset by Penguin Books
Printed in Great Britain by Clays Ltd, St Ives plc

ISBN: 978-0-718-15817-0

www.greenpenguin.co.uk

MIX
Paper from
responsible sources
FSC
www.fsc.org   FSC™ C018179

Penguin Books is committed to a sustainable
future for our business, our readers and our
planet. This book is made from paper certified
by the Forest Stewardship Council.

To My Angel, My Saviour, My Zachary.
Who is and always will be the love of my life. For ever
and always. My Bubba. I love you to the moon and
stars and back!!! X

Prologue

'Grow up!' the nurse snaps. 'You're a mother now. You can't cry.'

Tears stream down my face. I can't stop sobbing. I feel so alone.

I want my mum so much, but the nurse has sent her home, along with the rest of my family. 'No visitors allowed at this time of night!'

I have no one to talk to, no one to comfort me. I'm so unhappy. I've just been through the longest, most agonizing labour – hours and hours of pain, cramps and panic – during which the baby got stressed and I was told to push at the wrong moment. Is it any wonder I'm crying my eyes out? Why doesn't the nurse have any sympathy for me? Would it be too much for her to give me a word or two of gentle reassurance?

All around me, babies are wailing and crying. There isn't a quiet baby on the whole ward. There's something wriggling and screaming in a box next to my bed, but I have no idea what to do with it. I don't know what to do with a baby. Am I supposed to feed it? I'm so tired and drained of energy, just completely overwhelmed by exhaustion. I've been awake and in pain for so long that it feels like my mind has left my body and is floating somewhere near the ceiling. If I had even an ounce of energy left, I would snatch up my baby, run out of this hospital and never, ever come back.

Another nurse comes to see me. 'Have you fed him?' she asks curtly.

I shake my head and start sobbing again. None of the nurses are being at all friendly. I feel as though they are looking at me disapprovingly. I'm sure I know what they're thinking. To them I'm just another unmarried teenager having a baby, another statistic, a kid with a kid, a hopeless case. I know how they're judging me because I also used to be judgmental about teenage mothers. I couldn't understand why girls wanted to have babies so young when they had their whole lives ahead of them, especially if they weren't properly settled in a relationship. How do you have a life? How do you go out? I thought when I saw them.

But at least I felt sorry for them – unlike the nurses in this hospital, who purse their lips and stare at me with cold, old-fashioned eyes.

'Why aren't you feeding him?' the nurse asks, her voice as sharp as a dagger.

'Because I don't know how to!' I sob. No one has shown me what to do; no one has bothered to take the time to sit down with me and give me a lesson in breastfeeding.

I reach down into the box and pick up my baby. My heart races in panic as I look at him. What do I do with him? How on earth am I going to cope? I raise his head up to my breast and bring his mouth close to my nipple. Nothing happens. I try to coax him to feed, but he doesn't react. All he does is wail, his eyes scrunched up, his tiny fists balled, his face a picture of anger and frustration. Poor little thing. I start sobbing again and he cries even harder. He must be able to sense my sadness and I'm sure it's making him sad, too.

I'm so miserable and confused. It feels like my life is over.

What is left for me now, apart from being a mother to the tiny screaming baby in my arms? All my hopes and ambitions have been destroyed. I can't go to college any more; I'll never fulfil my dreams of being a singer. I'll never work in musical theatre, or go to university, or even become a teacher. I'm just a nothing now, a big zero, a teenage mum with a kid to look after. I've got no other role to play.

Even worse, I'm only eighteen years old and while all my friends are going out and enjoying themselves, I'll be stuck at home with a baby. Although I've got the best parents in the world and a really supportive family, this child is my responsibility. So I can't ring up my girlfriends and say, 'Hey, let's all go to Ibiza!' I can't drop everything at a moment's notice and rush off to a new club with my mates. I can't even go to the pub for a few hours.

This is it. My life's over, I keep thinking. I'll just be a mother and then I'll die. No career, no boyfriend, no fun. Just duty, duty, duty.

I have absolutely no idea how wrong I am – or how different everything will be in just a few months' time. At my lowest point, at my most miserable and dejected, I can't foresee that my baby Zach will turn out to be the greatest blessing I could ever have.

Instead of my life being over, it's just beginning. All the good things are about to come my way. My dreams will come true; I will fulfil my ambitions; and there will be a happy ending. And it's all because of the little screaming thing I'm holding in my arms, my darling baby Zachary. But right now, I haven't a clue about any of these things. How on earth could I possibly know?

Chapter 1

I've always had to do everything first, or so my mum says. I try everything too early; I do everything too soon. I was born prematurely, I grew up before my time, I had boobs before everyone else, I kissed a boy too young, I had a baby in my teens and I tried for *The X Factor* before I was ready. That's me. Always in a rush! Mum says the one thing I definitely mustn't do is die too early; everything else she can just about put up with.

I was obviously in a real hurry to come into the world, because I was born six weeks premature. In fact, I tried to come out even earlier than that, although no one realized it at the time. My mum started to bleed about two and a half months before I was due, but the doctors at Rush Green Hospital told her it was probably just a urine infection and advised her to go back to work.

A couple of weeks later she started feeling a lot worse. When she got home from work one evening, it was like a tap had been turned on. But at the hospital, the doctors couldn't find anything wrong with her. They did several scans, but it wasn't clear what was going on or why she was bleeding. 'We're going to have to keep you in,' they told her, shaking their heads.

They gave her a bed in the delivery section of the labour ward and she wasn't allowed to move from the bed; she couldn't go anywhere or do anything. By now the bleeding was continuous, but they still couldn't work out where it was coming from or what was wrong. She spent four whole weeks lying on that bed, surrounded by women screaming as they gave birth. It drove her insane. There were more scans, but still no diagnosis. Meanwhile the blood kept flowing and she became weaker and weaker.

On 4 October 1989 everything went mad. Mum was really ill by now. She was losing blood by the bucketload, and when the doctors did a scan they saw me drowning in her blood inside the womb. 'Caesarean, now!' they yelled.

Someone rushed at Mum, waving a consent form and a pen. 'Sign this,' he said. Then she was rushed into surgery with my dad following frantically behind.

'I'm sorry, Mr Solomon, you can't come any further,' they told him when they arrived at the operating theatre.

'But she's my wife!' Dad protested. Two sets of doors slammed in his face.

He waited in agony, desperate to know what was going on. The ten minutes or so that my mum was in surgery were the longest ten minutes of his life. What on earth is happening? he wondered.

Meanwhile, in the operating theatre, a surgeon quickly cut Mum open and took me out, along with a whole jumble of her organs. Then he stuffed all her insides back in again and stitched her up. We both nearly died in the process. It was touch and go whether we would survive. When they wheeled my mum out of surgery, she was grey, like a corpse. She looked so lifeless that my dad wasn't sure if she was still alive.

Me and my mum didn't see each other again for nearly two weeks. I was whisked off to the special care ward, where I was put into an incubator, with tubes coming out of me, while Mum was on a permanent transfusion of just about everything they could give her.

About five days after I was born, the nurses took a photograph of me so that Mum could see what I looked like. She was still completely out of it, though, so she could hardly register it. She was a lot better by the end of the second week and one of the nurses brought me in to her, so that she could see me in the flesh. But the nurse only rested me on her before taking me away again.

We were in hospital for about four weeks before we went home – they had to make sure I was developing properly and Mum needed to be brought back to the living. We still weren't seeing much of each other. Sometimes they were able to wheel her in to special care during the day, but I don't think it was for very long.

Finally the doctors found out why she'd bled so much. The placenta surrounding me had been tearing away from the womb lining for months. The chances of it happening were at least one in a million; it was really rare, which Mum said made me pretty special. It was so unusual that the doctors were able to assure her it wouldn't happen again.

So that was my dramatic arrival into the world. Sadly, I wasn't a nice-looking baby, because like all premature babies, I had see-through skin. I weighed 4.4 pounds, roughly the same as two bags of sugar, and I was tiny. I could fit into my auntie's hand, and my head was the length of her little finger.

My dad used to come and see me in hospital, sometimes bringing my eighteen-month-old sister Jemma with him. Dad found it very upsetting that he wasn't allowed to pick me up and cuddle me. The nurses would only let him hold my hand and stare at me adoringly, making gurgling noises. He says it was the strangest feeling. He's a very affectionate parent, so it went against all his paternal instincts.

I wouldn't blame my sister if she resented me for crashing

into her life – she can't have been too pleased that I took her mum away from her for a whole eight weeks. Perhaps this planted the seed for the rivalry that sprang up between us in the years to come, which was always focused on how much attention we got from our mum and dad. Because I was so tiny and fragile, all eyes were often on me, and I grew up to be a real attention seeker – it's obvious I still am, seeing what I do now!

My sister was really sweet with me when me and Mum came out of hospital. Mum took a while to recover and she relied on Jemma to help her out, even though she was only a toddler. She would sit Jemma in the armchair at home, lay me on her lap and give her a bottle to feed me with. Apparently, my sister nursed me like a little mum. She often had me on her lap while my mum was washing up. Maybe that's why she's so good with children now: she's training to be a children's nurse, studying paediatrics at university.

Premature babies often have quite serious health problems, but I thrived. I grew bigger and bigger and even ended up outgrowing my sister. The doctors said I would lag behind and that my organs would be small and might not develop very well. However, I'm the biggest girl in my family – I outgrew all my girl cousins in height – so I didn't fit the premature profile at all.

Because I was born so early, my mum was always telling me I was incredibly special, which probably gave me the confidence to go for the things I've gone for in life. 'See, they all said you couldn't, and you did,' she was always saying. Mind you, she also used to say, 'You were trouble even before you came out . . .' so I suppose there are two sides to everything!

I was really sporty too: when I grew older, I swam for

Dagenham and Redbridge, I ran for the school and I was in the netball and rounders teams. I was also pretty bright, and I don't mean that in a big-headed way. I didn't want to be, but I was quite smart without even realizing. It makes you wonder what I would have been like if I'd stayed inside my mum for another six weeks. Superwoman, he he!

Even though the doctors had told my mum to give her body a rest from having children for a while, just two years after my action-packed entry into the world, my younger brother Matthew arrived in 1991, making me the middle child. My earliest memory is a really random one from around the time he was born, when our next-door neighbour looked after me and my sister while our mum was in hospital. All I remember from that time is our neighbour's pink slippers, which had fluffy bobbles on them. That's my very first memory. Those slippers really must have made an impact on me! I always associate them with my brother now. Whenever I think of him, it's the first thing I think of: slippers!

Me and my brother and sister are all really close in age, which made life a little difficult when we were small, especially between me and my sister as we argued so much. It seemed like everything was so much better for her, because she was the oldest, and my brother was really spoiled, because he was the boy and the youngest. I thought I was really hard done by, even though I wasn't.

My mum says that after having my sister and me, she wouldn't have stopped until she had a boy. So she was thrilled when she had my brother. Knowing that he was going to be her last child meant she treasured him even more, which made me and my sister think, What's so good about him? As a result we were always fighting for attention.

Me and my sister resented each other from very early on. There's a family video of me in a bouncy chair, so young that I'm hardly alert, being given a present at Christmas. You can see Jemma reacting furiously, '*No!* Why is she getting that?' The outrage is written all over her face. Her present was bigger than mine, but mine was the one she wanted.

Mum told her to be nice to me and give me a kiss. 'OK,' she lisped, toddling over to me. Unfortunately, as she went to kiss me, she fell and whacked me in the face! That sums up our relationship as children, really.

My dad used to video everything, so we have films of us brushing our teeth all through childhood. He was always there with his camera; it was so embarrassing. In the Christmas videos that he made every year, you can see me and my sister looking daggers at each other as we open our presents. 'Why has she got the Barbie house? It's so unfair!'

My favourite Christmas present ever was a plastic kitchen, which I was given when I was about five. I was so happy with it, that was a really good Christmas for me. The only problem was that Jemma kept putting her hamster in it, which drove me mad. 'Stop! You're making it dirty!' I'd yell. I got really angry about it. But then I got used to it and started including the hamster in my play. My favourite trick was to put it in my toy frying pan and pretend to cook it.

It was often possessions that caused Jemma and me to squabble. She'd get a hamster and I would think, Ugh! She got a hamster! I'd get a fiver from my dad and she'd think, Ugh! Why did she get a fiver? I was really jealous when she got a job. 'I want a job!' I said, but I wasn't allowed to get one until I was fourteen, so I used to get money from my dad instead, and that just made Jemma think, Ugh! I'm working for my money! We really got on each other's nerves.

I was really competitive and I always wanted to win. When we played games in class, like who could do the crossword puzzle first, I'd make a huge effort to make sure it was me. I was really beastie in netball, too, being tall for my age. 'We have to win!' I'd tell the rest of the team. I was determined to come out on top.

So it's not surprising that I was always vying for the upper hand with my sister, as well as competing for space. We shared a room with my brother in the same house in Dagenham that my mum still lives in today. I don't know how we all squeezed in, because there were five of us in a two-bedroom house, but it was home and I'm still very attached to it. It's only two bedrooms, but a happy two bedrooms, and I found it very hard to leave when I finally moved out.

My parents moved to Dagenham before I was born. By then they'd been together for six years and married for three. My mum, Fiona, came to London from the Forest of Dean, Gloucestershire, when she was eighteen. The daughter of a Church of England vicar, she was working as a student nurse and living in nurses' lodgings in Victoria when she met my dad, David, at the Empire nightclub in Leicester Square. It was one of her haunts, apparently, and Dad used to take photographs there every night.

Mum and Dad quickly fell in love and decided to get married. My dad is Jewish and ideally he wanted Mum to convert to Judaism, but he didn't put any pressure on her. It wasn't going to affect whether they stayed together or not, and Mum wouldn't have converted just for the sake of getting married, but when she looked into what it meant, she decided it was what she wanted after all. It takes five years to become an Orthodox Jew, but Mum went the Progressive route, which takes two years.

When she and my dad went up to the Forest of Dean to announce that they wanted to get married and that she was converting to Judaism, her parents were lovely about it. Her dad said, 'At the end of the day, we all believe in the same god, in our different ways. If you're happy and this is what you want to do, then do it.' I loved my granddad; he was such a kind and generous person. He passed away recently at the age of ninety and we all miss him. Amazing, ninety! Please God I live until I'm ninety! What a joy that would be. My mum's mum is still alive and we often see her. We all love Grandma; she's lovely.

Dad's family were very accepting of my mum, too, and there were no issues there whatsoever. My dad is the grandson of Iraqi Jews who were coffee merchants in Burma and fled to Calcutta when the Japanese invaded. They then moved to London in the 1950s. My grandfather died of heart failure when Dad was a young boy, leaving my nana with four children to bring up. It must have been really hard for her, but if anyone could do it, my nana could. She was an amazing person, the daughter of Polish emigrants to London in the early twentieth century. My dad was very close to her; we all were. She's not with us any more, sadly, but I have great memories of her.

Mum and Dad had a traditional Jewish wedding in September 1986 at the North London Progressive Synagogue near Stamford Hill. Twelve years and three kids later, they divorced when I was nine. I don't remember much about life before they split up, except the big occasions like Christmas, birthdays and holidays. For New Year, we used to go to Butlin's in Skegness or Bognor Regis; whichever was the cheapest, I suppose.

In the summer we'd all meet up at Butlin's or Pontins – my nan and my cousins and everyone – or sometimes we'd go camping. My dad's family all live in Hackney, London, and I've got eight cousins on my dad's side, so there were sometimes as many as eleven kids on holiday. We're all around the same age and we lived in each other's pockets, which was brilliant. I loved it. We went through everything together.

At Pontins we all stayed in one chalet, or in two chalets if there were too many of us, and the kids would all be in together. It was brilliant. The adults could never get us to go to sleep. We seemed to spend most of our waking hours following a man dressed up in a crocodile outfit, who was known as 'Captain Croc'. At the kids' disco, we did routines to 'Agadoo', 'Oops Upside Your Head' and 'Silver Lining', and then the crocodile would appear and do 'The Crocodile Song'.

We went go-carting; did dive bombs in the pool, which had a wave machine; trampolined; played on the pirate ship in the playground and tried our luck on the 2p slot machines. The only thing I never liked going on was the bouncy castle, because of the loose black strings that were attached to the floor. They used to fly about when the other kids jumped and I was convinced they were spiders.

I was terrified of spiders, so when my dad put me on there I used to cry my eyes out and scream, 'Get me off! It's got spiders on it.'

My dad used to go totally mad, because he didn't want us to be afraid of anything in life. 'Go on! Get on that bouncy castle!' he would tell me.

'No, Dad, *no*! There are spiders!'

It was a proper phobia. I just couldn't overcome it. It wasn't a learned fear, because no one else in my family was scared of spiders and none of my friends were either. It wasn't cool to be scared of anything. But I must have naturally and intuitively been frightened, because I didn't even like to go barefoot in the grass in case I stepped on one.

A big highlight of the holiday camps was the gift shop. Everything on the shelves was glow-in-the-dark, and we'd go in there and gasp in wonder. We were all allowed to choose one thing each at the end of the holiday and I chose luminous ceiling stars. I remember one year when we went camping, all the girl cousins bought false nails at the local shop. We loved them, even though they were the worst false nails ever and used to flick off if you touched anything.

My dad's mum was always at the centre of things. She was the best nana in the world, and the most Jewish. I mean, you'd walk into her flat and she'd be making chicken soup! Everyone had to have some. She was a little bit deaf and sometimes she couldn't hear you. 'WHAT DID YOU SAY?' she would boom.

She was so funny, just the nicest lady, and my dad adored her. Everyone who met her loved her. She was a real Jewish *bubbe*. When I say that she had a heart of gold, I really mean it. I've never met anyone like her, not my mum, not my step-mum. She had barely a penny, yet she would give everything to her grandchildren. She'd lived in the same flat all her life and wouldn't move; she would rather give everything she had to us.

As far as she was concerned she had everything in the world, whereas to someone else it would seem as if she had nothing. They might think, Oh dear, that poor lady! But she would have said to them, 'Trust me, I've got all I need in the whole wide world.' She had her family around her the whole time. We visited her every Friday for dinner, without fail.

Sadly, we saw a lot less of my mum's family, because her brother and sisters live all over the place. One of my aunties on my mum's side lives in Scotland and the other is in Canada. Still, there were enough of us on my dad's side to make up for it. We certainly weren't short of relatives. We had wonderful holidays with Grandma and Grandad in Wales and the Forest of Dean. I have very happy memories of swimming in rivers and chestnut picking, and going to our favourite places, the Giant's Chair and Eastnor Castle.

It's hard to know exactly why my mum and dad split up. They've never said anything about it in front of us, because they're not like that, so we've had to piece it together for ourselves over the years. I used to ask my mum about it, but she'd only say, 'One day I'll tell you.' But I don't think she would ever say anything that she thought would change my attitude towards my dad, and he's the same; he would never say anything that might change my opinion of my mum. Maybe there will come a time when they think they can tell us without being judged, but maybe not.

I do know that my dad spent a lot of time working. He had just started a company with his brother called White Weddings, a photography business catering for Jewish bar mitzvahs and weddings. He set up a tiny shop in the Blackhorse Road in North London and put everything into it, as you have to when you're just starting out. He had been passionate about photography since he was a kid, and he's an established photographer now. It was all he ever wanted to do; he even had a dark room at home, at my nana's house, when he was growing up.

My mum has never had a bad word to say about my dad. I just think that he left her on her own to do everything, and she reached a point when she'd had enough. She threatened divorce, assuming he wouldn't take her seriously. I think she expected him to say they could work it out and to promise that he'd spend more time with her, but sadly that didn't happen and so my parents divorced.

Dad went to find another house, and we didn't ask any questions. Mum just said, 'We're not together any more.' That was it. Everyone was sad, especially Matthew. I remember him being really, really upset, even though he was only seven and I don't think he really understood what had happened. He became very quiet and you could see the sadness in his face. My mum would cuddle him when she was feeling upset, so in a way he had to carry her sadness, which must have been tough for him.

My mum never cried in front of us, but we always knew when she was crying, because she'd turn on the hoover and we wouldn't be allowed downstairs while she was hoovering. She was so sad. It broke her heart that our lives would never be the same again.

I can't imagine how awful she must have felt. I haven't been with my boyfriend, Aaron, for ever, but I really like him and Zach loves him and he loves Zach. And I know that if he was really bugging me and I said, 'Fine! We're not together any more!' and he left and didn't come back, I'd be heartbroken.

We didn't see my dad for a little while after they decided to get divorced. Time wasn't the same then as it is now, so it's hard to judge how long it was exactly. If he went away for a month or two now, I would say, 'Where the heck have you been?' But back then none of us thought much about it. We didn't ask him where he'd been and he didn't say.

Dad managed to find a house in our road, which was brilliant as we got to spend a lot more time with him. I especially remember Wednesdays, when Dad took us to the swimming pool just around the corner. We loved going there because it had a fantastic tube slide. You couldn't go down it without an adult, so we spent most of our time waiting at the side for him, while all the big kids went down before us, shouting, 'Come on, Dad! Hurry up! It's our go now!'

Life went on and we all got used to the new situation. We had to, because nothing was ever discussed. No one explained exactly why our parents had split up, so we just got on with it. Looking back, I think it was quite confusing for us. As a child, you don't understand why adults behave in the way they do. You don't realize that a divorce is about the adult relationship breaking down; you think it must be something to do with you and that maybe you're the one who has done something wrong. All that confusion and hurt built up inside me and stayed there, unexpressed. It didn't come out until years later, by which time it had turned into anger.

For the moment, though, outwardly at least, I was happy enough. I enjoyed going to John Perry Primary School, just down the road. It wasn't hard to be happy there, because at primary school all you do is make sarcophaguses out of pasta or papier mâché, and other fun things like that. You have a Christmas party and everyone brings in a pack of biscuits; you take in a tin of beans for harvest festival. What's not to like?

By now I'd decided I wanted to be a singer, because it struck me as a really cool thing to do. When we were in the car with the radio on, I'd think, Wow! I'd love to sing on the radio. I loved Eva Cassidy, especially when she sang 'Over The Rainbow'. I thought she had the best voice in the world.

My mum listened to The Carpenters all the time and I loved them, too. Karen Carpenter had the most distinctive voice, so beautiful and velvety. I like it when you can tell who's singing, no matter what the track is, and you can always tell when it's Karen Carpenter singing.

'You can be a singer if you want to,' Mum would say.

I didn't get very far with my performing career at primary school, though. Every year, I'd audition for the nativity play, hoping to be cast as a shepherd, which was a really good part, but every year I ended up being a sheep, with one line: 'Baa!'

'Dad, I'm a sheep,' I'd say every year.

'Wow! You're a sheep!' everyone would yell enthusiastically, but I wasn't happy.

In the last year, we were allowed to take part in a concert in the school hall. My friends Charlie, Rebecca, Gemma and me made up a dance to 'It Wasn't Me' by Shaggy. We were eleven years old and had no idea what the lyrics meant, but everyone cheered us and I really liked the feeling it gave me.

I was always a little bit into boys, even at primary school. There was a boy called Bradley Wiggins in my class and I used to tell my mum I loved him. 'Mum, I love Bradley Wiggins.'

'Stacey, you don't love him,' she'd say.

'I do, Mum, I do.'

He didn't love me back, though. He didn't even like me. He used to find me funny, but he liked a girl called Rosie. Unlike me, she was really pretty, with long blonde hair and pink cheeks. I was a pretty toddler – I looked like a mini version of my mum – but I didn't blossom as I grew older. I had gappy teeth, glasses, the lot.

My friend Gemma lived opposite Bradley Wiggins and

she fancied him, too. He was the class pin-up – everyone loved him. When I stayed the night at Gemma's house, we used to lie awake planning how we'd sneak out of the window, run across the road to Bradley's house, break in, slip past his mum and wake him up. But we never seemed to get beyond drawing the map to his house or deciding what we'd do if we got into his bedroom and woke him up. We just fell asleep on the map!

I have a vivid memory of something that happened in class one day, when I was being an idiot and not listening to the teacher. I was pulling faces and messing around and Bradley was really laughing. He was wetting himself, crying with laughter. Great, I thought excitedly. He finds me really funny.

He laughed and laughed and I laughed with him, thinking I was hilarious. Then I felt a tap on my shoulder and turned round to find the teacher – Mrs Twiglet, we used to call her – standing behind me. She'd been there for ages, all the time I wasn't listening, all the time I was happily thinking that Bradley was laughing at me because I was so funny, when in fact he was laughing because I was about to get into trouble. I was heartbroken. Oh no, I'm in trouble *and* he was laughing *at* me. Darn! Of all the things that happened at primary school, that moment really sticks out in my head.

Then one day a rumour went round: 'Bradley Wiggins is moving!'

'What? Bradley Wiggins is moving?'

'Yes, Bradley Wiggins is moving. To Kent.' Me and Gemma burst into tears. We were heartbroken. My first love was leaving Dagenham. It was a crushing blow.

After that, I was always in love with some boy or another. I never went through a tomboy stage.

'I love that boy,' I'd tell my mum.

'Shut up,' she'd say. 'You don't.'

Like a lot of girls, I used to dream about meeting my Prince Charming. I loved Disney films and was determined to turn my life into a Disney fantasy. My mum showed us Disney films from a young age and I liked them all; my favourites were *Beauty and the Beast*, *Aladdin* and *Cinderella*. *Beauty and the Beast* was the big one. I think it was the colours that made it so vivid for me: that bright red rose and her yellow dress when they fall in love. All the stories inspired me to write little poems and songs, which I pasted into my scrapbooks. I loved writing my feelings, thoughts and dreams down, and I still do to this day. My dad even framed one of my poems once, because I won a prize for it in a competition at school.

We enjoyed all the classics like *The Wizard of Oz* and *The Sound of Music*, and I discovered that Disney was a wonderful escape for me when I wanted to forget about everything. It still is today. It's another place, a happy place, with happy endings. You can't be scared when you're watching a Disney film. I particularly identified with Disney's Aladdin, because someone calls him 'a diamond in the rough' and that's what my dad always used to call me.

By now, my dad had had a couple of girlfriends. Like Mum, he was upset about the divorce, but instead of staying in and being sad like she did, he started dating, although he tried to hide it from us.

Then, in the summer of 2000, when I was ten, he introduced me and my brother and sister to someone new. 'This is Karen, everyone,' he said when we were at his house one Saturday. Karen was dark-haired and pretty, with blue eyes, and she had a deep tan because she used to live in Israel. I thought she looked really young, although she's actually older than my mum.

At first we felt weird about it because we didn't realize Dad had been with Karen for a while. When they moved in together, soon after that – along with Karen's three children, Aaron, Samantha and Ray – everything seemed to be happening really quickly. My sister hated my dad for seeing someone else, and didn't want to be a part of any of it. Jemma used to say exactly what she thought in front of Karen and it made everyone feel really awkward. Karen was really good about it, though. 'It's understandable,' she'd say sympathetically. 'She's just trying to get used to the idea. It'll take time.' Karen's three kids hated my dad, too, at first, so it worked both ways.

I soon got over my initial wariness, and when they announced they were getting married I got really excited about the wedding. 'I'm going to be a bridesmaid!' I sang, skipping around the house. It was like something out of Disney. I liked Karen, who seemed like a really nice lady, and I *loved* Ray, her youngest son, who was quite a lot older than me and really good looking. I enjoyed making new friends, and he seemed incredibly cool.

Like me, Jemma was a bridesmaid at the wedding, but she wasn't too happy about it. She said Dad was out of order for getting married again and she cried all day. My poor dad. He was only trying to move on with his life. I thought it was a really great day. All my family were there, including my mum. We wouldn't have gone without my mum. I would have hated the idea of her sitting at home while we all celebrated my dad getting married. It sounds odd, but it didn't occur to me that Mum would find it painful. Me and my brother were a bit naive about things like that, or maybe we were just burying our own conflicted feelings. I think my sister was more aware of how Mum might feel, which was why she reacted in the way she did. Luckily, my mum isn't a bitter person and she was able to leave the past behind. She would never not like Karen just because she was with my dad. She and Karen have always got on well, because they're both really good people.

A few years later, when Karen got pregnant with Josh, I was thrilled at the prospect of having a little baby brother. 'I can't believe you're happy about it, Stace!' my sister said. She hadn't wanted them to get married or have a child. Karen already had three children and Jemma felt that was quite enough. She was also worried that Josh would feel isolated, being so much younger than his brothers and sisters.

Not long after Dad and Karen got married, my sister left primary school and started a really good music and arts school in Elm Park called Abbs Cross School and Arts College. She got in because she was brilliant at music – she played the saxophone and piano really well. I was fast discovering that it was hard to be as good as my sister. She wasn't naturally smart, but she worked really hard in her lessons and got very good results, so when I got home from school, my parents were always saying, 'Well, we hope you've done as well as Jemma.' Oh my gosh! I was bright, but I hated being compared to her the whole time. It was so annoying.

I really resented that she was so good at everything. I hate you! I'd think. We went to baton-twirling classes together and she was even really good at that, whereas I was the clumsiest clod. I hated that. She was also a real daddy's girl; she looked like my dad and could wind him round her little finger, whereas I was the spitting image of my mum.

When it was my turn to leave primary school, I was accepted by Abbs Cross because Jemma was there, but I really didn't want to go. I wanted to go to the normal school around the corner. Still, I had to go because it was such a good school.

OK, I thought, but I'm not going to be like Jemma. I wanted to be the complete opposite of her. If she was good, then I would be bad. In fact, I would be really naughty.

Chapter 2

On my first day at secondary school in September 2001, I sat next to a girl called Louise. We were in assembly when Mr Mayo, the head teacher, came in. 'Mayo-nnaise!' I burst out after he'd been introduced. I found it really funny. 'Egg mayo!' I shouted. 'Tuna mayo!'

Louise laughed, but she must have thought, Freak!

Everyone else must have wondered, Who is this idiot? But being an idiot was my way of making friends, and it seemed to work. Me and Louise ended up spending the whole day together and we went on to become really good mates.

I tried to be funny and say funny things because I didn't know any other way of making friends. As I've said, I wasn't a pretty kid, and I didn't blossom as I reached my teens either. As well as wearing glasses, I had braces and was a lot broader than I am now. I also had a big Jewish 'fro on my head, since there was no such thing as straighteners in those days. A Jew'fro! It wasn't attractive.

I remember thinking, Gosh, I'm so ugly that I'll have to be funny and loud to be socially accepted. I thought I didn't have anything else to offer; I was a right minger! Even worse, I was ugly *and* clever; there's nothing less acceptable at school than that combination. If I hadn't been funny I wouldn't have had any friends at all. To be fair, though, at least I wasn't spotty. Can you imagine that? Braces, glasses *and* spotty! Now that would have been unfortunate.

I'd wanted to be the funny lovable one from an early age, and I was always loud. My sister wasn't like me at all. She was much cooler and more reserved. She was never bothered about making friends; it just happened naturally. Whereas having lots of friends was really important for me and I went out of my way to make as many as I could.

'Why do you feel the need to be friends with everyone?' my dad used to say. 'Not everybody is going to love you in life.'

People will always say, 'You can't please everyone.' But I don't agree. Why can't you please everyone? If you're genuinely nice to people, there's no reason why they won't all like you. And even if someone isn't the nicest person, I'll still like them, because you have to accept that everybody has their good and bad characteristics. Of course, when people are nasty, you don't necessarily aspire to have them as your friends. I'm talking about befriending people you actually want as friends.

'Whatever!' I'd say. 'You can't please them all, but I'll give it a go.' I was obsessed with making people laugh and making people happy. I liked to please everyone. I'd be naughty to please my friends, but then I'd do my homework to please my parents and teachers.

During my first week at Abbs Cross, all the teachers greeted me delightedly with the words, 'Ah, Jemma's sister.'

Yeah, that's me. I have a name, thanks! I thought.

Secondary school was very different from primary school. Instead of turning up with a tin of beans for Harvest Festival, you had to bring in a ruler and a compass. I forgot my pencil case all the time, which instantly meant trouble. I was really scatty: I was always losing my homework on the way to school and I regularly lost my blazer and bag, too. I remember thinking, Oh well, we won't be making sarcopha-guses out of pasta here!

I got into trouble from the start because I would not be told what to do. When everyone sat down for the register, I would stand up. I found it funny. I gave up trying to please the teachers and focused on making friends instead. No one could say to me, 'Stacey, do your work now,' because I'd just say, 'No, I don't want to.' I was awful. It wasn't long before me and Louise were split up and banned from sitting next to each other in class.

I also refused to wear my uniform properly. According to the rules, you had to have your top button done up and your tie straight. Most people would undo their top button and wear their tie short, but I didn't wear a tie at all, and I wore all my shirt buttons undone to reveal a vest underneath, with a cheeky slogan printed on it. It was just ridiculous.

You weren't allowed patterned tights, but I still wore them. You weren't allowed to wear your hair down, either, so I did. I rebelled in every way. I'd pull my skirt right up and I wore make-up, heels and jewellery – and when I say jewel-lery, you could have jumped through the hoops I wore in my ears, and they had huge balls hanging off them, too. I wore massive gold rings, as well, and a necklace with a big doll on the end of it.

'Not only are you not wearing your uniform properly, but you're wearing the most ridiculous things,' my mum would say. And she was right. I just wouldn't wear what I was sup-posed to wear, so I was always being sent home.

Until then, Mum and Dad had been very strict. When we were little, Mum had never let us play out in the street because it was dangerous. If we wanted to play, we had to go into the back garden. But you can't invite everyone in off the street to play in your back garden, can you? It was really frustrating. 'I want to play out!' I'd say. It felt like everyone was out there except me. But when I went to my friends' houses I didn't mention to their parents that I wasn't allowed out. That way at least I got to play in *their* streets.

My mum tried to tell me off, but I didn't listen. 'Oh, whatever!' I'd say dismissively. 'I just don't care. What are you going to do? *Make me* go in there with my uniform on properly? No one can force me to do anything.'

I had worked out that I could do whatever I wanted, because my dad wasn't around to stop me and my mum couldn't physically force me. After all, I was 5 feet 8 by the time I was twelve. If my dad had been there he could have put me in the car, made me wear my uniform properly and robbed me of my jewellery, but my mum wasn't physically strong, so all she could do was tell me off until she was blue in the face. I took no notice, though. I just walked out of the door, saying, 'See ya!'

I remember a teacher I didn't get on with looking me up and down and saying, 'You look like a lady of the night. You'll probably end up as one, too.'

What the heck is that? I thought. You're really getting on my nerves. I don't even know what language you're speaking.

I told my mum. 'What?' she said, shocked. He was basically saying that I look like a prostitute!

He used to make comments like that all the time. He was one of those teachers who hates kids. 'Children!' he used to say.

You'd think, Gosh, you're a teacher! How can you hate children?

I got in trouble for being late to school all the time.

'Solomon!' My name would echo through the hall. 'What time do you call this?'

'Sorry, sir!'

'You've missed reception. Go to your class. Hurry up. You're late.'

I used to get lots of detentions, but detentions were fun, because all my friends were there. Detention was either after school or in the lunch hour, depending on how bad you'd been. If you were really bad, it would be after school; if it was just because you were late, it was at lunchtime, when you still had ten minutes at the end to get your food, so it didn't really matter. You just sat there having a laugh with your mates, throwing balls of paper at the teacher.

Everyone was scared of Mr Mayo, our head teacher, apart from me. I didn't respect authority in any way, and I didn't foresee the consequences of my bad behaviour, especially as I always got good results. What's the big deal? I thought. I can do whatever I want. I'm going to pass my exams anyway.

My sister looked down on me for being bad and that made me want to be even worse. The funny thing was that I always got better results than she did in exams. She had to work really hard, whereas for some reason it was less effort for me. You can imagine how much she hated that. 'How come you don't have to do any work?' she'd complain.

We still didn't get on and we argued about everything, especially clothes and friends. I was constantly asking to borrow her clothes and I'd go mad if she wouldn't let me. She always had better things than me; she was allowed a mobile phone first, everything. Ugh, I hate you! You've got everything! I'd think. She had her reasons for hating me back. For one, I stole her clothes when she wouldn't lend them to me. And she really didn't like it when I hung out with people from her year, which was inevitable, because I was only one year below her. We were always arguing about that.

Why couldn't we just get on? I think it was all about fighting to be your own person. We each had very strong, distinct personalities, and rather than accepting each other's differences, we both insisted our way was right. It was a huge clash between two very different people. One of the only times we put aside our differences was when we both wanted to be in the school's Christmas concert. We knew that the only way we'd get a slot was by offering something special, like a sister act, so I sang, 'From This Moment On' by Shania Twain, with Jemma accompanying me on the piano.

We didn't fight all the time, of course. There was another side to our relationship; there always is with sisters. Despite all our arguments, we were fiercely loyal to each other. Jemma was very protective of me. Not physically, because I was the physical one: if anyone was ever horrible to her, I would step in and say, 'Don't go near my sister!' As much as I hated her, there was no way I would allow anyone to threaten her or be mean to her. That was just the way I was.

Jemma was protective in a different way: if she sensed that something was going to upset me, she would try to shield me from it. As much as we argued over clothes and stupid things like that, she would never have said anything to hurt me, because she knew how emotional I was.

She was very aware of what people were saying around me and she always looked out for my feelings. If someone didn't realize how sensitive I was and said something hurtful, she would tell them how wrong they were. I was aware of what she was doing and, as much as I resented her, I appreciated it.

Jemma was brilliant at music and went to Austria and France with the music department, which may sound good, but I much preferred the idea of being behind the bike shed at school in England! Our mum had taught us all how to play the piano at home and then signed us up for lessons. I'd done my piano exams up to grade six; I was really good at the drums and I'd played violin up to grade three. But I wasn't interested in hanging out in the music department, like Jemma was.

My best subjects at school were biology, maths and English literature, but strangely I wasn't so good at the things I loved, like music and drama, even though I really wanted to do well at them. It wasn't cool to be into music and drama among my friends at Abbs Cross – they were into street culture, so pop was seen as really naff. As a result I stopped going to my piano lessons and dreaming about being a singer, and when people asked me what I wanted to be when I was older, I'd say, 'I don't care. I don't want to be anything.'

I wasn't very good at French, but I really liked Mr Wheatley, my French teacher, so I behaved well in his class. Funnily enough, if I wasn't good at a subject, I wanted to improve, so I'd try much harder in those lessons.

One of the big problems with school, for me, was that they would teach us something one day and then go over it the next, by which time I'd already picked it up. 'I know what you're talking about. I really don't need to be here,' I'd say arrogantly. 'Why should I bother? I just need to come to my exams and that's it. I'm going to pass and you know it.'

If I saw a kid with that attitude now, I'd think they were so rude. The teachers were only trying to do their job, and they must have hated the way everyone around me suffered because of my bad behaviour. Nevertheless, I still flew through my exams. They couldn't stand that, and I ended up making enemies of all my teachers, as well as my mum.

It was around about now that me and my mum started having a really tough time. I couldn't get on with her. I didn't want to do the things she wanted me to do and when she told me not to do something, I'd say, 'Why can't I do it? *You* do what you want.' I couldn't agree with her about anything and I must have put her through such a terrible time.

I think I was aware of her unhappiness over the divorce from my dad, but I couldn't admit it, not even to myself. It's her fault! She divorced him! I'd think. What's she got to be unhappy about? She told him to go.

When you're a kid, you don't want to worry about your mum. You want her to be the one you turn to. After you've watched something scary, she's the one you call out to in the night, the one who makes you feel safe again. As long as I've got my mum, I'll always be all right, you think. Nothing bad will ever happen to me if my mum's around. It's only as you grow older that you realize she's not superwoman, she's a person like everyone else.

So I hated it when people said, 'Look at your mum. She's so thin.'

Shut up! She's not thin. There's nothing wrong with her, I'd think. I just dismissed their comments. 'She's fine,' I said. 'Stop fussing.'

My sister and brother weren't always very sympathetic to Mum either, and together we probably really ground her down at times. She must have had a terrible time: not only had Dad left without trying to get her back, her children blamed her for the break-up. What makes it worse is that I think she thought it was all her fault: Look what I've done! It's no wonder she didn't meet anyone else. I think she felt too guilty to go out and meet someone because she felt it was her sole responsibility to look after us. When I look back and think about how much she had to deal with, I feel so sorry for her.

I was less aware of my mum's feelings then, because I was having the time of my life. It was such a laugh hanging out with all my new friends, and I'd leave the house every morning at 7a.m. to meet them at Elm Park station, which was one stop on the tube from my house. Opposite the station there was an alleyway, where we'd sit on a set of steps for at least an hour before school started, chatting, laughing and eating sweets and bacon rolls. There were loads of us, about twelve or thirteen kids, and it was a really great gang. Even though we met up really early, we'd still stroll into school late most days. I'm not going to lie: I really loved my friends and they came first, before school, family, everything.

We spent most of our time talking complete rubbish, though: 'Oh yeah, I hate him!'

'Do you? Do you really?'

'Who do you fancy?' We constantly fancied someone new.

'Who's going over the park on Friday?' Friday night was park night.

You never kissed anyone at that age, but you had boyfriends that you'd meet at Harrow Lodge Park, which was one or two stops from me on the District Line. Your boyfriend was always older and you thought you were really cool as you went to meet him. And then, of course, you gave your report on what had happened on the alleyway steps the following Monday.

'I met Dan over the park.'

'Oh my God! Dan! What happened?'

Of course, nothing ever happened, because we were only little kids, especially in the first year at school. Some people started snogging when we were thirteen and fourteen, but no one did it in the first year, and even when we were older, none of us had the guts to go further than a snog. Still, everyone asked, 'Then what?' Since it never amounted to anything, they'd say, 'Oh, you're rubbish!' Then it would be, 'He doesn't like you. Dump him! Chuck him!' It was all about taking the mickey.

We'd write our names in 3D on the walls and doodle pictures for hours. 'In a hundred years' time, we'll be famous because of this wall,' we'd declare because we thought our doodles were so great. They've probably been painted over now, though!

We sometimes spoke in made-up foreign languages when people walked past, for a joke, even though we couldn't even speak English properly. 'I bet they think we're speaking French,' we'd whisper to one another. What idiots! I have no idea why we did it. We must have looked like a bunch of weirdos.

There weren't enough things to do to use up all our energy, so we danced on the steps, swung on the poles, drew on the walls and talked about complete rubbish for hours. It was just the best and I loved it. Thinking of it now really makes me smile. I would definitely go back and do it again, even at twenty-one years old, with a kid. I'd love to go back to school.

I had never enjoyed myself as much. My life opened up and everything was a laugh, exactly how it should be. I don't think anyone should take their life too seriously, because it's so much better when you're having fun, when it's a laugh and everyone's laughing with you. It's just great seeing your friends every day. These days, you say to your mates, 'Yeah,

yeah, see you tomorrow' but you never do, do you? Empty promises. 'Yes, see you soon.' But at school you see them all the time. It's brilliant.

There was always loads of banter, and running jokes that continued all term. So if someone did something embarrassing, like farting in class, they would never live it down: 'All right, love? Farting again, are you?' No one forgot it. We constantly took the mickey.

My best friends were Jade and Joely. We were together in every class, because the register goes in alphabetical order and their surnames also began with 'S' – we got on really well from the start. Jade was well advanced. She knew how to smoke and wear make-up and everything. She had a chest infection before anyone else, that chesty cough that you only associate with adults. How did she get that cough? you'd think. In the mornings before school, Jade was the one who bought the fags, because she looked the oldest. She'd buy ten Sovereign, which were only something like £1.50 at the time.

At school, we hung out in the girls' toilets, messing around for hours. While me and Joely sat by the taps, wetting paper towels and throwing them everywhere, Jade sat on the toilet having a fag, taking rapid drags and fanning the smoke away. I've never seen anyone smoke a cigarette so quickly; somehow she managed to inhale smoke and breathe it out of her nose simultaneously. I still don't know how she did it.

I tried smoking, but I wasn't very good at it, not like Jade. I really wanted to be cool, but I'd take a drag and think, This is just disgusting! Whereas it was like an accessory to Jade; she wore it so well. I didn't know how to hold a cigarette properly or light it in the right way; I just don't think I was born for it. I'd have one if everyone else was having one, though. 'Yeah, OK, me, please! Don't forget about me!' I'd say, even though they all knew I didn't really smoke.

They probably thought, Poor thing, trying to fit in.

Joely was a big tomboy. She's now a hairdresser and the girliest girl you've ever seen, but at school she was the total opposite. She would never, ever roll her skirt up, made no effort to look pretty and scraped her hair back so she looked like a boy. She played football with the boys and walked around in shin pads even when she wasn't playing. All the boys loved Joely, because she wasn't like the other girls. 'Come on, Jo,' they'd call to her, 'come and play football.'

Why do they love her? I thought. She's like a boy.

Jade, on the other hand, liked to make herself look pretty and always wore foundation and mascara. There was usually an orange ring of foundation around her collar, which fascinated me, because I only ever experimented with eyeliner and mascara at that age. Jade was quite tall and broad and she looked good. She protected us, because she was hard and people were in awe of her. 'Yeah, whatever. Don't care about no one. No one can tell me nothing,' she'd say. Everyone was a little bit scared of Jade, so they were really nice to her and sucked up to her all the time. She had two older sisters, who were in the top years, so she was someone you just wouldn't mess with. She had that kind of reputation.

She lived in a flat opposite the station and I thought that was really cool: she lives in Elm Park! Even though I only lived one stop away, I still had to get on the train to go there. It felt like a right journey to me, really far away, whereas Jade and Joely could walk to see each other, because they lived across the road from one another. I was really jealous of that.

I used to spend loads of time at Jade's flat. The block was really cool: every flat had a balcony, where people kept all their stuff, and everyone was always outside. 'All right, love? How you doing? Want a cup of tea?' It was as friendly as the street where I live, but in a more enclosed area, with everyone talking to everyone else and all the flats joined together, so that you could climb through a window from one person's house to the next.

Everything about it seemed really cool to me, from the metal stairs leading up to the flats to the view of the train tracks from the windows. And Jade's dad was so cool. He let us do whatever we wanted. There were shops underneath, so you could go and get your bacon roll, your fizzy drink or crackling candy, which we loved. You could shout at people down below from the flat and no one cared, whereas for some reason it just didn't feel right to do that from a house.

Me and Joely often used to sit outside Jade's flat, waiting for her to get ready. She took ages, because she used to put on all that blusher and mascara, even though no one else cared much about make-up. While we were waiting, we'd chew some gum, take it out of our mouths, throw it on the floor and watch the people walk past and step on it. We found it so funny. We'd scream with laughter as people looked back at us as if to say, 'What the heck are you laughing at?' little knowing that they were walking away with chewing gum stretching between the pavement and the sole of their shoe. Every time I see Joely, I say, 'Do you remember the chewing gum . . . ?' It was such a laugh that I think I'd go back and do it now if I could put on a morph suit, so that no one could see who I was.

I was somewhere between Jade and Joely; I wanted to be

a bit of both. They were like my other half; they were the best of me. I was the one who made us all laugh: 'Let's go somewhere!' I'd suggest out of the blue. 'Let's walk out of school now. Let's go to the park. Let's go!'

'Come on, then!' they'd shout and we'd all run out of school, maybe ten or twenty of us, and head for the first place we could think of. It was 20p to go on the bus then, so we'd get our 20p pieces together and yell, 'Let's all go to Romford!' It was just so good. We'd be wetting ourselves, sitting on top of the bus at the back, playing music; Jade would spark up another fag and she'd usually get away with it. We had such a good time. We didn't go far, only to Romford, Hornchurch or maybe Rainham. Rainham was a bit of a hotspot. When we were thirteen and fourteen we'd go to the Cherry Tree pub, which was the only pub that would let us in.

My first kiss was when I was thirteen with a boy called Michael, the geekiest, cutest little guy. The teachers used to take the mickey out of him because he had the same name as a notorious murderer. He lived in Elm Park and was the first boy to have Dance Mat on PlayStation. Dance Mat is the game where you put a mat on the floor, place your feet on the arrows and dance along to the directions on screen. It's so good. Arrows come up on the screen: right, left, up and down. If the arrow goes up, you put your feet forward; if it goes down, you put them back. It's a bit like aerobics, and perhaps not the most attractive thing to do in front of someone you really fancy!

One Friday after school, me, Joely and our friend Cally went over to Michael's house before we went over the park. We played Dance Mat while he was changing his clothes and getting ready. You had to put your good clothes on before you went over the park – you couldn't go to Harrow

Lodge Park in your school uniform. That would have been embarrassing.

So first you went home and put your tracksuit bottoms on – your best Adidas ones, with the least number of fag-burn holes in them. For some reason people found it hilariously funny to come up and burn your clothes with a fag, hence the holes. My tracksuit bottoms were blue with white stripes down the side. Then you wore your best Nike trainers or Reebok Workouts, which had to be crystal white. You couldn't have dirty trainers. Again, that would have been embarrassing. You wore some sort of vest top and a tracksuit jacket to complete the look, and then you looked really good. You also had to pull your socks over the bottom of your tracksuit, right the way up.

Flares came in, and jeans, but we never wore them. We cringed at flared jeans. It wasn't cool to wear a dress, either. If you saw someone in a dress, you'd think, What a slag!

I'd even wear a tracksuit when we went to see my grandma. My parents would be like, 'You look nice, but you'd look really lovely in a skirt . . .'

'I don't care! I love my clothes,' I'd say.

My mum would have done anything to get me in a pair of jeans and a nice top from Adams, and my nana would have loved to see me in a nice flowery dress, but she never did. Me and my brother and sister always attracted loads of attention when we went to see Mum's parents in the Forest of Dean, dressed in our tracksuits. The Forest of Dean is the opposite to Dagenham; it's full of trees, rivers and lakes, and everyone there is beautiful and posh. People would look at us as if to say, 'Who's that bunch of ragamuffins?'

You wore your jogging bottoms on your hips, rolled over at the top, with your label out, so you could prove they were real. If they were fake Adidas, it was really embarrassing. If someone only had two lines down the side, people would say, 'Oh dear, they've only got two lines! Horrendous!' So you couldn't buy any old pair. They had to be Adidas or Reebok, which were expensive, something like £30. It had to be Christmas or my birthday for my mum to buy me a pair of Adidas bottoms and I'd wear them for months and months before I got a new pair.

The idea of saying, 'We're going over the park with a bottle of Lambrini,' has become a teen cliché. People say it to take the mickey. But when I hear those words, I think, Shut up! Those were my best years. I had the time of my life.

You'd have about £2.50 on you for the night and you'd all go in £1 on a few bottles of White Lightning. You'd spend £1 on a chip butty and then you'd have 50p left over to spend on sweets or go in on another bottle. I don't remember getting drunk, though. It was more a case of getting hyper and being loud. 'Come on, everyone! Wheeee!'

We'd walk around in a gang and you'd always try to walk next to the boy you fancied. Sometimes you'd get to walk off with him and when you came back, everyone would ask, 'What did you say? What happened?'

Again, there was never anything to report. 'Well, we er . . . walked.'

Sometimes you'd dare your friends to snog a boy. 'Go on!' you'd say. 'I dare you. Snog him.'

'Eurgh, no!'

Or you'd point someone out as you were walking around and say, 'See if you can get with him tonight.'

'OK!'

Usually we'd stay there for hours, until ten or eleven o'clock at night, when our parents would ring us saying,

'Where are you?' My mum hated me going to the park, because she knew exactly what me and my mates got up to there, so I usually pretended I was at a friend's house. Once my dad caught me out, though, when he rang my friend's mum to see if I was there. 'Er, she's just popped to the park,' she said. Furious, he came and got me. It was so embarrassing in front of all my friends.

I listened to what everyone else was listening to, which was garage mainly, and a bit of drum and bass. I still love that music now as it reminds me of being a kid. My friends were always doing MC battles against a backing track. They used to get really into it. It was so good.

Back to my first proper kiss: when Michael was dressed and ready, we left his house for the park. He was my boyfriend, so obviously I had to kiss him. I think it was his first kiss as well. It happened as we were sitting on the grass, and afterwards I stood up and said, 'OK, see you later.' I don't think either of us really knew what we were doing. It was more like, 'OK, cool, see ya.' I went out with him for a few weeks, not very long. Relationships didn't last long at school.

'Yeah, we're going out now, everyone!' you'd announce. Then the next minute you'd be saying, 'We're just friends now, everyone. It's all over.' It was never serious for us until we were older. In our early teens it was just a bit of fun.

I had several boyfriends at Abbs Cross, but my favourite was a boy called Ross, who was in the same year as me. He came well after Michael and I really liked him. We were good friends for a long time and then finally he became my boyfriend, which lasted about two weeks!

I'd fancied him for ages and used to hang out where all his friends were. 'All right. What you doing? Where's everyone going?'

They must have thought, Go away!

But boys didn't matter all that much. They were mainly just something to talk about with your mates. My best times were with my friends, either at the park or wandering around the streets, doing stupid things. We'd go to a petrol station and buy a bunch of sweets or some coal. What did we need coal for? We threw it in the lake or at each other. 'Yeah, this is good!' We were silly, really.

Life was so sweet, so perfect. I had it all worked out: I could do what I wanted and I got on with everyone. Whereas some of my friends often had people from other schools squaring up to them, I was friends with everyone. No one hated me. Everything was just how I wanted it to be and I absolutely loved my life.

Then one day my mum came home from a parents' evening looking very unhappy. The teachers hadn't had a good word to say about me. What's more, some people's parents had complained about me because I was disruptive in class and their children couldn't concentrate. 'This is really serious,' Mum said. 'It's got to stop. From now on, things are going to be different.'

'Whatever!' I said, knowing that she couldn't physically prevent me from doing what I wanted.

I didn't realize that she meant it this time, though, and I had no idea how much things were about to change.

Chapter 3

Sitting alone in my room, I stared miserably out of the window at the street below. It was six o'clock on a Friday evening and all my friends were out at the park. While they were messing around, having a laugh and flirting with people they fancied, I was stuck at home with nothing to do and no one to do it with. I wasn't allowed to go out; I wasn't allowed to do anything. I couldn't even text my mates because my dad had taken my phone away. It was so annoying. I hated it.

My life was completely different now. I couldn't do any of the things I loved doing. I wasn't allowed to meet my friends at Elm Park station early in the morning, because my mum had started driving me to school to make sure I got in on time. That meant I lost out on at least an hour of fun a day, if not more, and it drove me mad. I really, really missed having a laugh with my mates.

They just took the mick. 'See you tomorrow, yeah? At nine,' they'd say. 'Will your mum be driving you in again?'

Everything had changed the moment my dad stepped in. Until then he hadn't been involved. I think my parents had decided that if my mum was telling me off, I didn't need my dad telling me off as well. Also, Dad was busy moving house to Hornchurch, so he left everything to mum. But when the situation became too much for her to cope with, what with me disobeying her all the time and the teachers and parents complaining about me, Dad finally had to do something.

'Give me your phone,' he said to me one day when I was over at his house.

'What? Why?' I asked him.

'I'm taking it away,' he replied. 'Your mother and I don't want you using it any more and we don't want you seeing your friends outside of school.'

'What? *No*, Dad!' I yelled. But he ignored my pleas and confiscated it anyway.

He had a right go at me. 'You're going to behave from now on,' he told me. I was gutted. This was serious. Whereas I had no problem ignoring my mum, I didn't dare disobey my dad.

I was grounded for three months. I wasn't allowed to go anywhere after school; instead, I was picked up and taken home. I never got to see my friends, apart from at school, which meant I was totally behind on all the latest gossip. I had no idea what was going on or what the jokes were, and it made me feel completely left out.

I did everything I could to spend time with my mates during school hours, so instead of going to lessons, I'd say, 'Come on, let's go to the toilets!'

Until then, if I didn't turn up to lessons I was sent home. I didn't care, though, because instead of actually going home, I'd just walk out of the gate, go to the park and meet up with whoever was there. Now when I didn't turn up to a lesson, the teacher would report me to the head, who would ring my mum. Then my mum would come and pick me up and take me home. There was no escape.

I couldn't stand school any more. It was boring beyond belief to have to sit in lessons listening to someone repeat something they'd already told me three days in a row, especially as I couldn't let off steam with my mates before or after school. The upshot was I became more disruptive than

43

ever. I was constantly being sent out of class and given detention. My sister was appalled and didn't want anything to do with me. The teachers were always complaining about how naughty I was and she felt really awkward about it. It was a difficult time for her at home, too, because I was getting all the attention – even if it was negative – and of course Matthew suffered as well.

I didn't think about how I was affecting my brother and sister. I just needed to find a way to catch up on all the things I was missing out on with my mates, so I pleaded with Mum to let me go to the park after school. 'No,' she said. 'You've been naughty at school. You've been in detention. You are *not* going to the park.'

Jade thought of a way round it. 'Say you're staying round at mine and we'll do an all-nighter round the park,' she suggested.

My heart leapt at the thought – 'Yeah, let's do that!' I said – but my mum wouldn't let me stay at any of my friends' houses.

I started bunking off as often as I could. When Mum dropped me at school, I'd walk through the gate and wait for her to drive away before running out again and heading to the park. It was the only way I could have any freedom.

Mum stopped giving me dinner money and started making packed lunches for me to take to school, so I didn't have money for sweets or bacon rolls. 'What are you doing?' I screamed at her. 'I was having such a good time. Now I can't buy anything when I'm with my friends.' She interfered in every little thing.

It seemed really unfair, because, amazingly, I was still getting good results at school and wasn't failing anything. It didn't matter to me that I was disturbing other people's learning and being disrespectful to the teachers. I didn't understand that my parents were trying to lay down boundaries because I had none. I just felt that all these restrictions had been imposed on me for no reason and I really resented Mum and Dad for it, especially Mum.

In my mind, it was all my mum's fault. She was ruining my life, so I was mean and horrible to her. She had a nightmare with me. Half the time, I wouldn't talk to her. 'Whatever,' I'd say. 'Shut up. Go away. Leave me alone.' I can't believe I spoke to her like that. It was so rude. If someone told my mum to shut up today, I'd want to kill them, but I said it all the time back then.

It was really hard for Mum because she had to put everything aside to stop me from doing what I wanted to do. She was constantly leaving work early, or taking time out in the middle of the day to come and pick me up. Still, she felt it was worth all the hassle and inconvenience. Convinced that my friends were a bad influence on me, she wanted to protect me from them. In her mind it was worth doing for my sake, even though I hated her for it.

Meanwhile my behaviour at school became worse and worse. I didn't listen to the teachers, I just wanted to chat to my friends and make them laugh so they didn't forget me. Because I was so angry about all the restrictions on me, I talked back in class and was rude and obnoxious. It was beyond a joke and things were getting out of hand.

To be fair, my parents didn't entirely blame me for what was going on. My mum felt I'd got in with the wrong crowd and my dad was disappointed that the school couldn't discipline me or keep me interested in lessons. I didn't realize this at the time, though and felt they were blaming and punishing me unjustly.

45

Strangely, the person I found I could talk to about the problems I was having at home was my stepmum Karen, perhaps because she was an outsider and could take an objective, detached view. It was a bit like having your best friend's mum to turn to and I really appreciated that. It's funny, isn't it, we're brought up with the stereotype of the scary evil stepmum, but my experience was exactly the opposite. However, although she could listen and advise, there was nothing Karen could do about the storm that was brewing.

Everything came to a head one morning before school in November 2003, about a month after my fourteenth birthday. I was about to get in the car with Mum to be driven to school when the doorbell went. 'Can you get that?' Mum said. The bell went again and I answered it to find my dad standing on the doorstep.

What the heck is he doing here? I thought. He hadn't been to our house in a long time.

'Get in the car, Stacey,' Mum said. Dad got in beside her.

'Why are you coming?' I asked Dad. He said nothing. Oh, God! I thought. He was so irritating.

When we arrived at the school gates, Mum and Dad got out of the car. 'What the hell?' I said. 'Why are you at my school? Why are you here?'

'Come on,' my dad said gruffly. We walked through the school gates and I realized they were making a beeline for Mr Mayo's office. So I was heading for a telling-off. Big deal. The head teacher's assistant asked us to sit and wait outside his office for a few minutes. When we finally went in, Mr Mayo was waiting for us, with the deputy head teacher sat next to him.

'We're not happy with what's going on,' my dad said. 'If

46

you don't address our concerns about discipline at Abbs Cross, we're going to take Stacey away.'

Great. Wonderful, I thought, not really taking the situation seriously.

The meeting didn't take long. There was talk of me leaving school. There was more talk about my parents taking me away and putting me in another school. I crossed my arms and rolled my eyes. What were they going on about?

Then my dad dropped a bombshell. 'All right, she's leaving,' he said. 'Right now.'

My mouth dropped open. 'What?' I said. I was shocked. I thought it was just going to be a case of promising to do things differently, of agreeing to behave in class and treat my teachers with respect. I would say I was sorry and they would give me another chance and everything would go back to normal. So why was my dad suddenly saying he was taking me out of school? I hadn't even had a chance to defend myself.

'Thank you very much,' my dad said. 'And I'm sorry,' he added, standing up to leave, along with my mum. I stayed in my seat, looking from Mr Mayo to my dad in confusion. 'Come on, we're going,' Dad said, and I had no option but to leave with them.

On our way out, we passed a couple of my mates in the corridor. 'Where are you going?' they whispered. 'What are your mum and dad doing here?'

'I don't know,' I replied, feeling totally bewildered. 'I don't know where I'm going.'

As we got in the car I burst into tears. 'Why are you doing this?' I sobbed as my parents drove me home. 'I want to go back to school.'

'That school isn't good for you,' they said.

'All my friends are there!' I yelled. 'You can't separate me from my friends!' But the subject was closed.

Back at home they made me pack up some clothes. 'Why? Where are you taking me?' I screamed. I was hysterical now. I would have done anything to stay, but they weren't giving me a choice.

They bundled me back into the car and took me to my Auntie Mal's flat in Hackney. My mum just couldn't deal with me any more. I was too much heartache for her, so I was going to stay with Auntie Mal and my nana for a while.

I sobbed for the whole journey. I begged for my phone back, but my dad shook his head and said I was forbidden from getting in contact with any of my friends. I wasn't allowed to phone them, email them or write to them. 'Why? It's not fair!' I yelled.

'We only want the best for you, Stacey,' he said. 'You've got so much potential, but your friends are holding you back.'

So this was it, the end. After all the fun we'd had and all the growing up we'd done together, I wasn't even going to have a chance to say goodbye to my mates. The life I knew and loved was over, just like that. I didn't see or speak to my friends for years afterwards. It was really sad.

It took over an hour to get to Auntie Mal's. It felt like the other end of the earth. There was no chance I'd be bumping into any of my mates from Dagenham over here. Auntie Mal answered the door to her flat with a welcoming smile. 'Come on, then,' she said warmly as she greeted me. 'We'll have fun.'

My heart sank. 'Ugh!' I sighed as I reluctantly entered the flat. I don't want to be here; I *really* don't want to be here, I thought. I liked Auntie Mal a lot, but what was I going to do with her, day in, day out?

When my parents left, she showed me to the middle bedroom in the flat, which I was going to be sharing with her son Robert. I slumped down on my bed, feeling numb with shock, unable to take in what had happened over the last eight hours. I'd got up in the morning thinking I was going to school as usual, and now I was in disgrace, a long way from home, isolated from my friends and out of school for good. What was going on? As Auntie Mal left the room, closing the door to give me some privacy, tears poured down my face. I flung my head on the pillow and sobbed my heart out.

It tore me to pieces inside to think about my friends. What would they be doing now? I couldn't bear to imagine them having fun without me, at the park, at each other's houses, or just wandering around the streets. They didn't know I'd left Abbs Cross for good, so when would they start to miss me? Would they be wondering where I was yet? I pictured Jade and Joely having a laugh at Jade's flat, or over at the park with everyone else, sharing a bottle of White Lightning and daring each other to snog people. I thought about the alleyway opposite Elm Park station and the doodles on the walls. Every morning before school my mates would still be meeting up there, eating bacon rolls, swinging on the steps, drawing on the wall and laughing their heads off about who they fancied – without me. It destroyed me that I would never see them again. It was devastating.

I punched the pillow in anger and frustration. Why were my parents so mean to me? I didn't deserve it, I really didn't. OK, I was rude to my mum, but only because she was so horrible to me. It didn't occur to me to see things from my parents' point of view. I was your typical self-absorbed teenager, so I didn't give a thought to all the worry and heartache that

Mum and Dad had been going through. All I kept thinking was that it wasn't my fault! I just wanted to hang out with my friends – what was wrong with that? Everyone needs their mates, don't they? My thoughts brought me full circle. My life wouldn't be worth living without my friends. Overwhelmed by self-pity, I buried my face in the pillow and blubbed all over again. I felt like the unluckiest person in the world.

I cried until there were no tears left. Totally wretched and drained of energy, I fell asleep. When I woke up a couple of hours later I started crying again. How would I survive without my mates? I just didn't know. The days stretched ahead, bleak and empty. I wondered how long I'd be trapped in Hackney. My dad had said something about staying here to give my mum a rest, but surely I would have to go to school at some point? It was the middle of term, after all. They wouldn't be sending me anywhere in Hackney, I knew that much. The schools near my auntie's flat definitely didn't have the best reputation.

My auntie left me to myself at first and I spent days feeling sorry for myself and obsessing about how much I wanted to return to Dagenham. I felt like I was missing out on everything; all I could think about was how much fun everyone would be having without me.

Luckily, my auntie never judged me. She didn't care that I had kissed a boy or hadn't done my homework. It didn't bother her. She just wanted me to be happy. And I wasn't angry with her. I saw my parents as my jailers, not Auntie Mal. She's a lovely person and we've always got on well. She's my dad's oldest sister, and when their father died, she helped my nana raise my dad, uncle and auntie. Big and really pretty, with lovely dark skin and fair hair, she's six years older than my dad but has always looked really young.

I listened to everything she said, because she spoke sense. 'If you want to smoke, smoke,' she'd say. 'But it's not good for you.' That meant so much more than someone just shouting, 'DON'T SMOKE! YOU MUSTN'T SMOKE!' She was cool.

For three months I hadn't been allowed to go anywhere without my mum driving me, but my auntie trusted me to go and post her letters on my own. OK, she knew I didn't have any money to get on the tube and go back to Elm Park, but I still felt grateful to her for letting me out, even if it was just to go to the post box. Then one day, after I'd sat in my room being miserable for long enough, she said, 'Come on, let's go shopping.'

I think Auntie Mal felt sorry for me. She thought that perhaps my parents had handled the situation wrongly and that it was a bit much for a kid to take all her friends away and shove her in someone else's house. Rather than resolving the situation, my parents had just cut me off from my old life and made me start again. Wouldn't it have been better to sit down and discuss it first? Maybe they felt they couldn't get through to me, but at the time I felt they should have tried harder. Perhaps I'm not taking into account how much of a nightmare I was, though. They were tearing their hair out over me, while I was living in my own selfish bubble. They just didn't know what to do with me, so they did what they thought was best.

For me, the worst thing about it was that I'd had no choice; I wasn't given a second chance. I was sure that if I'd promised the head that I would change completely, if I had turned up for all my lessons, done my homework and started behaving, the school would have been happy enough to keep me on. I think they were just trying to scare me when they talked about letting me go, but my dad took them at their word and said, 'See you later.'

I wasn't given the opportunity to say, 'If you're going to take me away from everything I love, I'll stop being naughty and I'll sort it out.' They just took me away and then everything was gone.

Whether I could have behaved is another matter. Could I have changed? And how long would it have lasted if I had? I don't know. But perhaps I should have been given the chance to try. Anything would have been better than what I now faced: an empty life in limbo, with no friends and no school to go to.

Gradually I stopped moping, though, and started doing things with Auntie Mal. She was my nana's carer at the time, so we just did everyday things. It was probably quite fun for her to have me around, I suppose. She had a big collection of beads and sequins, so I'd sit and make bracelets in the kitchen with her – I love anything shiny! I helped her to cook and she taught me to make meringues. And sometimes she'd take me to the cinema, or to the shops.

My nan was also really good to me. She adored me and would have done anything for me. She never told me off. 'You've got to do what you've got to do,' she used to say. 'Do what you believe in.'

'Yeah, all right, Nana,' I'd say. I think her main worry was that I would fall out with my family, like my dad and my uncle had fallen out. It was very upsetting for Nana that her sons didn't get on and she didn't want any more rifts, so she never made me feel like I was in the wrong or took sides. 'As long as you know that everyone is here for you,' she'd say, waving her hands around. 'Your parents are doing this for a good reason. Now, eat!'

You felt loved when Nana was around. She was always pinching us and saying, 'Beautiful children. Gorgeous children.'

I stayed with Auntie Mal for a few weeks and then began dividing my time between her flat, Mum's house and Dad's house. It was a strange existence. For more than six months I wasn't allowed out to see a single friend. I was never left alone in the house, either, in case I rang a friend or ran away. It was awful, especially as I didn't enjoy spending time with my mum, dad, sister or brother, because I was so angry with them all. I don't think they were that keen on seeing me, either, at the time because I wasn't very pleasant. They were probably as relieved as I was every time I went back to Auntie Mal's.

I couldn't help thinking that life had been much more productive when I was sitting in class, not listening to my teachers. Now I just sat around sulking, thinking about how unlucky I was. For the first few months Abbs Cross sent me school work to do at home. But then I stopped bothering with it and they didn't chase me for it. There was no incentive for me to work out equations or write essays when I wasn't going into school.

It took my parents ages to find me another school. I couldn't get into any of the schools in the same borough as Abbs Cross, because they all wanted to know why I'd left my old school, and my dad had to be honest, obviously. As a result they all turned me down. It was inconvenient enough to take on a new student in the middle of the school year, let alone a naughty one.

My mum and dad went to several appeals boards to plead my case. They met the school teachers and governors and tried to persuade them to take me, but every time they got knocked back. Meanwhile, to their disgust, the local education authority didn't make a single enquiry as to why I wasn't attending school, or get in contact to see if I was OK. While the government were threatening to fine and jail parents whose kids persistently played truant, no one seemed in the least bit interested in the fact that I hadn't been to school for six months at the age of fourteen.

My parents felt like they were going round in circles and they were running out of options. My education had been on hold for far too long at a crucial time in my life. What on earth were they going to do? Some of my dad's relatives suggested sending me to a Jewish school. Most of my cousins had gone to the Jewish Free School in North London and they were all doing well. My dad wanted me to go to a Jewish school, so he decided to approach King Solomon High School.

In his letter to the school, Dad had to show that he was Jewish by proving that his mother was Jewish, because according to Jewish law, your mother has to be born Jewish in order for you to be Jewish. Of course, that meant that I wasn't technically Jewish, even though my mother had converted to Judaism.

These days I think that if you believe you're Jewish and you want to be Jewish, that should be the end of it, but at the time I couldn't have cared less. I just wasn't interested. Now I love being Jewish, although I don't think it matters what religion you are, as long as you interpret the message in a good way.

The way I interpret it is, if you're good to everyone around you and treat everyone as you'd like to be treated, you'll be fine. Even if you don't get everything you want in this world, we're all going to die and go to the same place. So as long as you're good, everything will work out.

I like the Jewish traditions because they bring you close as a family. When we celebrate Hanukkah, the Jewish holiday that falls around Christmas time, we incorporate Christmas into it, because I don't think you can miss out a national tradition like Christmas. My mum's house is the Christmas house in our family. Me, my brother and sister all sleep there on Christmas Eve in our old bedroom, with Zach, of course. Christmas isn't even about religion half the time; like Hanukkah, though, it brings the family and the whole nation together. It's lovely when Zach and I are lighting the Hanukkah candles together and it's lovely when we're opening presents under the Christmas tree and having a roast turkey dinner, too.

If you're all coming together, I think you can take a bit from every religion. After all, your religion doesn't determine whether you're a nice person or not – that's down to whether you're a good person deep down. Otherwise, you could celebrate Christmas or Hanukkah every day all year long and it wouldn't mean a thing.

Unfortunately, just like all the other schools, King Solomon wrote back to say there wasn't a place for me. By now, my parents were absolutely desperate, so my mum and Karen went to the appeal at King Solomon, with the rabbi from Dad's and Karen's synagogue, who supported my application. My dad couldn't go because he was photographing a wedding that day. Mum, Karen and the rabbi sat in front of a long table of representatives from the school, plus the appeal board judges, who were there to listen to both sides, and Mum did all the talking.

The next day the appeal board rang her. 'Your appeal for your daughter to attend King Solomon was so sincere and heartfelt that there was no way we could turn it down,' she was told. She nearly collapsed with relief. At last I would be going to school again.

As soon as the decision was made, the staff at King Solomon bent over backwards to welcome me. 'No matter what has gone on,' the acting head told Mum, 'from this day forward, Stacey is a part of this school and a part of our community. We will look after her and do everything we can for her.'

I think I was the first 'non-Jewish' person to attend King Solomon. I started in May 2004, two days before everyone took their SATS. I went backwards and forwards between Hackney and Dagenham to sort out my school uniform and equipment, then finally, the day before I started school, I went home for good.

I was really excited. After months of doing nothing, I couldn't wait to do something – anything. I was desperate to get back out into the world and be someone again, at last.

Chapter 4

I honestly believe that you make your own universe. If you believe something strongly enough, it will happen. So I walked into my new school thinking, I'm going to work hard and I'm going to make friends.

I had to make friends, because my friends are my life. My best times are when I drive round to a friend's house and sit on the kitchen counter, chatting. We talk about rubbish and end up rolling around on the floor laughing about stupid things. Those are the moments I always remember. I don't remember sitting at home on my own watching a film.

If you walk into a room thinking, Right, I'm going to make friends with everyone, people might be a bit off with you at first. But if you really believe it and think, I'm going to be nice to everyone, there's no reason why everyone in the room can't like you, as long as you're not bitchy and you don't talk behind anyone's back.

I tried to look pretty on my first day at King Solomon: my mum straightened my hair and I put it in a pony. One of my old schoolfriends recently told me that everyone was spying on me through the classroom window as I walked in. 'She's got nice legs,' they said. They all remember it, but at the time I didn't have a clue they were checking me out.

It's hard enough starting at a new school, but King Solomon was the complete opposite of my old school, so it took a bit of adjusting. It wasn't cool to smoke. It wasn't cool not to work or be disruptive in class. You were cool if you had never smoked a cigarette in your life. You were cool if you were really clever and got the best results, and no one bunked school. 'No way! We're not getting into trouble,' they'd say.

In spite of everything that had happened, I probably still went in with a bit of attitude on the first day, but I soon realized I'd have to change completely if I wanted to be accepted. 'No, I've never smoked,' I assured everyone. It was a half truth, as I hadn't *properly* smoked and I didn't enjoy it when I tried it, so for me it was a plus that no one liked smoking.

As I started school on a random day, two days before the SATS exams, I had to sit the exams, too, and I passed them all with flying colours, even though I don't know how. 'Ugh! See what you can do!' my parents said in exasperation.

When I was congratulated on doing well at school, I was so happy because it was cool to be clever there!

I was still cheeky and funny, and I still answered back to the teachers. But at King Solomon they reacted differently. 'Funny! Good one!' they'd say when I made a joke in class, 'Now answer this question ...' The teachers at my old school would just have said, 'You're not funny and you're not clever. Get out!'

I got in with a nice group of girls from the start, and they included the really popular girls. Yes! I thought. I'm going to be with the popular girls! Before long I was going to Lauren G's house on Fridays (at a Jewish school, you finish early on Fridays). We'd get McDonald's, go back to her house and read magazines.

It was a whole new experience for me. In the past it had always been, Get your pack of fags, get your bottle of White Lightning and we'll all go over the park. Whereas now it was, Get your *Heat* magazine and your McDonald's and we'll all compare make-up and clothes. It was the complete opposite of what I'd known before, but I really enjoyed it. It felt good to be growing up and I was the right age to be doing girly things. Everything was falling into place.

The first party I was invited to was at Lauren A's house. This was something else new. We didn't have parties at Abbs Cross. Instead, a friend would ring up and say, 'Come round.' Then everyone would pitch up to their house, pile in and sit around the kitchen, drinking, smoking and talking rubbish. It wasn't considered a party.

At King Solomon you'd be invited to a 'house party', where everyone watched films and you sat next to the boys on the sofa, thinking, Wow! I'm sitting next to Alex! People ordered in takeaways and we'd all eat together. It was really cool.

People drank, but instead of White Lightning and Lambrini, they drank WKD and Smirnoff Ice, which were £3 a bottle. Where am I going to get £3 from? I thought in a panic. I had to save up £1 every day from my dinner money so I could afford a Smirnoff Ice to take to the next house party. Luckily, people shared their takeaways, so at least I didn't have to come up with money for food as well.

You had to dress nicely for a house party, in jeans and a really good vest top. I got really flustered about it the week before Lauren's party. What am I going to wear? I thought, as all I had was jogging bottoms.

'I really need jeans!' I told my dad in a flap, so he bought me a pair at the market. They were a bit small for me and really tight, so my muffin top hung over the edge, but I still thought they were cool, because they made me look like I had a bum – and I don't have a bum! Luckily I was OK for shoes. We didn't wear high heels until we were about fifteen or sixteen and that was only when we went out. If you went to a friend's house, you wore trainers or Converse.

Some of the kids at King Solomon had a lot of money, or at least their parents did. I thought my Reebok and Adidas jogging bottoms were expensive, but the girls in my class wore £300 Victoria Beckham jeans. Oh my God! I thought. They wore Tiffany bracelets and jewellery from Links of London, which I'd never even heard of. My friend Melissa had a pair of Tiffany cross earrings and a check Burberry bag with black trim!

A girl in the year below us had the most incredible wardrobe of designer clothes you've ever seen, from Vivienne Westwood to Ralph Lauren, Gucci and Juicy Couture. Her dad owned a designer outlet with stores in every major shopping centre in the south, from Lakeside and Bluewater to Canary Wharf. It was the biggest deal. You can't imagine. She was the best-dressed, most popular girl in her year.

There might have been some snobbery about money among people's parents, but it wasn't that bad amongst the kids. I think the parents wanted their kids to go to a good school and wear designer stuff, but the kids just seemed normal. I didn't have expensive jeans or tops or a Burberry bag, but no one was bothered. I was still friends with everyone. I didn't care too much, either. Occasionally I'd think, I wish I had that Burberry bag; one day I'm going to have one, or, I love those Tiffany earrings, but it wasn't a really big deal.

Sometimes we'd all go shopping in Romford on a Friday, which was really fun. It never bothered me when my friends bought clothes, but I was always amazed at how expensive everything was in places like Topshop. It was a long way from BHS or Primark, where my mum took me shopping.

My friends always had loads of money on them – enough to buy clothes and McDonald's and pay their bus fare. They often had £50 on them – at the age of fourteen! Looking back, I think that's strange as it's a lot of money. Even now I don't go out with £50. But when I was a kid, I thought, Cool!

I always had enough for a McDonald's, though. Either I'd save up during the week, or about once a month I'd ask my mum for £5 on a Friday, and she'd give it to me if she had it. I didn't get pocket money because I'd spend it on rubbish, so there was no point in letting me have any. Sometimes I did a few hours' work at the children's nursery where my sister worked. I wasn't allowed to do much, though, because of my age, so it was stuff like ticking the register and answering the phone.

I also used to babysit a schoolfriend's little sister, who was called Courtney. She was the sweetest little girl and I adored looking after her. She loved me and always wanted me to babysit her. I'll never forget the first time I went to their house in Chigwell. It was the biggest house I'd ever seen in my whole life; it was like something out of a film, with a marble hall five times the size of our front room and a sweeping staircase leading up to the first floor. There was a front room for the kids and a front room for the adults, a computer room for the kids and a computer room for the adults; there was a patio and a huge garden with pools at the end of it and lights everywhere. The bedrooms were enormous. One of the girls' rooms actually had stairs connecting one part of her bedroom to another. The kids had quad bikes and the dad had an Aston Martin. It was incredible.

I was blown away. It was amazing, like a palace. I felt like Cinderella the babysitter and I used to daydream that one day I'd own a house like that and have loads of kids and someone to babysit them. One day a prince will fall in love with me, I'd think, lost in my own little world.

Chigwell is full of houses like that. It's even better than Hampstead. Loughton and Epping are the same. You'd never imagine there'd be houses like that there, but there are loads of beautiful mansions behind massive gates. It's just unbelievable.

All my schoolfriends seemed to have gates outside their houses, so when you went round to see someone, you had to wait for them to open the gates and let you in. The houses were all enormous, with kitchens the size of my house. There was always a sunbed room and at least one swimming pool, if not two or three, and there were gardeners to look after the huge gardens. It was a different life altogether. Everyone was well off.

It was typical of the Jewish community, where the mentality is that you have to do well at school, make money or marry someone who is going to make money, buy a house in a nice area and send your kids to school in a nice area. Nothing less will do. I met mums who would struggle to get by and go without themselves in order to send their kids to a good school.

Nobody could really be bothered to come to my house, because it was two bus rides away from school. Sometimes I stayed with my dad in Hornchurch, but I always felt more rooted in Dagenham. I didn't particularly enjoy living with my dad, because it didn't feel like my house. I never felt like I could settle there; I couldn't chuck my stuff about or throw my dirty knickers on the floor, because my dad wasn't doing my washing, his wife was.

As lovely as Karen is, I didn't feel as comfortable there as

I did at home with Mum. I couldn't say, 'Mu-um, make a drink!' I had to be polite and say, 'May I make myself a drink?' It just wasn't home and I'm a really homely person.

My brother and sister spent quite a lot of time living at my dad's. They were always going backwards and forwards, neither here nor there. We'd all be together at my mum's house around twice a week and we always did at least one day a week with my dad, me included. Me and Jemma still argued about everything. It's weird to think that five or six years ago, we could hardly even sit in the same room together.

Unfortunately, at Dad's house we shared a room. Then one day we came home to find a wall down the middle of the bedroom. My dad had had enough of us arguing, so he'd built a wall to keep us separate. What the heck is that about? we thought. It was bang in the middle of the window, dividing the light on either side. It wasn't appropriate at all. That's when we realized that everyone was sick to death of us fighting.

We tended to get on better on family holidays, especially when Karen's children were there. I remember one fun holiday in Wales when seven of us squashed into a caravan. Me, Jemma, Matthew, Ray and Sam slept in the bedroom and my dad and Karen had a pull-out bed in the main room.

On the last night of the holiday, us kids thought we'd sneak out and go and party. Before everyone went to sleep, we put a chair underneath the bedroom window in preparation. Then, when we were sure that Dad and Karen were asleep, we opened the window and snuck out. The caravan shook as each of us jumped out of the window and landed on the grass below. We were terrified that my dad or Karen would wake up, but to our relief, we all made it out without being caught. Then, when we were about ten steps away from the caravan, I looked back and saw what I thought was a silhouette at the window. 'Oh no, Karen's up!' I whispered.

'I can see her, too,' Jemma said.

We froze. Panicked, we ran back to the caravan and climbed in through the window, shaking the caravan even harder in the rush. Back inside, we lay in bed, petrified, waiting to be told off. But nothing happened. After a while, Jemma said, 'We must have been seeing things. It was nobody.'

We all relaxed and I went to get a drink from the fridge. But as I opened the fridge door, Karen yelled, 'What are you doing?' She hadn't noticed the caravan shaking as we jumped in and out, but she woke up the instant she heard the fridge door squeak!

My friends at King Solomon went on far more exotic holidays than me, of course, although that doesn't mean they were as much of a laugh. Most of them lived round the corner from school and were picked up by their mums at the end of the day. All the mums were really pretty, with high cheekbones, perfect eyebrows and immaculately done hair and nails, and after school they'd take their kids to the nearby David Lloyd gym. They were always down the David Lloyd; everybody seemed obsessed with it, though none of them ever exercised. They just sat in the café talking while their kids swam or played tennis.

Oh God! They're off to the David Lloyd again, I'd think. I hated it because it would cost me £12.50 to get in there as a guest, which obviously I couldn't afford. Where was I going to get £12.50 from? My mates used to try and sneak me in – sometimes we'd get away with it and sometimes we wouldn't. I didn't even want to go that much, because it was boring sitting in the café watching people play tennis. You also had to dress up to go in there, even though it was a gym.

People wouldn't wear their tracksuits; they'd wear really nice clothes. And you'd think, What the heck? This is supposed to be a gym, but everybody's in jeans!

Sometimes I used to wish my friends had less money and that we could do normal things. I much preferred it when we went to someone's house and all each of us needed to have fun was a bottle of Smirnoff Ice and a magazine.

At school, though, we were all equal, and I continued to do well. I think my parents had said to the teachers, 'She knows too much, so challenge her and keep her stimulated.' As a result, I enjoyed lessons, because as soon as I'd picked something up and started saying, 'Yeah, whatever, I know it,' the teachers would say, 'OK, try this, then.' That was all I needed: to be given something new to think about.

In Maths they put me in the top class, where they'd sometimes give us A Level questions on mechanics and engineering, things that we'd never need to know, just to challenge us. 'OK, I'll do it,' I'd say. 'Go on, watch this.'

I had some great teachers. I really struggled when I did Biology A/S Level and the Biology teacher once stayed behind after school to go through a whole topic with me until I understood it. We were there until seven o'clock, but he wouldn't go home before he'd made sure I understood everything. I really appreciated that.

Miss Pinnion, the head of year, was also very good to me. If I did something bad, she'd say, 'OK, I'm not going to send you home. Come and help me with this instead,' because she didn't want me to get into trouble at home.

Discipline was much less of a problem at King Solomon than it had been at Abbs Cross. I was always a little bit cautious of my head teacher. He never shouted, but he just had to look at me and I'd think, Whoops! We didn't have detention, but we could be sent to isolation. In isolation, you sat in a booth facing a wall and wrote out a chunk of the dictionary all day. I went there a couple of times, but only when I'd been really naughty.

At Abbs Cross, my friends had laughed at me for playing the piano, so after a while I'd hidden the fact that I had any musical ability. Oh my God, this is so not cool, I thought during music and drama lessons. But at King Solomon people were impressed if you were good at the piano and singing. Everyone was into music and drama and it was really cool to be a performer. As a result I began to enjoy singing, acting and music again. Luckily, I don't think you ever forget how to play the piano, so I was able to pick up where I'd left off.

I had completely forgotten how much I loved singing, too. I liked acting and had fun in drama, but I absolutely loved singing. I loved the feeling I had when I was up on stage. And I loved the feeling I had afterwards, when people clapped. Wow! They're clapping! They like me! I'd think, flushed with excitement.

On Saturdays I went to Paul's Theatre School in Hornchurch with my brother and sister, where we used to sing and make up stories. It was all right, but it wasn't really me. I don't think I'm very 'drama school'. I probably would have enjoyed it when I was younger, but at least when I sang everyone said, 'You've got a lovely voice.'

At school, the kids in my music class often put on concerts in the school hall at lunchtime. Hardly anyone ever came to watch – sometimes there were only two people in the audience – but it didn't matter to us, because we'd do anything to get up on stage and sing with the microphone. You could sing whatever you wanted, so I often chose my favourite song, 'Over The Rainbow' – the Eva Cassidy version, of course. Everyone probably thought, Get a new song, Stace! but I just loved that track. I used to love organizing the concerts as well, deciding who went first and which songs would be good to sing.

'I'm going to be a singer,' I started saying to my mum, who hadn't heard those words for a while.

Once we did an after-school concert, a mini variety show with people singing, dancing and performing sketches. All our parents and friends came and the hall was packed out. It was really fun. I wore my best jeans and a glittery top and went out on stage thinking I looked really cool. Afterwards, my music teacher told my mum that I had the X factor!

I was loving school now. It's really difficult when I look back now to know whether my parents did the right thing or not by taking me away from Abbs Cross. There is an argument for both sides. One part of me thinks it was the right decision, because I went on to have a brilliant time at King Solomon. I made some really good friends, got on well with the teachers and probably got much better results than I would have done at my old school, but at the same time I'm sure I would have been happy if I'd stayed at Abbs Cross, too. It's a weird one. It was probably worth it, but perhaps it could have been handled differently, although now I'm older I understand what a difficult situation my parents felt they were in and I think they did the best they could.

I had a lot of friends who were boys, but my best friend at the time was a boy called Adam. What I liked about my male friends – people like Adam, Alex (aka 'Ali C') and Jamie – was that they were so funny. They made me laugh all the time. They were stupid funny and slapstick funny, but they were also clever funny. They were always making up words and playing around with language and meaning.

I used to feel really cool being friends with the boys. They all had massive houses and threw lots of house parties. I wasn't seriously attracted to any of them, because I was far more developed than they were. Me and Adam went out for about two weeks and then realized it was gross and went back to being friends. The thing was, I was really tall, with big boobs and hips, so I didn't look like a teenager, I looked much older. The boys in my year were all shorter than me, so I didn't look right with any of them. Boys mature slower than girls, so I wasn't interested in them as boyfriends. I just wanted to be friends.

I had loads of best girlfriends, too: Natasha, Jessica, Anya, Lauren, Mel and Haley. And along with all the girls in my year, I fancied three boys in the sixth form called Adam, Lee and Joel. They were two years older and *so* good looking!

At the end of year 10, I went to Israel on a school trip. It was a big thing for my family to send me to Israel and I was desperate not to miss out. 'You have to go,' my dad said, and my mum was really keen as well, so we all saved up for it, me by working at my sister's nursery and babysitting. That was such a good holiday! All my friends went; there were about fifty of us staying in youth hostels all over the country. It was just the best experience. One minute we were in Midreshet Ben-Gurion in the Negev desert, the next minute we were in Jerusalem at the Western Wall. All of us.

Israel is a fantastic, beautiful country. People think it's all fighting and bombs, but it really isn't. One of my best memories is of going to Eilat, which is by the sea, and going out on the marina to see all the dolphins. It was the most unbelievable day. Jerusalem was amazing, too. We happened to visit the Western Wall (also known as the 'Wailing Wall') on the anniversary of the destruction of the Holy Temple in Roman times. It's a very holy day, when Jewish people traditionally come to the wall to lament the loss of the temple, among other events in Jewish history. It was quite overwhelming to see the queues of weeping people everywhere, slipping notes and prayers into the crevices in the wall. I felt very moved to be there. It's amazing to think that more than a million notes are placed in the wall each year. We were told to write something that we were thankful for and then fold it up and put it in the wall. 'I'm thankful I'm alive!' I wrote.

Death is the only thing I'm properly scared of. As long as I'm alive, I feel I can do anything and be anything. I'm having such a great time and everything is so good that the only thing that scares me is being struck down dead. It's the one thing I'm afraid of in the whole world. I just don't want my life to end.

We spent two weeks travelling around Israel and I enjoyed every minute. The exchange rate at the time meant that everything seemed very cheap. I had £100 spending money, which was around a thousand shekels, and as nothing seemed to cost more than five shekels, or 50p, I felt really rich. My friends and I bought friendship bracelets and the boys kept giving us sweets and presents because they had loads of money. It made us feel really special.

We met a group of Americans at one of the youth hostels. They were doing the same thing as us: travelling around and seeing the sights. Our teachers were very watchful of us and made sure that the boys and girls never mixed during the night. There was a girls' dorm and a boys' dorm and the teachers constantly checked that the boys didn't go near the girls' dorm. But, of course, they didn't check the American camp, so the American boys would sneak over to our dorm every night without getting caught.

One evening I ended up getting off with a boy called Noah. Oh my God, he was so ugly! The tallest, lankiest, ugliest kid! I guess I found him interesting because he was American. Ah, these Americans! I thought. I was going out with Adam at the time and unfortunately he found out about Noah. I don't know who told him, but it definitely wasn't me. Adam was really upset and didn't talk to me for the rest of the holiday, which I was gutted about. Luckily, we made it up when we got back to school and were best friends again after that.

Everyone went home after two weeks, but I stayed on for an extra week and went to visit Karen's best friend on the kibbutz where she and her family were living. Before she met my dad, Karen had also lived there. It's a modern kibbutz, with new housing; it's more like a village than anything else, and my dad has a house there now.

I had a brilliant time there, even though I'd never met any of the people before. 'Hello, Dad and Karen have told me a lot about you,' I kept saying on the first day. I spent the week hanging out with all the kids on the beach. It felt like such a safe environment; it's not dangerous for kids to play out, like it is in England, and everybody stayed at the beach until 4 a.m. without having to worry. It was really cool and I could easily have stayed there for the rest of the summer holidays.

It was great going back to school the following autumn. I was so happy at King Solomon, and things were a lot better at home, too. I was getting on well with my mum and dad and was being much nicer to Jemma and Matthew.

It may sound stupid, but the highlight of that year for me

was being invited to a party thrown by Lee in the sixth form! I was really excited when he invited me and told me to bring a friend. I was the coolest girl in my year for that one day: 'Oh my God, are you really going to Lee's party?' I don't know why I was invited, to be honest. We weren't that cool in my year. I took along my friend Thalia, who was quite old for her age, too. She was the first girl at King Solomon to try smoking, so she was kind of on my level.

The party was at the King George pub near Hangman's Hill in Loughton. They say that Hangman's Hill is haunted: if you drive your car up there and stall, some supernatural power drags you up to the top. I've never been up there because I'm too scared. Fortunately the pub wasn't actually on the hill, so that was all right. It was a pub with a swimming pool out the back. It was all so posh over in Loughton, such a different world! I felt so cool as me and Talia walked into the party. I remember it vividly. All the older lot were there, and the older girls looked shocked, as if to say, 'What are *they* doing here?' They weren't very friendly but we didn't care. We felt so good just being there.

I spent quite a lot of time at the party with a boy called Adam, who I'd fancied for ages. He was going out with a really pretty, popular girl, but a few weeks later he dumped her and got with me. I felt like the coolest girl in the world.

From then onwards I became good friends with Lee, Joel and Adam. Lee had the biggest house, opposite Ali C's. His dad had a Porsche with gull wing doors that opened upwards. Once when we went round to see him, he pretended it was his. 'And this is mine,' he said proudly, showing us into the garage.

'Get off my car!' his dad yelled from the house.

'Aha!' we said, laughing.

The following year I passed all my GCSEs. I got thirteen, a mixture of As, Bs and a couple of Cs, including English Literature and English Language, Maths, Triple Science, Music, Drama and Textiles and Sewing. Some of them I really worked hard at, others I didn't bother so much with, but I still passed. I think I just got lucky.

That was the first year I auditioned for *The X Factor*, aged sixteen. The auditions were held at Wembley and I was one of the last people to be seen. My mum came with me and we queued for hours, from six in the morning until ten at night. We sat and waited, sat and waited, in a queue of 30,000 people, listening to everyone singing and practising their moves. My mum was so good to stay with me all that time. It must have been even more boring for her than it was for me.

Finally, it was time for my audition, and I sang 'Over The Rainbow' – of course.

'Sorry, no,' I was told after I'd sung a couple of lines. 'Not this year.'

'OK, thank you. Bye,' I said. It was so funny. I was such a geek.

Mum was waiting for me. 'I didn't get through,' I said.

She just smiled at me and said, 'Oh well, come on then.' After sixteen hours of waiting and less than two minutes auditioning, we left. Dream over; back to school.

By now, all my friends seemed to have lost their virginity. People at school were always talking about having done it. If you were still a virgin, as I was, you'd just sit there, saying nothing. You wouldn't admit that you hadn't, but you wouldn't say that you had, either. You'd just nod and smile and stay silent.

One weekend I went to an adventure holiday centre,

where we all went canoeing and climbing and stuff. On the first night, some of us got drunk and I found myself going into a bedroom in one of the dorms with a boy on the trip. The dorm was deserted. We didn't speak. Nothing was agreed between us – there was no exchange of words – but that night I think I lost my virginity to him, although I was never really sure if we'd done it properly. I had no idea what to do.

Now I could sit around with my friends at school and say that I'd done it, even though I wasn't truly certain that I had. Is that it? I wondered. Did I really do it? Is that what everybody else does? Since me and him were never going to discuss it, I was never going to find out. I couldn't ask my friends, because although they all used to talk about it, I don't think any of them really knew what they were on about, so I just left it at that.

I decided to stay on at King Solomon for the sixth form. Sadly, the gorgeous older boys had all left school now – Ah, the older boys have gone! – and they weren't cool outside of school, weirdly, because they weren't the older boys any more. They were just men. They were so attractive in the enclosed school environment, but out in the real world you thought, There has to be someone better!

I chose to do Biology, Maths, English Literature and Law A Levels, partly to please my mum, who really wanted me to go to university and on to a career that would earn me lots of money. But my heart wasn't in it, even though I loved English Literature and Biology. The problem was that I wasn't singing any more, because I wasn't studying music, and I really wanted to sing. It wasn't long before I began to feel restless. I enjoyed writing and analysing plays and books, like *The Merchant of Venice* and *Great Expectations*, and I enjoyed learning about the cell structure of plants – it was all really interesting – but I didn't want to be a writer or a biologist, I wanted to be a singer. It sounds crazy, but I would have been happier if my A Level subjects had just been hobbies.

When I stayed with my dad in Hornchurch, I often bumped into my friend Lauren. We'd lost contact when she left King Solomon after GCSEs to study music and drama at Havering College, just nearby. Havering had a good music department and she was enjoying herself there. We met up a couple of times and became close again and I started thinking about leaving King Solomon and joining her at Havering College.

I looked into it and found out that I could take a diploma in Musical Theatre, which would be the equivalent of taking three A Levels. I would have to wait until the following September before I could sign up for the course, but it sounded fantastic and I decided that it would definitely be worth the wait. Oh my God! I thought. I can study something I'm really passionate about and still go to university afterwards.

'Mum,' I said, halfway through my first year in the sixth form. 'I really want to go to Havering College to do Musical Theatre.' I was banking on the fact that she had always said there was something about my personality that was different, and that from an early age something had told her I wasn't going to be your average nine-to-five girl.

There was a long pause. 'It sounds like a good idea,' she said, 'as long as you stick it out and get your diploma, because that will give you choices.'

In the meantime, I needed to support myself, so I got a job in a massive fish and chip shop called Oh My Cod! just down the road from the college. I loved it, and eventually I got Lauren a job there, too, which made it even more fun.

The owners of Oh My Cod! were Turkish and Greek – they sold fish and chips on the Greek side of the shop and kebabs on the Turkish side. Me and Lauren always worked on the fish and chip side. I got to know a lot of the regulars well and I always remembered what they ordered so they really liked me. 'Two cod and chips, with extra vinegar?' I'd say, and I used to throw in extra gherkins, too, which pleased them.

The people who worked at Oh My Cod! were all really nice, and they often used to cook us grilled fish for supper. Sometimes on a Friday night we'd turn up with a Mars Bar and they'd deep fry it for us. Delicious, but not very healthy, I know!

It didn't bother me that I constantly stank of fish and chips: my hair, my clothes, everything. My parents used to hate it, but I didn't mind. I'd just jump in the shower after work and go out. It was a bit of a pain having long hair, but often I'd put it in plaits and go out without drying it. There wasn't time to bother with a hairdryer, I just wanted to get out!

I tried again for *The X Factor* that year, but it was the same old story. I sat in the queue for ages, with my mum – yes, she came again, the saint! – and I sang 'Over The Rainbow' again.

'Thank you, but no,' they said. 'See you next year.'

'OK,' I said, and we went home.

Despite my *X Factor* failures, this was a very happy time for me. My job was fun, I was having a really good time with my friends and it was great to have my own money at last. Life was opening up and I was really looking forward to

September, when my course would start. Then everything would be perfect and I would finally be doing what I wanted. I forgot that life rarely goes according to plan.

Chapter 5

'You know what?' Lauren said. 'We need to find a good night out.' Now that Lauren and I were working we could afford to dress up and make a night of it.

The old brewery in Romford had been a hangout of ours at school, back when it was dark, dingy and deserted. Now it had been done up and turned into a shopping centre and leisure complex, with restaurants, a cinema and a bowling alley with a bar. One night me and Lauren were drinking in the bowling bar when we noticed a sign saying, 'Karaoke Every Wednesday'.

'That's it!' Lauren said. 'We have to come here every Wednesday.'

So we did, and it was so good that we went on meeting there every Wednesday for ages. During that time, we met loads of great people and built up a massive group of friends. Our mate Elise used to come with her boyfriend, and he'd sometimes bring along his brother, Dean. Dean's best friends were Phil, Wonky and Steve, and Phil brought along his girlfriend Sam. The group just grew from there and it was the best fun.

I really liked Phil and Sam. Phil loved singing karaoke, especially 'How To Save A Life' by The Fray and 'New Shoes' by Paolo Nutini. Sam wasn't a singer, though, and she never sang; she just hung out with everyone and talked. The only time I ever heard her sing was one night when we all went to Brannigan's, a club in Romford, and Sam was the designated driver. We sang at the tops of our voices in the car on the way home. It was hilarious. We were all trying to be the loudest and Sam was shouting the words as she drove.

Quite a few of Lauren's friends from college started coming along to the karaoke and I got on with all of them. The only person I had a problem with was Elise's boyfriend's brother, Dean. He was often very cool with me and used to ignore me a lot of the time. It infuriated me, because I had a laugh with everyone else. But Dean made it obvious that I annoyed him. He was always telling me to go away and I hated it.

Tall and skinny, Dean was two years older than me and reminded me of the chimney sweep in *Mary Poppins*: cap on, dirty face, just a real boy. He was a car body worker who sprayed cars and worked on their exteriors, like Kenickie in *Grease*. He was definitely more Kenickie than Danny.

My strongest memory of Dean from those early days at the karaoke bar is of him playing pool, wearing a polo and jeans, with a grandad hat on his head and a fag in his mouth (back then, you could smoke indoors). I'd take the mickey out of him and tell him he looked like a grandad. 'So?' he'd reply coolly, making it clear that I got on his nerves.

Something about his attitude intrigued me. The more he ignored me, the more I wanted him to like me. But he really irritated me as well. I could never make up my mind about him. I used to look at his cap and think, I hate your grandad hat! Even though I liked it really.

Dean hated going to the karaoke, but his brother used to drag him along for support because he was seeing Elise. 'I've got to go and see her; come with me, please,' he'd say.

Elise used to ring me up and say, 'You coming out?'

'Is Dean coming?' I'd ask, and I'd hear her say, 'Are you coming, Dean?'

'No,' would come his voice down the phone, 'I ain't coming.'

Oh, I'd think, feeling disappointed. He's not coming.

Occasionally we played pool together at the bar, and after he beat me, he'd say, 'You can buy me a drink now.'

'No! What the hell!' I'd splutter angrily. 'Why would I do that when you ignore me the whole time?'

This went on for months and it really started to bug me. Why don't you fancy me? I thought, as it dawned on me how much I fancied him. I really like you!

I used to sing karaoke in the hope that he was watching me, but he never cared whether I was singing or not. 'Did you see me?' I'd say breathlessly after I'd finished a song.

'No,' he'd reply shortly, and if I was lucky he might add, 'Sorry, I was playing pool.'

It just made me like him even more. I'll go out with him one day, I decided. But in the meantime, I was always telling my friends, 'I really like him, but he doesn't like me. It's so unfair.'

'Don't bother,' Elise told me. 'He's not interested in having a girlfriend. I've never seen him even look at a girl.'

Several girls were obsessed with him, and the less interested he was in them, the more they seemed to fancy him. I suppose girls must like a cool guy, because they were all over him, myself included. He's not even that good looking, I thought angrily. The situation became more and more frustrating.

Then, after months of ignoring me, he suddenly changed his mind. It was March 2007 and one night Lauren said to him, 'Don't you like her? Come on, you like her really, don't you?'

And he said, 'Yes.'

'What?' I screeched when she told me.

I immediately texted him. 'I heard you like me!'

'I might do,' he texted back. 'You're all right, ain't you?' It wasn't the most romantic message in the world, but it made my heart leap.

He asked me to his house, which was just around the corner. Everyone knows his family around where I live. He introduced me to them and they were really friendly. 'All right?' they said. Dean was really nice to me, too, and straight away he said, 'Let's go out.'

The next time I saw him he said, 'So, are you my girl-friend, or what?'

'Yes!' I said. I was really excited about it. I'd fancied him for such a long time and now at last it had happened.

All our friends were amazed. 'Oh my God!' they kept saying, when they saw us out together. It was a really big deal as no one had seen him with anyone before.

I didn't sleep with Dean straight away. I waited a month, partly because I felt a bit insecure about his feelings for me. He'd been distant with me for so long that I couldn't help wondering why he'd suddenly changed his mind and decided to go out with me. It made me wary. I know a month doesn't sound like a long time, but in the scale of my life it was. Dean was only the second person I'd slept with, so making up my mind to sleep with him was a big deal for me. We used con-doms from the start and never, ever had unprotected sex.

He was really nice, but he wasn't all over me. He wasn't that kind of guy. We had a good time, but he didn't tell me he loved me or anything; he was too cool to be openly affectionate. Of course, that made me determined to make him like me more. Come on, LOVE ME! I thought.

I always tried to be at my best when I was around him. At the time I was really good at pool and he seemed to find that cool. Yes, he thinks I'm good at pool! I'd think. I was on the pool table all the time, challenging his friends.

It was like a game, really, or a school romance. I'd see him at the karaoke and think, Oooh, there he is! At least now he clapped when I sang a song. Everyone clapped when you sang, so I would have been devastated if I'd turned round to find that he wasn't.

I tried to be as cool as I could. I couldn't be needy or ask him why he wasn't more affectionate – that would have made me cringe. 'You don't need to ask those questions,' I told myself. 'Just be cool and eventually he'll come round.' To be honest, I think I was more obsessed with him than I was in love with him. I really wanted to make him like me.

I'd save up my money, so that I had cash when I saw him and could pay for things. I really wanted to show him that, Yup, I earn my own money, and for him to see that I was self-sufficient and didn't need anyone.

He probably just thought, Ah, bless her! But he stayed with me, so he must have liked it. I loved it when we went to the cinema together, because he wasn't as detached when we were on our own. It was so exciting for me. Yes, I've got him to myself! And when we were watching a film at his house, I'd cuddle up to him a bit. If no one was around, he was more relaxed about that sort of thing. We often stayed in and watched films with my mum, as well. They got on well, which was good.

As the summer went on, me and Dean became really close. Sometimes we'd go and hang out at his best friend Phil's house. Phil was building a bar at the end of the house, with a line of bottles with optics and a pool table. Everyone was impressed by this bar and we had such a laugh ordering crazy cocktails from 'Phil the bartender'. His parents were always really welcoming and so we ended up going there quite a lot.

In August, I went to Tenerife on a girls' holiday for two weeks. There were eight of us and we were definitely going to have a good time, but as we got off the plane after we landed, I suddenly felt sick. 'Oh no, I feel ill,' I said.

'You need a drink!' one of my mates suggested.

We immediately started drinking anything and everything: vodka, rum, brandy, whatever. We'd order a massive fish bowl cocktail, usually a Blue Lagoon or a Sex on the Beach, then we'd all dip a straw in and that was it, we were on our way! When you're on holiday, anything goes, doesn't it? Especially when you're seventeen. We had such a good time. At night we'd go out clubbing wearing nothing but a vest and shorts. Everybody would be off their face. Then in the day we'd lie on sunbeds doing absolutely nothing, dead to the world, blind to the sunshine.

I was obviously overdoing it, though, because I was sick every morning when I woke up. I must have drunk too much last night. I mustn't do that again, I'd think. I would resolve to go easy on the cocktails that evening, but then I'd sleep through the whole day on my sunbed and at night time I'd suddenly wake up. 'What are we drinking?' I'd yell. 'Come on, girls!' I seemed to follow the same pattern every day for the whole two weeks: feeling sick all day and great all night.

When we got back from Tenerife, I enrolled at college. At last, after a six-month wait! I was really excited about the course, but while I was standing in the long queue for the enrollment office, I suddenly came over all dizzy. 'Why is it so hot?' I asked the person behind me. I felt flushed and weak, my vision went fuzzy and my head was spinning, so I had to sit down. This is awful! I thought.

After a few minutes, my head cleared and I started to feel better. I went back to my place in the queue and eventually signed up to my course. But I still didn't feel right, so I went home and slept for a couple of hours. A couple of times in the days that followed, I felt dizzy and faint again. It was so weird. I'm never ill, so I couldn't understand it.

In the weeks to come, I threw myself into my course and studied hard. There were lots of different modules, including voice anatomy, singing, drama, history of drama, principles of drama, ballet, tap, street and contemporary dance. In principles of drama we learnt about the various theories of acting and acting methods, which I found fascinating, while in drama we'd pick a musical and study it. Sometimes we'd perform it, or scenes from it, too.

I chose to do Musical Theatre because I could get the equivalent of three A Levels out of it, which meant I could go to university if I wanted, to study English or Law. It was good to know I had that to fall back on. Once you have the right number of UCAS points, you can go and study anything, as long as you don't want to be a doctor or something that requires a specific qualification. My secret dream, though, was to get into RADA, even though I knew I wasn't good enough. Failing that, I was hoping to get really good results and go to university or get a job at a top musical theatre.

If I couldn't get into the West End or be a singer, I wanted to teach musical theatre. So I had to qualify in it. I would still love to be on the West End stage one day. I've seen lots of West End musicals, even the modern ones like *Dirty*

Dancing and *We Will Rock You*. I love them all. I love the energy and excitement of live theatre.

A couple of weeks after my enrolment I went out for lunch with my dad and Karen at a café near my college. 'I keep fainting,' I told them lightheartedly, then I went on to describe what had happened the day I'd enrolled. 'I was in the queue and I couldn't even stand up!' I found it funny. 'I thought I was going to die or something,' I added with a laugh.

'That's strange,' Karen said, leaning forward.

'Oh my God, what is that smell?' I said, recoiling from her. 'Eurgh! Your breath stinks! It's making me feel sick.'

'What does it smell of?' she asked curiously.

'Ugh!' I put my hand up to cover my nose. 'Onions!'

'But I haven't even eaten an onion for days,' she said.

'What could it be, then?' I asked. 'It's definitely onions.' We looked around the café for the source of the smell. There was a man on the other side of the room eating a hot dog with onions in it. 'Yuk, that stinks!' I exclaimed.

'I can't even smell it,' Karen said. 'What's wrong with you?'

'I don't know, I just can't stand that smell, I suppose,' I said. 'Can we leave?'

Karen glanced at my dad and then back at me. 'Of course,' she said.

A couple of days later, I saw her again. My dad had just bought a flat to rent out and she was having the carpets laid. I was hanging about, not doing anything – definitely not helping! – and out of the blue Karen said, 'I think you're pregnant.' She didn't refer to what had happened in the café or on the day I'd enrolled, she just said, 'I think you're pregnant.'

I was stunned. 'What are you talking about?' I said, frowning.

'I think you're pregnant,' she repeated.

'Don't be so stupid!' I said, and then for some reason I started crying.

'Why are you crying?' she asked gently.

'I don't know. I don't want to be pregnant. I'm not pregnant. I don't even know why I'm crying,' I sobbed. 'I'm definitely not pregnant because I've had my period.' I broke down and cried hysterically.

'Whatever you say,' she said, and she left it at that.

The next time I went round to Dad's house, she came into my room holding out a pregnancy test. 'If you're sure you're not pregnant, prove it,' she challenged.

'Go away,' I said angrily. 'Leave me alone.'

'Come on,' she insisted. 'Let's settle this now.'

Reluctantly, I took the test from her and followed the instructions, weeing on the end of the stick for three seconds. Before I'd even put it on the side to wait for the results, a blue cross appeared in the test window, signifying a positive result. It was so quick. I was pregnant.

'Huh?' I mumbled, unable to believe my eyes. It couldn't be true. It had to be a mistake.

Karen just looked at me without saying anything. 'But I can't be pregnant!' I burst out. 'I've been getting my period as usual. I've been having heavy periods.'

'You're pregnant, Stacey,' she said, pointing at the test. 'Whatever you say, you're pregnant.'

'No!' I howled. 'I can't be!' Tears started pouring down my cheeks. It didn't add up. I was still getting my period every month. Me and Dean had never once had unprotected sex. Plus, I hadn't got any bigger or heavier, although it wouldn't have surprised me if I had, because I was eating fried food almost every night at the fish and chip shop and drinking loads.

I was in so much denial. 'The test must be wrong,' I insisted.

'Fine, we'd better go to the doctor, then,' Karen replied. We went to my GP the next day. He didn't even bother to give me a pregnancy test. He simply had to feel my belly to be sure that there was a baby there, because the foetus was already so developed. 'Yes, you're definitely pregnant,' he said.

On a subconscious level, I think I must have known – perhaps I'd known for a while. Looking back, it suddenly seemed obvious why I'd felt so sick in the mornings on holiday in Tenerife. Now I understood why I'd been feeling faint for the past couple of weeks. Even so, I couldn't blame myself for not realizing. If you've never been pregnant before, how would you know? I had no idea what it felt like. And believe me, if you don't know better, a baby kicking in the early stages feels just like wind! Karen had spotted the symptoms because she'd had my little brother two years earlier and it was still fresh in her mind. My mum was less likely to notice because it had been sixteen years since she'd had her last child.

Back home, Karen said, 'You've got to tell your dad. I'm not keeping this a secret from him.'

I had no choice, so I went to find my dad. He was sitting in front of his computer. 'Dad, I'm pregnant,' I said.

'You'd better not be,' he said without turning round.

OK, that's one out of the way, I thought. 'Well, I am, so see you!' I said.

He turned round to face me. 'What do you want?' he said impatiently. It was obvious that he thought I was just trying

86

to get his attention. 'Hurry up and tell me, what do you want?'

'Dad, I *am* pregnant,' I said.

He erupted. He was really angry. 'How could you let this happen?' he yelled. 'How could you be so stupid?' But my dad's the kind of person who gets angry and then gets over it and says, 'Where are we going to go from here? What are we going to do?'

Telling my mum was much worse. As soon as she heard, her face fell and she looked sad beyond belief. 'I'm really, really sorry,' she said dully. She stretched her arms out. 'Come on, give me a cuddle.'

I couldn't bear it; I would have much preferred her to get angry and shout at me. 'Hate me, Mum!' I told her. 'Tell me that what I've done is really awful. Tell me I'm rubbish. Tell me I'm the worst daughter in the world.'

'No,' she said. 'I'm just sad for you.'

'But why? Aren't children supposed to be a blessing?'

She sighed. 'You'd just got into college, you were getting your life on track and doing the things you wanted to do, but now that's all going to change. I just feel really sad for you.' She knew how much I loved being a kid, how much I loved living my life without responsibilities, floating in and out of home, going here, there and everywhere. 'It just means that nothing can be the same again, which is going to be really tough for you,' she said. 'I wish I could make it different, but I can't.'

I knew she was right and it was devastating to hear. I could no longer be the girl who said, 'Let's all go to Ibiza, everyone!' I just couldn't be that girl any more. I was going to have to change completely.

Chapter 6

I cried my eyes out for days. I was completely and utterly miserable. I really didn't want this to be happening to me just when I felt like I'd sorted everything out in my life. I was at college; I had a job; I had great friends and I had the boyfriend I really, really wanted. I couldn't bear to think how he would react when I told him I was pregnant.

I rang him from my dad's house and said, 'Are you coming round?' Then when he arrived, I said, 'Let's go out.' As we walked up the road, I took a deep breath and said, 'I'm pregnant.'

There was a long pause. Poor thing, he was probably so shocked that words completely failed him. What would I have said in his situation? I'm sure I wouldn't have known how to deal with it either.

Neither of us could get our heads round it. We just couldn't process it. At seventeen and nineteen we were both so young, and it was so unexpected. We had no idea what to do, no idea at all. It was too much, too soon.

My mum and dad didn't advise me one way or the other. They were worried that I might blame them if they swayed my opinion, especially if I regretted my decision later. All the same, I desperately wanted someone to give me some advice.

I didn't know what to do. My mum and dad told me they would support whatever decision I made, but I felt very confused. There were so many negatives to having a baby: I would have to leave college, stop going out with my mates and give up work and my independence. What were the positives? I tried my hardest, but I couldn't think of any. So I asked my mum to make an appointment at a termination clinic.

Mum made inquiries and first we went to a walk-in centre in Barking, where we talked everything through. I explained the circumstances: I was seventeen, at college, and the pregnancy was a total accident. What else could I do, apart from have a termination? To my relief, the counsellor I saw made it very clear that I wasn't being judged. She was there to help and advise me so that I could make the right decision.

A week later, me, Mum, Dad, Karen and Dean all piled into my dad's car and drove to a termination clinic in Essex. It was a really awkward journey. No one said much; we just listened to the radio and pretended everything was normal. When we arrived, Dad wanted to come into the clinic, but they would only allow one person in with me, so I took Mum. Dad, Karen and Dean waited in a café nearby.

At the clinic, me and Mum had a very brief discussion with a counsellor to make sure this was what I really wanted. Next, we were shown into a consultant's room, where I was given a scan. The screen was turned away from me so I couldn't see the image, but the consultant called my mum over, saying, 'Come and take a look.'

I watched Mum's face as she looked at the screen. Her expression changed completely. Although she was struggling not to show her emotions, she looked really sentimental and upset. I don't think she'd expected to see what appeared to be a well-formed baby, with arms and legs.

Of all the people I could have come with, I had to bring my mum, I thought. 'Stop it,' I said. 'I'm not looking, and it's not helping that you're making that face.' Then I saw that she had tears in her eyes. For goodness sake!

The consultant measured the baby and told us it was around four and a half months old. It had hands and a face and a brain. Because it was so developed, having a termination would be more complicated than if it had been earlier on in the pregnancy. He explained the procedure to me and it sounded really awful.

I was horrified beyond belief. There's no way on earth I'm going to do that, I thought. I don't think anyone in their right mind would. To be honest, I still don't think I could have done it even if they'd said, 'OK, no problem, we can do it the easy way.' All I needed to hear was that they were going to kill it. The harsh reality of that fact changed my mind. I couldn't do it, I just couldn't. There wasn't one bone in my body that could have gone through with that. No, I thought. No.

'I can't do it, Mum,' I said.

She smiled. 'Come on, let's go,' she said, and we got up and left.

'Is that it?' my dad asked when we joined them in the café where they were waiting. 'All over?' He assumed I'd had the termination already.

'I didn't do it, Dad,' I said tearfully.

You should have seen the smiles on Dad's and Karen's faces when they heard that! They were overjoyed. It was the best news they'd ever heard. I was really surprised as they hadn't given me any hint that they didn't want me to have a termination.

My dad started crying his eyes out. 'Oh, thank God!' he kept saying. My mum looked really relieved.

'Mum, Dad, Karen? Why didn't you tell me?' I said, looking at each of them in turn. 'No one told me!'

'We couldn't,' they said. 'It's your decision, don't you see? You have to do what you have to do.' Not for love nor money would they have told me that I was about to go and do the most horrendous thing.

It was a really emotional scene in that café. My mum was happy because, after looking at the scan and seeing the baby, she already loved it. Karen was happy because she was thinking that her two-year-old Josh, my half-brother, would have someone his own age to play with. My dad was happy for the same reason, and also because he just didn't want me to have an abortion. Out of my whole family — all the cousins, even though some of them are six and seven years older than me — I was the first person to be pregnant with a grandchild, so I would have been killing the only grandchild in the family.

I didn't feel happy like they did, though. I didn't know how I felt. I still didn't want a baby; it's just that I didn't want to kill it. Right, I'm not killing it, but what the hell am I going to do? I thought.

I looked at Dean. 'Sorry, I just couldn't go through with it,' I said to him.

'You need to do whatever you think is best,' he said, 'and I'll support you.'

A few days after I'd been to the clinic, it was my eighteenth birthday. Everybody was turning eighteen that year and they were going out to massive clubs like Ministry of Sound, but I couldn't drink and I couldn't go anywhere to celebrate, so I did nothing. That's when it really hit home how much my life was changing. My birthday didn't mean a thing now. I wasn't allowed to have fun any more. There would be no more carefree evenings out, no laughing all night with my friends; from now on my life would be nothing, nothing, nothingness. I hated it. On my birthday I sat at home, pregnant, wallowing in self-pity.

I even had to leave college because a quarter of the course was dance, so I wasn't allowed to stay on for Health and Safety reasons. I tried to argue with them. 'But I've been doing it while I was pregnant,' I protested.

'Yes, but no one knew. Sorry, but we can't keep you on in the knowledge that you're pregnant.'

So that was it. Suddenly I felt as if I had nothing to give, so I started cutting myself off from people. I isolated myself and went a bit weird. I didn't want to speak to anyone and I definitely didn't want to tell people I was having a baby. I was embarrassed. I didn't tell my friends for ages. In the past I'd been really judgmental of teenagers who had kids. Other people would say, 'Look at her, a kid with a kid,' and I'd look over and think, Yes, you are a bit young. But mostly I'd think, How do you go out? What do you do all day? Poor you!

I kept wondering if it was my fault that I'd got pregnant, and I still don't know. The fact is that condoms are only 98 per cent safe, so there's always a 2 per cent chance that they won't work. Perhaps I should have been on the pill or had a contraceptive injection or implant. I don't know. I had a nagging feeling that I hadn't done everything I could have done to avoid getting pregnant, although it was too late for regrets now.

As the woman, I'm the one who should have been more bothered about pregnancy. A man can get someone pregnant and leave. He doesn't have to stay. He doesn't have a bond with his child during pregnancy, whereas a woman does, almost from the minute it's conceived – although that wasn't the case with me! I should have been more scared of the consequences, because I was the one who could be left pregnant and alone, having to decide whether to get rid of the baby or not. No man will ever be in that situation. It's not his decision to make.

I should have thought about it more and been more cautious. Dean was my first proper boyfriend and I should have gone to my mum for advice about contraception. I know that she would have taken me to the chemist and got me the pill – she's so supportive and always has been – but I didn't want to talk to her about sex or even mention it, because I was too embarrassed. So I didn't think about it and used whatever was there, which was condoms.

Talking about sex makes me cringe, even to this day. Unless it's the person I'm doing it with, when it's the total opposite – I'm completely different in that situation. But otherwise I think, It's not your business. Go away! In my view, there are things you talk about and things you don't. I find it uncomfortable being around the kind of people who describe their sex lives in detail. 'And then I did this . . . and then he did that.'

How embarrassing. Where do I look? I think. Kill me now. Swallow me up in a hole. I find it so crude and I'd rather they didn't say anything, because I just don't want to know. It's funny, I've got a baby, so I've obviously had sex. Everyone in the maternity ward at the hospital where I gave birth has seen my noony, but I still cannot talk about it.

As long as I could disguise my bump, I still went out occasionally. One night Lauren tempted me out to a pub near her house in Chigwell and we soon settled into a chat. She was in the middle of telling me a story about one of her teachers at college when my phone rang.

'It's Dean,' I said as I looked at the caller ID. 'Hello?' I said.

He didn't say hello back. He sounded really upset, but I couldn't catch what he was saying. I didn't get it. I looked at Lauren and smirked slightly, as if to say, 'What is going on?' Dean wasn't making any sense.

'Come on, what's wrong?' I kept asking. I had no idea that the news he was about to give me would shake me to the core. I was completely unprepared for what was coming; I didn't expect it at all. It took him about ten minutes to calm down, then finally he managed to get the words out. Our friends Phil and Sam, from the karaoke nights, had been killed in a car crash. It was a head-on collision and they'd died straightaway because they weren't wearing seat belts.

I heard the words, but their meaning was lost on me. I just couldn't take in what he was saying. 'It can't be true,' I said. There was no way I could believe it. Phil and Sam were our friends; Phil was Dean's best friend in the world. They couldn't be dead. It wasn't possible. 'You're joking,' I said, hoping against hope that it wasn't true.

But he was serious. He was at the hospital. It wasn't a joke; there hadn't been a mix-up. Phil and Sam were dead.

'Shall I come down?' I asked, in a haze of shock and disbelief.

'No,' he said. Phil and Sam had died before they'd arrived at the hospital, so there wasn't any point in anyone being there, apart from their parents.

I can't remember how the phone call ended, but I do know that I then had to tell Lauren. She was as shocked as I was. Neither of us knew what to say. I phoned my mum. Everything was a blur. The words sounded all wrong as they came out of my mouth. '*Sam and Phil are dead, they're dead.*' I couldn't believe I was saying them. 'Mum, can I sleep in your bed tonight?' I asked. I found it hard to sleep that night. I just lay awake, staring at the ceiling in total shock.

The next day, I went to where the accident had happened. I couldn't believe my eyes when we got there. I'd never seen anything like it in my life. There were fields of flowers laid out around the lamppost where the cars had crashed, more flowers than I've ever seen before. So many people were grieving for Phil and Sam. I sat next to the lamppost for ages, keeping a vigil, paying my respects. I remember Phil's mum and dad kept coming backwards and forwards. They were really cut up, just in bits. I felt for them so much.

Sam and Phil's friends met up constantly in the days leading up to the funerals. No one knew what else to do with themselves. We didn't know what to say to each other – we just didn't get it – but we needed to be together, mourning together. The weird thing was that I kept expecting Phil and Sam to walk in and join us at any moment. It didn't sink in that I would never see them again.

When someone dies, it's horrible, but when someone dies young, it's worse than anything. They were nineteen years old. It was so, so sad. When something like that happens, it makes you realize that you can die at any time. Until then, you think, I can do anything. I can jump off anything. I can go anywhere. But when Phil and Sam died, it brought home to me how close life and death really are.

Phil's body was laid out at a funeral director's just round the corner from my house, and since me and Lauren hadn't had a chance to say goodbye or anything, we went to see him. But I will never, ever go and see someone in an open coffin again and I will never let my children go. Phil looked so different, so pale and old. It was really weird and I didn't like seeing him like that at all.

The funerals took place quite soon afterwards and they were packed; there were hundreds and hundreds of people at both of them. Phil's funeral was so awful, so sad. It was just terrible to see his mum and dad. The church was completely full, with people standing in the aisles and spilling out through the doors. There were hundreds of friends and relatives; I've never seen a funeral like it.

The funeral of a young person is very different to other funerals. My grandad's funeral in 2010 was much more of a celebration, because he'd lived a long, happy life and was a longstanding, active member of his community in the Forest of Dean, where he'd been a teacher and a vicar. Representatives from the British Legion were there, because he'd served in the RAF, and there were past members of his congregation and ex-pupils all present to pay their respects. Grandad had buried a lot of his friends, so the funeral wasn't packed out with his mates, like Phil and Sam's, but neither was there the choking sense of horror and tragedy that everyone feels when their loved ones die before their time.

At Sam's funeral I sang her favourite song, 'Wind Beneath My Wings', in the church. Everyone was crying and I had to block out my feelings to concentrate on getting through it and keeping my voice from wavering. I wanted to do the best for her and all the people who loved her so much. It was horrible, heartbreaking, just the saddest day ever.

What was strange, though, was that I didn't feel properly sad until a few weeks afterwards, because it all felt so unreal. It was only when I went to ring Phil and Sam to see if they were coming to karaoke that the reality sank in, or if I saw something funny that I wanted to text one of them about.

I'd start to ring them and then realize that I couldn't. I couldn't ring them, text them or see them ever again. It was the oddest thing.

I was still going to the karaoke, but it wasn't the same now that Phil and Sam weren't there, and as the weeks passed I became more and more conscious of being pregnant. Dean didn't tell anyone, because I'd asked him not to, and I was skinny enough to get away with it, so no one had guessed yet.

In the end, I told my closest friends my news: the two Laurens, Dana and Mel. They were really good to me, even though I was the worst company. I don't remember a lot between then and the day I went into labour. It was all nothingness, a blur of boredom and depression. When my bump started to show, I stopped going out altogether and spent the days just sitting at home in complete blankness, feeling miserable. My friends would come round and do nothing with me, just sit there and watch me being miserable. I was horrible to be with, but they stuck by me.

Dana even gave up drinking and clubbing to support me. She sat at home with me when everyone else was out, being pregnant with me. 'We'll go next year,' she'd say reassuringly. 'We'll do it all next year.' What a great friend.

Nothing could cheer me up. Not my friends, who came round and spent endless days and evenings keeping me company; not my sister, who was all excited about the baby and kept trying to get me interested in buying baby clothes, and not my mum, who said, 'If we're having a baby, we need to decorate the house and freshen it up.'

I just sat there, an ever-expanding lump, while Mum cheerily painted and decorated around me. I shut out all Mum's positive comments about the baby, I ignored my sister's growing excitement and I barely responded to Dean and my friends when they came round to keep me company. I just stared at the TV thinking, This is it now. My life is over.

Chapter 7

It was six o'clock on a Friday morning and I was asleep on a mattress on the bedroom floor, with my mum sleeping next to me. Dreams were swirling around my head, haunting images of a pram with no baby in it and a baby without a face.

Suddenly I woke up, feeling weird. 'Mum, I'm really uncomfortable,' I complained. She just laughed. Of course I was uncomfortable: I was the size of a house, I was nine months pregnant and the baby was nine days overdue.

I knew for sure that it was a boy now. I'd decided to call him Zachary, which is my favourite boy's name. I was thankful it wasn't a girl. 'Please God, don't let it be a girl,' I'd prayed when I first found out I was pregnant, because I shuddered at the thought of having to deal with a teenager like me. Having a boy would be a whole lot easier, surely.

Zach was so late coming that the hospital had arranged to induce me the next day. He was either going to come out naturally or they were going to force him out. I was dreading it. I kept having dreams about my bump suddenly falling off. Where did it go? Where's my bump?

And how on earth would I cope once he was out? I had no idea what to do with a baby. It was such a daunting responsibility. What if I was no good? What if I made some terrible mistake? In my dreams, I was constantly leaving him places and losing him.

I turned over on the mattress. 'I really can't sleep, Mum,' I said. 'I think there's something wrong.'

'You'll be all right,' she reassured me.

Alarm bells rang in my head. Normally she would have said something like, 'OK, well, let's get you down to the hospital and have you checked out.' What was going on?

Then it dawned on me: She knows! She knew what was coming, which was why she was ignoring my discomfort. 'Mum,' I said, 'I'm in labour, aren't I?'

'No,' she said and she laughed again.

But I could tell I was from the way she was acting. This is it, I thought, my heart pounding with fear. Here goes. Oh no, Mum!

I wanted my mum with me all the time now. I felt scared when I was on my own, so I needed her close, especially at night. She was really supportive, so if she didn't actually sleep next to me, she would be in and out to check on me.

A slow, dull ache spread across my stomach and I felt a spasm of pain. It had finally come, the moment I was dreading. What would happen? I hadn't been to antenatal classes, but I knew to expect pain. I knew that someone was going to ask me to push at some point, after which I'd be giving birth. I knew all of this. I also knew that I was going to have contractions, which would feel like bad period cramps.

A bolt of pain shot up my back. 'Mum!' I called out. 'It hurts!'

'It must be a contraction,' my mum said. 'Hang on, it'll be over soon.'

Oh. My. God. Who said that contractions would feel like a period pain? What a lie! This was pain on another level altogether, like nothing I'd ever known before. And it just got worse and worse and worse. My belly was one big cramping ache. And something was pressing against my back, grinding against my spine from the inside. It hurt so much.

Originally I'd wanted to have a home birth, so I stayed at home, in awful, awful pain, for about eight hours. I lay on the floor; I sat in the bath; I tried every room and every position, just trying to get comfortable. The midwife came round to give me gas and air while I was in the bath, which helped a bit. I told her I didn't want to go to hospital. It was the last thing I wanted, because nobody is allowed in there with you and you never get out.

While the midwife was with me, my dad and Karen turned up with my sister and brothers. Everyone came round. Oh my goodness, I had a houseful of people! Meanwhile, I was upstairs in the bath, thinking, Help!

'Go away!' I shouted.

Time crawled along and the pain got worse. I was in agony. Things weren't going how they should: my cervix wasn't dilating fast enough – only a centimetre every couple of hours – and it just wasn't happening. Then the baby started to get stressed, so all of a sudden it was an emergency. An ambulance arrived, its lights flashing, and I was helped into the back of it. By this point I didn't care about anything except stopping the pain. I wasn't worried about the baby. It was just, 'Get it out of me, because it's hurting!'

Half my family came with me to the hospital, where I was wheeled straight into the maternity ward. In no time, they were sticking a needle into my back and giving me an epidural to ease the pain. The epidural didn't do much, though, because I had a 'back labour' as opposed to a 'front labour', apparently. With a back labour, the awkward position of the baby puts pressure on your back, which means that all the pain is centred there. With a front labour, the pain is more spread out.

'I can still feel it!' I yelled.

'Where?' the anaesthetist asked.

'All the way down my back!'

With a back labour, nothing can get rid of the pain, not even an epidural. An epidural numbs the pain so that it's maybe half as bad, but nothing gets rid of it completely. With a front labour, it's completely different. You have a crunching pain at the front and sides that is completely numbed by an epidural, so you can just rest until the contractions get really close to each other.

Now I was on the bed and I couldn't move. At least my mum and Dean were with me, being supportive. I was only allowed two people in the delivery room, so my dad, sister and brothers had to stay in the waiting room. 'Don't leave me alone, will you, Mum?' I said. The midwives were nice, but I was scared of the nurses. They seemed unfriendly, disapproving, and not at all gentle or kind. I definitely got the impression that some of them were judging me: 'Here she comes: another pathetic, hopeless teenage mother!'

Thankfully the nurses left us alone after I'd been given the epidural. They're not interested until you're ready to push. An anaesthetist popped in every hour or so, to make sure the epidural was OK, but that was it. People come to measure the dilation of the cervix and they're there when the head is coming out, but that's it.

After a couple of hours, I was told that I was probably going to be given a Caesarean because everything was taking so long. But first they were going to try to induce me. They put a drip in my arm, which fed me drugs that would trigger the birth, and about an hour later, Zach started coming out. By now I was so exhausted I could hardly move. I'd gone into labour on Friday morning and it was nearly Sunday.

What do I do?' I asked frantically, although I wasn't sure

I could do anything. I started pushing, but I couldn't feel a thing. I had no sense of when my contractions were coming. 'I don't even know if I'm pushing,' I said. 'Am I pushing? Am I not pushing? Should I be doing it now? What the hell! What is this about?'

'Push,' said the midwife, and a few seconds later Zach came out. But she must have told me to push at the wrong time, because I tore from front to back, all the way down.

They took Zach away and cleaned him up before bringing him back to me, but before I could even see him, they were sewing me up for what seemed like ages and ages. Oh God, it was so horrendous. I was lying on my back, drenched in sweat and completely zonked out, while someone sewed me from top to bottom.

Apparently, women forget how bad labour is once it's over. Well, I'm telling you now, I am never going to forget it! Never, ever, ever! I can't believe that nobody warned me what it would be like. No one said, 'It's the most horrendous thing you will ever go through and you will feel like you're going to die.'

Why didn't my mum warn me? I suppose she didn't want to freak me out. She just said, 'You'll be all right.' So I thought, What the heck! I'll be all right, then. I'll just squeeze it out and go. But oh my goodness, that's not what happens. It is so, so harrowing.

Zach was born at 23:32 on 21 March 2008. I had hated every single second of my long, long labour. It was disgusting. When they finally gave him to me, I didn't even want to hold him. I just thought, Get me some food!

My dad, Karen and Dean came in to see us. My dad had his video camera with him, as usual, but he managed to put it down for a few seconds to hold the baby and coo over him. My dad loves kids. He took a lovely picture of Dean holding Zach, which I still have, along with lots of photos of me looking knackered. At the time, I was barely aware of anyone except my mum. I was completely wrapped up in myself and my unhappiness.

'Can someone get me some toast?' I asked. But I wasn't allowed any food yet, because I was still attached to the drip. Next, I was told that everybody had to leave. It was midnight, way past visiting hours. 'Oh no!' I cried out, feeling completely panicked. I was going to be left on my own. 'Please can my mum stay?' I begged. 'Just my mum? Please let her stay.'

'No visitors allowed,' the nurse said briskly. 'Everyone out, now.'

'OK, Stacey, I'm going to go now,' my mum said softly, taking my hand. 'But I'll be back as soon as they let me, don't you worry.'

'Mum,' I cried. 'Please don't leave me.' But although she wanted to stay, she had to go.

I was devastated. I was completely alone, apart from the baby lying next to me in a box. 'What am I supposed to do with it?' I wondered. To my dismay, I was told that I had to spend the next three days in hospital, because the baby had pooed inside me when it got stressed during labour and they had to make sure I was clean before I went home.

They moved me out of the delivery room and put me in a bed on the ward. Every single baby on that ward was crying; there wasn't one quiet baby. So it's not like you just have *your* baby crying; you have ten other babies screaming their heads off, too. My baby wouldn't stop crying. It just wouldn't stop! And neither could I. I just hated it. I hated it so much.

I didn't feel motherly. I didn't want to breastfeed Zach, but I knew I had to, even though I had no idea how to breastfeed and nobody showed me what to do. I lifted him up to my boob, but he didn't do anything. Nothing was happening. It was so weird. Why am I doing this? I thought, still crying constantly.

One of the nurses came in. 'Come on, you can't cry,' she said sternly. 'Grow up. You're a mother now.'

Her words just made me cry even more. 'But I can't do anything,' I sobbed. 'I can't move, I can't walk, I can't wee.' She just tutted and walked away.

A couple of hours later, another nurse came in to see me. 'Come on,' she said coldly. 'Why aren't you feeding him? Why aren't you changing him? Why aren't you bathing him?'

'Because I don't know how!' I said tearfully. It was true. I didn't know what to do and I didn't know what he wanted. I needed my mum to teach me. I really needed my mum.

The epidural had numbed me all over, so I couldn't tell if I needed a wee or not. Do I need the toilet? I wondered. Something – a weird feeling of pressure – told me I did. I tried to move, but my legs wouldn't respond. Assuming it was still the effect of the epidural, I rang the bell for a nurse. 'Yes?' she said when she arrived, her expression completely devoid of care or sympathy.

'I'm really sorry but I think I need the toilet,' I said.

She pointed to a door. 'It's over there, love,' she said coolly, before turning and walking off. She didn't bother to look at the notes at the end of my bed.

I suddenly felt very anxious. If I was supposed to walk to the toilet on my own, did that mean the epidural should have worn off? I thought it was supposed to take twenty-four hours. I tried to move my legs again. Nothing. Oh my

God, I'm supposed to walk now and I can't move, I thought, aware that paralysis was one of the risks of having an epidural. Maybe I'm paralysed? I rang the bell for the nurse again and again.

Eventually she came back. 'What's wrong?' she said stonily.

'I can't move. I've had an epidural,' I wailed.

She gave me a hard look. 'Then why didn't you say so?'

'I'm sorry,' I sobbed, feeling small and stupid. Although, as the nurse, wasn't she supposed to read my notes at the end of the bed, where it said I'd had an epidural? I was her patient, in her care; wasn't she supposed to be looking after me? But she didn't seem to have an ounce of sympathy for me. She just wasn't interested.

The nurses were so old-fashioned and crazy in their attitude towards me. They didn't seem to have any compassion and they didn't recognize that I was going through the biggest change in my life. It was simply a case of, 'You're having a baby, deal with it. We'll get it out for you and make sure it's healthy, but that's it.'

Maybe when you've been working as a nurse for a long time and you see life and death, day in, day out, you become a bit of a stone. You don't have much emotion left. That's why I think young nurses are often the best, because they still have the passion that inspired them to go into nursing in the first place. They want to make people feel better and cheer them up.

These nurses were really hard and I felt they were judging me. Yes, perhaps young women shouldn't get pregnant outside of marriage, but whatever your morals and values are, your patients are still people, and everyone ought to be treated well in hospital.

I felt so hopeless, like I was nothing. I didn't want a baby.

I really didn't. I went on crying and crying because I just couldn't stop. Obviously, a baby doesn't take to you straight-away, so he wouldn't feed from me and I didn't have a clue how to make him feed. I became hysterical, to the extent that I was crying so much I couldn't breathe.

It must have made Zach so sad, because the more I cried, the more he screamed, and his screaming really distressed me. I've never felt that upset, not in my entire life. It made it worse to think that my crying was causing him anguish, but I just couldn't stop myself. No one came to talk to me or comfort me, nobody came to help, so I sat up with this baby screaming at me, crying my eyes out. It was the craziest, saddest scene.

The next thing I remember was waking up to find my mum there. Thank God! She was holding Zach, who was still crying. The nurses had taken him away from me at some point, because I must have fallen asleep on him or some-thing. I was so exhausted. I couldn't understand why they didn't appreciate how exhausted I was. I'd been pushing him out for days. All I needed was to go to sleep, but they wouldn't help me.

Seeing my mum, I burst into tears. 'Please can I go home?' I begged. 'Please don't leave me here again!'

'I'm here now,' she said, cooing at Zach. She was looking down at him adoringly. 'Who's a beautiful baby?' she asked him, happiness lighting up her face. It had been ages since I'd seen her look so happy. 'He's absolutely perfect,' she said delightedly.

'Mum, I feel so awful,' I sobbed. 'Please take me home. I hate it here.'

But the nurses shooed her away again later and I was left alone for another night. I cried constantly during the three nights I was in hospital. It was so horrendous. I've never been as sad as I was then, all on my own, with a curtain around my bed and a screaming baby by my side.

The nurses didn't get any nicer as time went by either. They took no notice when I said, 'Please, I want to go home. Please, I *need* to go home.' At best, they would just huff impatiently before turning their backs.

A friend of mine from school is a nurse, and she's lost count of the sick children she's looked after whose parents don't even bother to come and visit them. Imagine that. How terrible. There are all these young mums whose babies get ill and they just shove them in hospital and leave them there.

Seeing it from a nurse's perspective, it might not be easy to feel optimistic about the prospects of a sobbing eighteen-year-old girl and her newborn baby. Maybe they thought, What's the betting that baby will be back here in a couple of months with no mum? They had hundreds of people in and out of those wards every week. Perhaps they'd seen it all before, or perhaps they were just so tired and overworked that their sympathy was all used up. Whatever the reason, it shouldn't have been that way. I needed emotional care just as much as physical care, but none of them were prepared – or able – to give it. Their cold, unfriendly attitude made me feel even more miserable and hopeless.

The nurses put me under a huge amount of pressure to breastfeed. 'He's not feeding,' I wailed. 'I can't breastfeed.'

'Of course you can,' they said, tutting with irritation. They'd probably had enough of new mums crying, but a kind word or two would have made such a difference to me. Looking back, I can see that I was going through more than just the baby blues – I was definitely suffering from post-natal depression, although I was unaware of it at the time. I'm surprised that the nurses didn't recognize it.

With the best will in the world, let me say that I will never, ever breastfeed again. One of the most depressing things about having a baby for me was that nobody else could wake up in the middle of the night and feed him. It had to be me. I couldn't leave him with my mum or stepmum for an afternoon and I couldn't go anywhere without getting my boob out. You can't take a break when you breastfeed. It's never-ending.

I felt like a human cow. I was just a thing that Zach ate. It was horrible and I hated it. Changing his nappy wasn't so bad, but it was the endless cycle of nappy-changing and feeding him again and again that got me down. Babies are never full up on breast milk. They want to be fed and fed and fed. Then it becomes a habit. They find it so comforting being on the breast that they never want to get off it. When you take them off, they scream because they want to be back on – not because they're hungry, but because it's comforting – and for the mum that's so difficult.

It's all right if you're the maternal type and want to walk around with your baby attached to your boob all day. My stepmum breastfed my little brother for a year and a half – by the time he was weened, he knew exactly what it was and could ask for it – but I didn't have the same instinct as her. I didn't have the drive to bond with my child through breastfeeding, although perhaps that was because I felt so low.

Through all this, there was no respite. I was so exhausted. Oh my God, I never want to feel like that again! 'It's so tiring,' people tell you, before you have a baby. All right. Whatever. Get over it. It's just a kid, you think to yourself. But, my goodness, I was so drained and depleted after what I'd been through that I didn't have an ounce of energy left. I couldn't do any of the normal things I used to do. It really hurt to wee, too, so to ease the pain I took a bottle of water to the toilet with me and poured cool water onto to my stitches while I weed. I didn't poo for about a week; I didn't dare. I was terrified of pushing in case my stitches ripped open again. My body was completely stressed out.

On top of all that, I couldn't sleep because there was a tiny constant presence next to me, demanding my attention twenty-four hours a day. Zach's needs seemed to be never-ending and I became more and more exhausted. I could sleep when he slept, but then he was awake again within twenty minutes. It got to a point where I just didn't know where I was, who I was talking to or what I was doing. I was in a daze. My life was a blur, and all the days seemed to merge into one.

'Help me,' I begged when Jemma came to see me. I felt utterly desperate and at my wits' end. I didn't know what to do; I just didn't have any energy left. If I had, I would have broken out of hospital and run home.

'Give him to me,' she said, reaching out to take Zach. She sat on the bed and cradled him in her arms. Looking down at the bedcover she said, 'Stacey, these bedclothes are filthy! Hasn't anyone changed them?'

The bed was really dirty. There was blood and everything on it. I'd been in there for nearly three days and no one had changed the sheets. 'Has Zach had a bath?' Jemma asked.

'No,' I said softly.

'That's terrible! Someone should have helped you. Go and ask them if you can give him a bath now,' she said.

After we'd bathed Zach, I quietly crept away for a few

minutes, in search of something to eat or just some time alone – I was happy just to look out of a window and do nothing.

While I was away, a couple of nurses came over to my bed. They didn't bother to ask Jemma if she was Zach's mum; they just checked him over and ticked a list. She went along with it, thinking, Aren't you even going to ask if I'm the child's mother? It was crazy, but I suppose it was understandable, because me and my sister look a bit alike and she was holding the baby.

It was all just routine to them as they moved on to the next bed and then the next. As they left, they said, 'You can go home at four o'clock.'

'Right, thanks,' Jemma said, thinking, OK, I'm not his mum, but go on, tell me anyway.

When I came back she gave me a rundown of everything that had been said. 'I know all of this because they think I'm his mum now,' she said with a laugh.

'Thanks, Jemma,' I said gratefully.

It was a relief to get home from the hospital, because at least I wasn't on my own any more. Physically, though, I felt totally disconnected, as if I was outside of my body. My thoughts and feelings didn't seem to be part of me any more; they were somewhere else in the distance, which I've since learned is a symptom of post-natal depression. Everything inside me felt different and I wasn't healing quickly enough. I was still a bit fat, which meant I couldn't really bend over, so my mum used to sterilize water and wash my stitches for me – I couldn't even reach them myself. Imagine your mum doing that for you when you're eighteen years old! Sometimes she would make me salt baths and I'd sit in them, wincing with pain. I had a lot of help from my mum.

She did everything for me. She looked after me like I was dying.

All the while I was so, so sad. I think anybody normal would have been sad in my situation. I felt as if I'd gone from having the best life in the world to everything being in ruins. I was fat, torn and sore. I had stretch marks all over my hips and boobs. I couldn't do anything or go anywhere. My life was one big nothing. I was helpless and trapped, and I felt like I was a hopeless mother. I used to cry all the time, cool silent tears of despair. I didn't even wonder if I would ever feel happy again; I was sure I never would be.

I don't remember a lot about that period of my life, because it seems like every day was the same, so in my mind it all merges into one long, unhappy day. When I look back, I don't feel like I was actually awake during that time. It's a really weird feeling, as if I wasn't really there. I remember not wanting to talk to anyone. I was really quiet and I took hardly any notice of the people who came and went. Dean was good with Zach and my friends, and often came to visit, but I was so miserable that I didn't want to see anyone. Me and Dean gradually drifted apart. Unfortunately, it just didn't work out between us, as having a boyfriend was the last thing on my mind. I just spoke to my mum and cried. Apart from that, nothing. I hated every second of my life.

I went through hell for three months. People would come round and I'd think, Go away! They'd bring presents for the baby and I'd think, Why does he need another white baby-gro? Why does he need another packet of socks? I will never go to see someone who's just had a baby without getting them something really nice, too, something that will make her think, Thank goodness someone has got me something for doing all that hard work.

Breastfeeding didn't get any easier as time went on. 'You're doing so well,' everyone told me. 'Keep going with it, keep going,' said the midwife, my mum and Karen. 'It's best for the baby.'

But I felt completely drained. My energy levels were as low as they could be and I found myself crying all the time. 'I don't want to do this any more,' I told my mum. 'I really don't want to do it.' It was depressing me too much and I was exhausted.

'You stop whenever you want to,' Mum said calmly.

'I can't do it,' I said, the tears rolling down my face. 'I know everybody wants me to, but I just can't do it any more. I can't keep waking up in the night. I haven't slept properly in three months.' I needed one solid night of sleep. 'Just one . . .' I said.

Mum could see that I had reached my limit, I think. 'You must do what you need to do,' she said.

I was so grateful to my mum for helping me so much. I just don't know what I would have done without her. I was living in a blur and it was such a comfort to know that she had everything under control. She was so loving and giving and I was so needy. Thank you, Mum.

Gradually I weaned Zach off the breast and onto the bottle. For the first few days of bottle feeding he was still up during the night, but now I had someone to help me out, and it was just the nicest feeling. I was so grateful. At three in the morning when Zach started crying, I could lie in bed and listen to my mum getting up and saying, 'Hello!'

I felt like crying. It was such a relief. She's there, I'd think. I can go back to sleep.

In one way, it didn't make too much difference, because I'd always wake when he cried anyway – that's a mother's instinct – but it was lovely not having to physically drag my aching, tired body out of bed to warm up a bottle, then feed him and try and keep my eyes open without rolling onto him and suffocating the poor boy. All of a sudden I was free again. Zach could be independent of me and other people could look after him.

It was a huge turning point for me. It wasn't just that after a couple of nights of proper sleep I felt so much better. Psychologically, I felt the worst was over. Energy surged back into my body and I thought, Yes, I can get my life sorted now. I can do anything! Life went from being dull and grey to being full of hope and promise and colour. 'That's it, I'm going back to college,' I decided. 'I'm going to make a new start.'

'Go away on holiday, just for one week,' my mum urged. 'Then Zach can get used to being without you and get accustomed to having a bottle. That way, everything will be settled for when you start college again.'

A holiday? 'Are you sure, Mum? Really?'

'Go on,' she said. It was the kindest, most generous thing she could have done for me.

Me, Dana, Lauren and Laura went straight to First Choice and booked the cheapest 18–30s holiday we could find. Two days later, I bound up my breasts to stop them leaking and we flew off to Kos in Greece.

What a difference sunshine makes, especially when you're having fun with your best mates! We had an amazing time. We made loads of friends, got really tanned, got drunk and went clubbing, none of which I had done in about a year. It was so brilliant: there were school uniform parties, all-night discos and pub crawls. It made me realize how incredibly low I'd been and how much I'd missed going out and having a good time.

We met a wicked bunch of people. They were staying in the same hotel and we ended up doing everything with them: swimming, dinner, going on the punch machine, bursting into their room and spraying shaving foam on their faces. We had a really good laugh and shared the same naughty, silly sense of humour. I got on unbelievably well with a guy called Paul. I called him 'Hoof' because he had the hairiest legs and looked like something out of Narnia, half man, half beast! I hardly had time to speak to his best friend, Aaron, because he made me laugh so much.

I didn't think I'd miss Zach while I was away, but I did. I kept thinking about him and I took his picture with me everywhere. Most days, I rang my mum and asked her to put the phone by his ear. 'Hello, munchkin, how are you?' I'd say. 'Miss you!'

'Na, na, na,' he'd gurgle. They were really short phone calls!

Then I'd rush off to find my friends again and laugh until I cried. It was the best feeling. At last my ordeal was over. I was back on track.

Chapter 8

Before you appear on a show like *The X Factor* or *I'm a Celebrity* you spend an afternoon with a psychiatrist, going through your whole life story from beginning to end, without leaving anything out. You have to be completely honest about everything or you can't go on the show. It's quite an interesting thing to do, actually, as it puts your life into perspective! And some of the questions they ask really make you think.

'It's intriguing how you went from being so angry as a teenager to being the way you are now,' the psychiatrist said when I went for my interview for *I'm a Celebrity* in September 2010. 'How did that happen?' she asked.

I honestly couldn't tell her at first. 'I don't know,' I said. 'I don't even know when I came to be this happy.'

'Do you think, perhaps, your life began to turn around when your parents took you out of one school and put you in another, more challenging school?'

I thought about it. My life definitely changed when I started at King Solomon, partly because the teachers were so encouraging. While I was there, I went from being rebellious and moody to being happier and more balanced, although maybe that was also partly to do with growing up. So, could I trace my positive outlook back to that time? Well, almost. But I couldn't forget that when I got pregnant at seventeen, I lost all my sparkle and motivation. I sank so low that all I could see was the negative side of life. What a joke! I thought. What a life. That's it: I'm going to be a mum and then I'm going to die. There wasn't a glimmer of positivity in me back then.

No, what changed everything was Zach. Beyond a shadow of a doubt, the reason I'm so happy and positive now is Zach. Because instead of my life ending when I had him, as I thought it would, he was the beginning of all things good and wonderful. Zach brought so much happiness and sunshine to everyone around him. He lit up all of our lives with his gorgeousness and sweet personality. It took me a little while to realize what an amazing gift he was, because I was exhausted and traumatized after he was born, but when it dawned on me just how lucky I was to have him, my attitude totally transformed.

The holiday in Kos helped me a lot. When I came back, feeling refreshed and in touch with myself again, I was thrilled to see my baby. As I lifted him into my arms and held him close for the first time in a week, I was overwhelmed by how much love I felt for him. 'Zach, my mooch, my munchkin!' I cried out. 'I'm home!' As he nestled in my arms, gurgling and wriggling, he looked up at me and smiled. It was the most angelic little chubby-faced smile I'd ever seen and it completely melted my heart. How could I ever have thought I didn't want you in my life? I wondered as I smothered him with kisses. It gave me so much joy just to be with him again.

From that moment, my priorities changed. Realizing how lucky I was to have my beautiful, healthy son, I felt so incredibly blessed. I didn't ever want to seem ungrateful or take anything for granted again, because I knew that, in Zach, I had the best thing in the world. Just as long as I don't die and nothing bad happens to him, I don't care what happens in my life, I thought. It was a liberating feeling. My son was the most important part of my life; nothing else mattered even half as much.

I was determined to be the best mother in the world. I was going to go back to college, get my qualifications and make something of myself, so that I could give him all the best things and great choices and a fantastic future. I pledged that I would never let him down.

Things were so much easier now that the burden of looking after him could be shared out and I didn't have to breastfeed him any more. My family were unbelievably supportive; I was so fortunate in that way. My mum, especially, couldn't get enough of Zach. She just adored him from the start.

It was great to see her happy again, happier than I'd ever seen her before, in fact. I don't think I'm exaggerating when I say that Zach turned her life around, too, and gave it meaning once more. She'd been stuck in a rut for years and he gave her a reason to live again. To be honest, it was a bit like he belonged to both of us. He wasn't just mine any more, he was mine and hers, because we could both feed him and look after him.

Now that I could leave him with other people, I couldn't wait to start college again in September. As soon as I was in full-time education, some of his childcare costs would be paid for by the government, and later on I got a part-time job in the bar of a nearby country club to help support us and pay for extra childcare. Zach was six months old when I started dropping him off at the college creche on my way into lessons, picking him up again at the end of the day. I didn't go and see him in the lunch hour, even though I always wanted to, because it used to unsettle him and he would cry until I came and picked him up again. As long as I didn't disturb him, he had a lovely time there.

After college, I'd take him straight home to my mum and then, three or four nights a week, I'd go to work. I worked as much as I could as I've always enjoyed working. What I didn't like was having so little time off to spend with Zach. I cherished the time I had with him. I was always telling him, 'I miss you, I miss you, I really want to kiss you.' Now he says it back to me: 'Miss me? Really want to kiss me?' But of course he was only a baby then, so he just gurgled.

I enjoyed my job, because it was really nice and social. I've always been a people person and at work I got to talk to everyone – mixing drinks was fun, too. Everyone was lively and happy because they were drinking, so the atmosphere was always good. And the wages meant that I was financially independent, which gave me a good feeling. The latest we'd ever finish was half three in the morning, because the parties on Fridays and Saturdays would finish at one or two o'clock and then we'd have to clear up.

Occasionally, I did shifts at a wedding venue, where I used to clean the toilets after everyone had gone home. I often found myself wiping away traces of cocaine from the cistern lids, which disgusted me, because the idea of someone putting something up their nose is hideous. It's the most unattractive thing. You should have seen the bride at one of the weddings I worked at. She had white powder all over her nose. I don't feel strongly about many things, but that just made me sick. She was taking charlie at her wedding!

I wasn't aware of anyone using hard drugs at either of the schools I went to. I never saw anything other than weed when I was younger. Weed was a laughing drug. Then everyone grew out of it and it wasn't cool to do it any more. It was like, 'Get a life!' It was a kiddies' drug. None of my old schoolfriends do it now. I think it would be sad if they did, because it reminds me of being thirteen years old over the park. It's not cool any more.

No one at King Solomon smoked weed, to my knowledge. But when they left school after the sixth form, some of them ended up trying different things. I didn't see charlie or pills until I went clubbing, when I thought, Oh God, people actually do this? It scared me a bit. I've never tried it in my life. I felt very uncomfortable when people were taking coke or pills anywhere near me.

I remember someone showing me a YouTube clip of Amy Winehouse taking coke and I just didn't want to look. 'Get it off!' I said. Everything about it is hideous: the way people are; how they get right in your face; the way they talk to you; how they sweat; the way their jaws grind. There's nothing worse. Honestly, I'm so appalled by it. Then they get angry, because coke's a really angry drug. It's a serious drug and I hate it. Weed is serious but coke changes your whole personality. You get addicted to it and you can't get away from it.

Cocaine's such a rich person's drug. You never saw it at Time & Envy, the club in Romford I went to when I was sixteen and seventeen, because people couldn't afford it. But at the more expensive clubs, you wouldn't see anything else. Everyone was covered in white. When you don't have money, I suppose you go for pills, but pills are more of a rave thing, whereas clubbing finishes at three and you just walk home drunk. Or that's how it was for me and my friends. Everybody smoked and drank loads, but that was it.

My worst nightmare is to be out of control. I've never passed out in my life. I've never been completely off my face, like out of control. You'll never see me puke up after drinking too much. Although I might throw up the next day when it's coming out of my system. You know when I've had a drink because it's the only time I swear. It never even crosses my mind to swear unless I'm having a drink with my friends and I know I'm allowed to, because Zach isn't around.

All right, I've maybe kissed someone when I've been drunk and afterwards thought, Gross! Why did I kiss him? I remember I kissed this one boy who I thought was really good looking at the time. I got his number and arranged to meet him the next day. What a shock I had when he came to the door! He wasn't anything like I remembered, or if he was, he wasn't good looking any more. My sister was standing at the window laughing at me as I left the house. I turned round and gave her a look as if to say, 'I hate you. I really hate you!' It was so embarrassing. I had to spend the whole day with him.

When I look back at my life before Zach, it seems so different. I was just a child then. Afterwards I had adult responsibilities, and going out with boys was the last thing on my mind. But even though I was working hard and studying, I was really enjoying life again, because Zach made everything worthwhile. I looked forward to waking up every day and having my morning cuddle with him. It made me laugh to put him in the bath and watch him splash around with a happy smile on his face. Best of all was bedtime, when I sang him soft lullabies to send him off to sleep. I loved him more and more each day, more than I could ever have believed I could love anyone.

And now I had a whole new group of friends from my holiday in Kos. I added them all as friends on Facebook and we had a right laugh online. After a little while, Paul's best friend Aaron started messaging me. 'Where do you lot live, then?' I asked. I knew they were from Essex, but we hadn't got further than that.

'Right by Lakeside,' he replied, referring to the massive shopping centre in Grays, Essex.

Well, you can imagine. I was like, 'Lakeside! Lakeside!' Because it's my favourite place. 'I love Lakeside,' I admitted.

'You should come,' he suggested.

I wanted to, but although Lakeside was only a few minutes by car down the A13 from my house, I didn't drive and you couldn't get there by bus. 'Ah, I haven't got a car,' I said regretfully. Hint, hint.

'I'll pick you up and take you, then,' he offered.

'OK.'

After that, Aaron often used to text me on a Wednesday to ask, 'What are you doing? Do you want to come to Lakeside?'

'Yes,' I'd always reply.

He'd come and pick me up in his rickety Berlingo van. It was the oldest, ugliest thing, but I loved it. We weren't seeing each other or anything – it was just a friendship – but we started to get close. I never spoke to him about Zach, though. I think he must have known I had a baby son, because I'm sure everyone on holiday had noticed that I had a photo of Zach with me, but I never mentioned him and Zach never came shopping with us. It was just me and Aaron. Once a week, I could forget that I was a mother and have some fun without any responsibility.

I really liked Aaron and we became good friends. He was only a year older than me and we enjoyed being silly together, staying up until four in the morning watching boxing, or going clubbing together, just me and him. Once or twice we found ourselves kissing in front of the telly, or when he dropped me home, but it was just a bit of fun. I didn't think

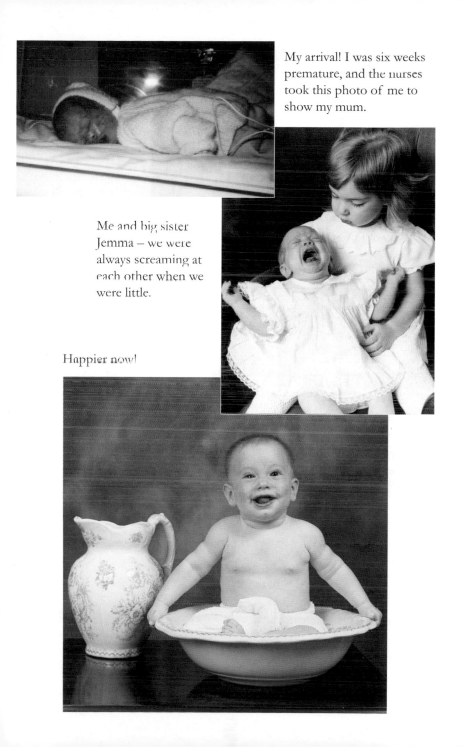

My arrival! I was six weeks premature, and the nurses took this photo of me to show my mum.

Me and big sister Jemma – we were always screaming at each other when we were little.

Happier now!

Nana, me and Jemma
– her pride and joys!

Butter wouldn't melt . . .

Practising my dance moves.

Nana loved coming with us to Pontins, it was always a big family affair.

With our little
brother, Matthew.

Me, in one of my mum's
homemade dresses!

A trophy from my mum and dad
as I didn't win one myself.

Baton twirling,
ooo dear!

Still twirling those batons . . . A fun day out at Legoland. It wasn't all Pontins!

Me and Paul! Who would have thought?

A rare moment when we weren't squabbling.

Having fun at Dad's photographic studio.

This is what I looked like at drama school – I wonder why I never got any of the lead roles?

Me and my cousin Jo.

My Abbs Cross birthday in the shed.

Mazel Tov to my little brother.

Here come the girls . . . I was so excited to be a bridesmaid at Dad and Karen's wedding.

Already a show-off . . . Singing at Daddy and Karen's wedding.

The whole family!

K. S.! School two.

I performed in a school concert with my mates
Jess and Danni.

Prom Queen, yaay.

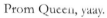

Ooo dear, bikini bod, ha ha!

At the Ice Bar in London for
a birthday party, wahooo!

Ahh . . . my beautiful
Zachary.

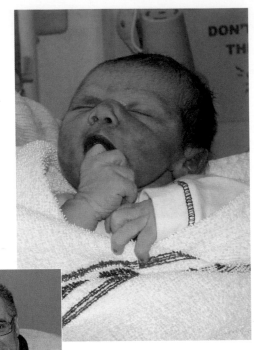

Just after having given
birth, and not looking
so pretty.

Nan and Daddy
with Zachary.

anything of it, or if I did I didn't say anything. He wasn't the type to bring it up either. He'd never say, 'I kissed you yesterday,' especially as he knew I wasn't interested in having a boyfriend. Anyway, it would have been embarrassing.

Quite a few times I told him, 'I don't want to be with anyone.'

'OK, whatever you want,' he said.

But I must have liked him more than I admitted to myself, because I really didn't need to go to Lakeside every Wednesday. We obviously liked each other, but something wasn't right. After everything that had gone on in my life over the previous year, getting involved with someone new was the last thing I wanted.

It wasn't just being with Aaron that I enjoyed, I loved being around his friends. They were my kind of people. They reminded me of my old school mates from Abbs Cross. Everyone was in a big group and had known each other for ever; meeting up was all about having a laugh and messing around, even though we weren't thirteen any more. This is what I used to be a part of, I thought. This is what I lost when I left Abbs Cross.

It made me want to get back in contact with my old friends, so it was brilliant when I bumped into Jade from Abbs Cross while I was shopping in Romford one day. 'Oh my God, how are you?' we screeched at each other. Soon afterwards, she arranged to get everyone together at a pub in Elm Park. It was so funny as none of them had changed. The pretty one was still the pretty one; the smoker still had the cigarettes; it was all exactly the same. They're still friends now and they still all go out together.

'Where've you been?' they asked. 'What have you been doing? Why did you leave us? You didn't even ring, nothing!'

I had to explain that my dad had taken me away from the school and the area and made me cut all ties with my friends. 'Oh well!' they said. 'Do you want a drink?' Suddenly it was as if we'd only seen each other yesterday.

I didn't have much time for socializing, though, because my days were super busy with Zach, college and work. My course was full of workshops and we constantly put on little shows for the class, so there was a lot of preparation to do. Our one big production was the Stephen Sondheim musical *Into the Woods*, which I love, because it's got all the fairy tales rolled into one. It was my ideal musical. I played the witch, which is a really funny role. Her songs are hilarious. She half sings, half rasps and she's extremely snappy and quick-witted. She was such fun to play.

The course combined lots of different elements, from studying plays to breaking down and analysing specific songs. So we put on *Jack the Ripper* for one module and sang 'Happy Ending' by Mica as a huge ensemble piece for another. It may have seemed a bit random at times, but it was brilliant and I learned so much about the essential elements of performance, singing and musical drama.

The months flew by and, before I knew it, the summer term was starting. It was April and the 2009 *X Factor* auditions were being held. I'd missed the auditions the year before, for obvious reasons, but now I felt it was the right time to try again. 'Well, you go on your own this time,' my mum said with a laugh. Not surprisingly, she couldn't face another sixteen-hour wait. She'd had enough of queueing with thousands of *X Factor* hopefuls to last a lifetime.

Some of my friends had decided to audition, too, so we got the train to the O2 Arena the night before and arrived around midnight. There were already hundreds of people there. We waited in the freezing cold all through the night until the morning, jumping around to keep ourselves warm and talking to other people in the queue to find out what they were doing and how long they'd been there.

The next morning the judges came out for a few minutes, which made the crowds cheer. Oh, please, just let us in, me and my friends thought. We don't care if we get through or not. We've been here for so long that we just want to come in.

Eventually we made it inside. The massive floor of the O2 Arena was dotted with polystyrene booths, each with a producer sitting inside, and you had to go into a booth and sing. Since I hadn't got through with 'Over The Rainbow' the last two times, I decided to sing something different – 'What A Wonderful World' – which is a song I've always loved singing.

After I'd sung a few lines, the producer said, 'Tell me a bit about yourself. You've got five seconds.'

'I'm nineteen and I'm a student from Dagenham,' I said. 'My son's called Zach. I'm really happy and excited to be here!' That was it.

'Yup,' she said. 'You're through.' Two of my friends, Lynette and Shakira, also got through, but unfortunately the others didn't.

The next stage was another audition with producers, this time at the Emirates Stadium. My mum came to that one. I sang the same song and got through again. After that, I was shown into another room, where I met some more producers. Then I was sent home to wait for a phone call to tell me whether or not I was through to the next stage. I had no idea if they liked me or not and I tried not to think about it too much. When the phone call came I was told, 'We'd really like you to come to an audition with Simon and the judges.'

'OK,' I said calmly, while thinking, What the heck! I put down the phone. 'Help! What do I wear?' I yelled at my mum.

After trying on everything in my wardrobe, I decided to wear a pair of blue shorts. 'They're a bit short,' my mum said cautiously.

'Yes, but I'll wear them with trainers,' I said. 'I won't wear them with heels.' So I wore shorts, trainers and a white polo that I was in love with at the time. Back then I used to love my polos; I dressed a bit like a boy golfer.

My family came with me to this audition, as we didn't think we'd be waiting around all day this time. Unfortunately, though, we waited and waited and waited, and I was the last person to be seen. It didn't show me as last on telly, but I was the last person in the whole room to go in. At one point someone said, 'Oh, we don't know if we're going to be able to see you today after all.'

'Oh no,' I said. 'Why not?' After sitting around all day with my family, burping Zach, getting baby sick on my top and baby food on my shorts, they weren't going to be able to see me? By now, Zach was not happy. He was crying his eyes out.

Eventually, a woman came in and said, 'Come on, we're going,' and I was escorted through to the stage, leaving Zach behind with my family, still crying his eyes out.

When I went on stage Simon Cowell said, 'Hello.'

'Hiya,' I replied.

'And what's your name?'

'Stacey.'

'Where are you from, Stacey?'

'Dagenham.'

'No!' he said, laughing. He asked me my age and then said, 'What's the dream here?

'Oh,' I said. 'To win this.'

'Yuh? Are you any good?'

'I hope so. You might not think I am.'

'Who has told you you're any good?'

'Sometimes my mum does, and my friends, obviously.'

Simon smirked. Oh no, he thinks I'm an idiot, I thought.

I started singing 'What A Wonderful World'. The audience seemed to like it, but Simon put his hand up quite early on in the song. Oh no, he thinks I'm rubbish! I thought.

All the judges were really nice. Cheryl spoke first. 'Do you know what?' she said. 'I don't know why I had a preconceived idea, but I didn't expect you to be that good.'

'Thank you,' I said, hardly able to believe what I was hearing. It was really strange to be standing there in front of these super famous people.

Louis was next. 'Stacey, I totally agree with Cheryl. I didn't expect your voice to be that good,' he said.

'I can't believe you're saying my name,' I burst out. Every one laughed, but I meant it. It felt weird to have people like Cheryl Cole and Louis Walsh calling me by name.

Dannii was the next to comment. 'It was a real surprise,' she said. 'It's so cute, your personality and the voice, and you didn't falter anywhere.'

So three of them liked me, but what was Simon Cowell going to say? 'I have to be honest with you, that performance really took me by surprise,' he said. 'I think that was really, really good.' Oh my God!

Each judge said yes to me going through to the next stage. 'Congratulations,' Simon said.

Yes! I thought, and I ran off the stage to find practically everyone in my family crying.

The presenter Dermot O'Leary came up and said, 'Well

done.' And every single producer, presenter and member of the crew was so nice to me.

'Do you want to go to the pod and talk about it with your family?' they said.

'Yeah!' I replied, and we all bundled into the pod and started talking at once, bubbling over with excitement.

And that was it for me and *The X Factor* . . . until the summer, when the next set of auditions would begin.

Soon after the *X Factor* audition, I went on an exchange programme to America with college. It was so good. We went to Ohio and Ohio came to London, and we put on the musical *Oh! What A Lovely War* over there and over here. In Ohio, we stayed in the college fire department, where we were surrounded by beefy men training to be firemen. We laughed so much when we were shown to our rooms. 'Wow! Does it get any better?' I didn't kiss anyone while I was away, though. I still wasn't interested in any of that. I was just having a really good time.

Oh! What a Lovely War is quite a weird musical to stage as it's very dark and political and controversial. It's a satire on World War One and features songs from that era, so while you're singing these supposedly uplifting songs about staying strong through tough times, footage of death and destruction is screened on the backdrop behind you. The cast wore Pierrot outfits and the idea was that you changed your hat to denote your character or military rank when you were singing, which was an interesting way of doing things.

It was great to see a bit of America, although we were in a rather remote, desolate part of Ohio; there was only ever one road, and lots of tumbleweed drifting around. It was the kind of lazy place you'd expect to see somebody rocking in a chair on their wooden porch listening to country music. In other words, it was a little bit scary. There were drive-thru banks and drive-thru liquor stores and everyone seemed to have a hot tub in their garden.

Not long after I got back from Ohio, I packed a suitcase with a week's worth of clothes and took the tube to Hammersmith in West London for the *X Factor* boot camp auditions. 'See you later, Mum. Bye, Zach.' The contestants stayed in a hotel near the Hammersmith Apollo, where the auditions were being held. I shared a room with a really nice girl called Ruth, a Scouser with a beautiful voice. We were friendly for the whole of boot camp and practised together all the time. When everyone else went down to the hotel bar, we stayed in our room together. 'No, we have to go to bed with our honey and lemon drinks!'

I didn't want to go down to the bar and shout and laugh and lose my voice. Well, I *did* want to go to the bar, where everyone was having a laugh, playing the piano, singing and drinking, but I didn't let myself. 'You're not going down there,' I told myself. I just couldn't. Being at boot camp was too good to be true and I wasn't going to risk ruining my chances. It meant so much to me to be there. So I went to bed at eight o'clock every night with my honey and lemon and my Walkman. As long as I had Ruth in the room with me, I didn't care. She was really good fun.

On the first day, we were divided into groups of three and given a list of songs to choose from. Each group had to break the song up into solo and ensemble parts. Ruth and I were grouped with a girl called Nastasia and we chose 'Use Somebody' by Kings of Leon as our song.

While we were rehearsing, I started to feel really nervous as I suddenly realized how serious this was. I was surrounded by 200 people who all wanted the same thing as me, and I thought every single one of them was better than I was. It made me feel sick to see how good they all were, all these people with amazing voices. It was the most horrible feeling. I hadn't really felt nervous before, but now I was confronted by the reality, I wanted to cry. I can't do it, I thought. I'm rubbish, nowhere near as good as everyone else here.

When I walked out on stage with Ruth and Nastasia on the second day, my heart was pounding so hard that I thought the judges would probably be able to hear it. I was trembling, a complete wreck. As we started singing, my mind went blank and I couldn't remember my words. I forgot everything I was supposed to be doing and sang terribly.

Afterwards, Simon Cowell said, 'I was disappointed in you, Stacey.'

I was close to tears. How awful. I felt like a complete failure. Worse, I couldn't bear the thought of having to go home, back to everyday life, with all my hopes and dreams dashed.

Me and Ruth got through but I wasn't happy. I was completely shaken up. I went outside, sat on the steps and called my mum. The moment I heard her voice I burst into tears. 'I can't do it, Mum!' I sobbed. 'I was too nervous and I forgot all my words. I really can't do it.'

'Don't be silly,' she soothed. 'You got through, didn't you?'

'But everything about it scares me. It means too much to me now. I keep thinking that if I don't get through, it's the end. That's what's making me so nervous.'

'You're fine, Stacey, you can do it,' she kept saying. 'Now go and do the next round.'

I must have been papped while I was pouring all my troubles out to her, because the next day there was a picture of me in the paper underneath a headline that labelled me an *X Factor* reject. I had to giggle when I saw it. But I got through! I thought.

I took Mum's words to heart and comforted myself with the thought that I hadn't been sent home, despite doing so badly in that round. 'I'll just have to do better the next time,' I told myself.

The following day we were whittled down to the last fifty. They put us into four different rooms in the hotel and told us that two rooms would get the thumbs up and two rooms wouldn't. I sat on the floor of the room I was in, wondering whether I was with the winners or losers. It was really nerve-racking. Suddenly we heard a massive cheer from one of the other rooms. So one group had got through. One down, one to go. Then we heard another massive cheer. My heart sank. Oh no, I thought. We didn't make it.

In fact, someone had said to the first room, 'Cheer again, so that the people in the other rooms think another room is through.' It was a clever trick — and it worked!

I wanted to leave as soon as I could, so I rang my sister. 'Can you come and get me?' I said, my voice cracking with emotion. 'I haven't got through.'

'I'm on my way,' she said.

The camera crew came into our room. 'Yes, we know we haven't got through,' we said. They must have been laughing behind the cameras.

'You're through!' someone said.

'What?'

I rang my sister again. 'Hold tight, we're not far away now,' she said.

'I'm not leaving now, after all, sorry. I got through!' I yelled at her. She was too pleased for me to be annoyed.

The next day it was non-stop filming. They film you

waking up and they film you walking down to lunch and there are individual interviews with each and every person. I didn't find it easy at all. During the week the pressure had been building day by day. You don't sleep properly or eat properly because you're so nervous. You're on a high one minute and a low the next. You rehearse until you're exhausted and then you have to wait around doing nothing much until you find out whether you've got through.

When they interview you, you're bombarded with questions: 'So what does it mean to you to get through? What's your son doing now? Where is he?' They're not trying to make you look silly; they just want to know everything you're thinking.

I didn't want to be one of those people who sobs. 'I'm not going to cry,' I told myself as I tried to keep up with the quick succession of questions.

'If you don't get through and nothing happens and you go back to your normal life, what will you do?'

'I'll just live a normal life, I suppose.'

'Do you feel bad that you've been away from Zach for a week?'

'Well, a little bit.'

'Do you think you did enough to get through?'

'I don't know.'

'Do you think this is going to be the end for you?'

'I don't know.'

Suddenly, in spite of everything, I found myself crying. 'Please don't put that in,' I asked, and they didn't. The crew were really good to me. They showed me with a big red face, but they didn't show me crying.

'I just want to be successful,' I said, 'and do something good.'

'What will you do if you don't get through?'

'This is my life,' I said. 'If I can't do this, I don't know what I'm going to do, although there's always Asda!' And that's the clip they showed.

Now I was one step away from the final twenty-four, but it was a massive step and I would have to calm down and stay focused to get through it. Our next task was to pick a song and sing it to the judges in front of a live audience. I chose 'There You'll Be' by Faith Hill and Ruth chose Christina Aguilera's 'Hurt'. We practised really hard all day and went to bed ridiculously early again. The following morning I got up, went on stage and sang my song in front of the judges, trying not to over think it. The audience helped by cheering really hard as each of us came out, but my mouth was like sand and I was visibly nervous.

Back at the hotel, I tried to go over my performance in my head. I had forgotten everything the minute I came off stage, so I didn't know whether I'd done well or not. I had a feeling I hadn't been great, but at least I didn't muck it up. This time, at least I'd remembered my words. So I went to bed, thinking, I did what I could and I was better than last time.

In the morning, we were told to line up in groups of five at the rear of the Hammersmith Apollo. As I got in line, I realized that Ruth was in another group. She'd gone in before me because my group was last.

Finally we went through the door into the building and trooped up on stage. 'Look, we may as well get this over with,' Simon said grimly.

Oh dear, I thought. That doesn't sound good.

Then, breaking into a grin, he added, 'You're through.'

My heart soared. 'What?' I looked at him for reassurance and he nodded. Wow! We really are through! Yes!

Sadly, Ruth hadn't made it. 'I haven't got through. I'm going home,' she said when I saw her. She was understandably upset and didn't want to hang around. I was gutted for her and knew I'd really miss her. She was a really nice, talented girl and it would have been great to be with her in the finals.

Everyone who did get through went upstairs at the Apollo and had pizza. Now the pressure was off, we all just ate and ate and ate. Back at the hotel, we were put in four rooms again: the girls in one, the boys in another, then the over twenty-fives and finally the groups. Now it was time to find out which judge we were being allotted.

My group, the girls, desperately wanted Dannii as she seemed like the nicest and friendliest of the judges. Throughout the audition process, she'd always stopped people to ask, 'How are you?' And she seemed very genuine.

We waited for ages, then the door finally opened and in walked Dannii. We surged forward and surrounded her, screaming and shouting about how glad we were that she was our judge. Poor thing. We practically fell on her, and she's so small and fragile that she probably thought she was going to die.

'We're going away. I can't wait for you to come,' she said, giving us one of her big smiles.

I immediately rang my sister. 'I got through!' I told her.

'Are you joking me? Are you joking me?'

'No!' I screamed. 'Can you come and pick me up?' I could have stayed one more night at the hotel if I'd wanted to, but I couldn't wait to get home to Zach.

It must have been about one in the morning by the time we got back but my mum was still waiting up for me. 'Mum, I did it,' I said.

134

'I knew you would,' she said. 'Well done you.'

I was so happy. It felt like a proper achievement to have come so far. No one really remembers who appears at boot camp, but if you get to the judges' houses, your friends are going to be impressed and say, 'Well done.' So I was proud of myself. I was in the last twenty-four out of 200,000. That's not bad going for a nineteen-year-old girl from Dagenham, I thought.

Chapter 9

One of my favourite possessions is a fluffy blue dolphin. I love it because it reminds me of one of the coolest weekends of my life, when I went to Dubai for the judges' houses stage of *The X Factor* with Dannii Minogue. That was one wicked weekend and I'll remember it for ever.

It started with a phone call telling us to meet at the airport. We were all there: me, Stacey McClean, Rachel Adedeji, Despina Pilavakis, Lucie Jones and Nicole Jackson — the girls! We had no idea where we were going, and when we found out it was Dubai, I was really excited. I'd never been anywhere like that in my life and I couldn't wait to see what it was like.

We stayed at the Atlantis, a massive, beautiful hotel on a man-made island off the coast of Dubai. It had marble floors and ceilings and mosaics and sculptures everywhere you looked. I shared a room with Stacey McClean. On our first day, Dannii took us to Aquaventure, the coolest water park in the world. It was mind-blowing. There was a slide that dropped you down under a tank of real sharks — it was the maddest thing. To top everything, Dannii arranged for us to swim with some dolphins, which is why I bought the fluffy dolphin as a souvenir at the airport on my way home. Oh my God! I'd always dreamed of swimming with dolphins, so it was just a dream come true, magical in every way. We got to ride them, kiss and cuddle them and dance with them. It was so good.

Dannii had given us our songs before we went to Dubai, so we'd had loads of time to practise them. I decided to sing 'Over The Rainbow' because I just love singing that song. First, though, it was time to find out who would be helping Dannii judge this round. We all met in the lobby of the Atlantis and were shown up to the biggest suite I've ever seen. The ceilings were something like 50 feet high and there was a massive front room. As we were standing there, gaping at the grandeur of it all, Dannii walked in with her sister Kylie. I opened my mouth in amazement and my heart kept skipping beats. Oh my goodness, I'm in a room with Dannii and Kylie Minogue!, I thought. It was such a good feeling.

Before we each did our bit in front of the Minogue sisters, we waited in a bedroom with a four-poster bed and five bathrooms surrounding it. Weirdly, I wasn't a bit nervous before I sang my song in front of Dannii and Kylie. I think it was because I was so pleased to have come this far and I wasn't thinking about what would happen next. 'I'm cool. I've come to Dubai. I've met Kylie Minogue. I've sung to Dannii and Kylie, and they are so cool.'

But I felt completely different when it came to decision time. I was a wreck. When you're watching it on telly, you just don't realize how intense it is. Yeah, you think, biggest day of your life, is it? But when you're actually there, believe me, it really does feel like the most important day of your life.

We each had to go up in a lift to Dannii's suite to find out whether or not we'd got through, and all the others went up before me. Once they're up there, they don't come back again, so I had no idea who was through and who wasn't. Oh no, I'm last again, I thought, sitting alone, crying my eyes out. I didn't think there was any way I could have got through, but, oh, I wanted it so badly. I'm definitely not through. Why else would I be last? Because I'm not through, I thought. I felt sick with nerves. Just tell me now, I kept thinking. Get it over with.

Finally, I got in the lift and went all the way up. At the top, I started walking down the corridor to where Dannii was. I was trembling and crying; I just couldn't calm myself down. It felt like the longest corridor in the world. When I got to the end, I walked through the doors into Dannii's enormous suite. The ceiling seemed higher than ever and I felt tiny underneath it.

Dannii was sitting on a blue velvet sofa in the middle of the room, wearing a beautiful red silk dress, her legs tucked under her. She had a really sad expression on her face and my heart plunged to the floor. Oh no. I haven't got through, I thought.

She called me over to the sofa and I sat down opposite her, feeling absolutely devastated. Her big blue eyes were full of sympathy for me.

'It's a really tough decision,' she said. 'All of you are so good.'

Tears were pouring down my face. My eyes were leaking like someone had turned a tap on. I couldn't control it; water just gushed out. I felt hysterical and at a really high pitch emotionally.

'From the first performance, you've blown us away with your personality and you've blown us away with your voice. You have to know that.'

It was like she was trying to console me for what was coming next. I nodded and sort of whimpered.

'Getting through the three months of the competition takes such strength. It's not just the voice. And I wouldn't want to put anyone through the intensity of it that just didn't have that self-belief.'

So she didn't think I was strong enough. She didn't think I had enough confidence or self-belief. I went on nodding and crying. I wiped the tears from my eyes for about the hundredth time. Wait, maybe she did think I was strong enough. Maybe she was just prolonging my agony. I had no idea. My body was so tense it felt like I might snap at any moment.

Dannii looked at me for several seconds without speaking, her eyes boring into me. She blinked very deliberately, and blinked again. I couldn't read her expression at all, but she seemed very sad and serious. Then she opened her mouth to speak. This was it, I just knew it. I scrunched up my face in anticipation.

'We *love* you! You're in my final top three!' she yelled, breaking into a grin. She reached over to hug me.

'Oh, thank you, thank you so much,' I said, smiling and crying at the same time.

I couldn't even hug her at first. I was thinking, Help me! Help me! I felt so weak, so happy and so shocked, I couldn't breathe properly. I couldn't believe I was in the final twelve. Not in a million years could I believe it. I didn't know what to do with myself. All the tension and anxiety was seeping out of my body; I was like a balloon deflating.

I walked back down the corridor crying and gasping for breath as Dermot said, 'Come on.'

I hugged and squeezed him. 'I'm going to get my teeth whitened,' I said joyfully when I finally found the breath to speak. I'd heard that when you get through to the live shows, you get your teeth whitened. I was thrilled, because I never could have afforded to get it done in real life.

I was in. Who would have thought it? I kept thinking.

The show's presenters, Holly Willoughby and Dermot, were so nice to me. When they hugged me, they really hugged me. 'I am so genuinely happy for you,' Holly said. They seemed as happy for me as I was. It was just the best feeling in the world to think that people really cared about me and wanted me to do good and be successful. I'd never experienced that before. It was the nicest thing. It's funny, but when people want me to do good, it makes me want to do good, even when it's people I don't know.

Next, I rang my mum, on camera. She was in the car with my little brother Josh and Zach, driving back from my dad's, when she heard her phone ringing, and she had to pull over to the side of the road to answer it.

When she picked up the phone, I could hear Josh yelling, 'I wanna talk to Stacey!'

'Shush a minute,' my mum said. 'Let me listen to what she's got to say.' Then the phone cut out, because it was bad reception. 'Ring me in five minutes,' Mum said when I called her back. I'm going to have to find somewhere else to park up.'

It was all being filmed and I had to ring her about five times in the end. Finally, I managed to tell her the good news, though. 'I've got through!'

'No,' she said softly. 'Did you really? Are you sure?'

'Mum, you're on telly,' I said. 'Scream or something.'

'Stacey, I'm in the car with two children in the car and you want me to scream down the phone?'

'Yes, I'm in the final twelve!' I yelled.

Finally she let out a massive scream. 'Wow!' She sounded so happy that I just wanted to cry all over again.

'Can I speak to Zach?' I asked. I was desperate to tell him,

140

even though he wouldn't understand. I wanted him to know that, more than anything, I wanted to succeed for his sake, so that I could make something of myself and give him the best upbringing I could.

'Da,' I heard him say in the background. That was his first word. 'No.' That was his second word.

All of a sudden, I just couldn't wait to get home. I was like, I need to be home now!

We didn't leave until the next day, though, which was tough on the girls who didn't get through. It was hard for me, Rachel and Lucie, too, because we were each sharing a room with one of them. They were devastated, of course, so the last thing you wanted to do was show how happy you were. If it was you, you wouldn't want someone jumping around for joy, so it was a case of being courteous until we got home. I carried on and pretended nothing had happened, because that way we didn't have to talk about it. There was no need to remind anyone of their disappointment, that was for sure.

When we arrived at Dubai airport and I thought back over the past few days, I shook my head in amazement. What a weekend! I'd swum with dolphins, visited the most incredible water park ever, met Kylie Minogue and made it through to the live shows of *The X Factor*. It doesn't get much better than that.

Back at home, everything went back to normal for a while, but my head was in the clouds, although I tried to keep myself down to earth. I felt so grateful for the way my life was turning around. I just couldn't believe my luck. It was so amazing to be given the opportunity to be a finalist on the biggest TV talent show in the country. It was unbelievable.

After my audition was shown on telly, suddenly there were photographers sitting outside the house and journalists asking me for interviews. Me and my mum were like, What's going on? I hadn't done anything yet. It was only my first audition. Then boot camp was shown and the attention increased even more.

Obviously I couldn't tell anyone I'd got through to the live shows because it was a secret, and all my family had to keep it secret, too. We were still in shock that I'd got so far and were too scared of something going wrong even to talk about it amongst ourselves. 'Let's just see what happens,' we said. We were determined to stay down to earth about it. We didn't want to get our hopes up only to have them dashed, and I wasn't going to let any of it go to my head.

I carried on going to college and tried to keep everything normal. My friends asked me what was happening, but I said, 'I don't know. I'll find out soon.' I just kept my head down, worked hard and passed my end-of-term exams.

The first week I was at *The X Factor* house in Hampstead, north London, we were on total lockdown, because nobody was allowed to know we were the final twelve. Then it came out and everything went absolutely mental. There were hundreds of *X Factor* fans outside the house all day, every day, just standing there taking pictures, and people would wait outside Wembley Studios all the time as well. It became crazier as each week went by and we were given more and more exposure. Hampstead is one of the most Jewish areas in the world, so I had hundreds of people on the street, stopping me and asking, 'Are you Jewish? Really?' They were so excited about it.

At first, I kept myself to myself in the house, and it took me a few weeks to start trusting anyone. I was lucky with my bedroom as I was sharing with Lucie and the girl group Kandy Rain, who were really nice girls, so when Kandy Rain were voted out and Lucie was voted out not long afterwards, I had this massive room to myself. It was the biggest room in the whole house, with a TV and a square bath in the en suite bathroom – the only en suite there was.

On the first live show I sang 'The Scientist' by Coldplay. To my disbelief, I was told that Robbie Williams would be mentoring me in the run-up to the show. Yes, Robbie Williams! I had no idea what to say or do when they pushed me into the room where he was waiting for me. I didn't know whether to smile or wave or what.

'You know when you see someone on telly and they're not like a real person? But now you're here and you're real. And I'm like, Oh my God!' I gushed. He must have thought I was a right idiot, but he was really nice to me and it was amazing when we sang together. We did a duet at the piano. He was very cuddly, the total opposite of Whitney Houston, who mentored us in the second week. It's weird to meet somebody you know you definitely can't cuddle or get too close to or say the wrong thing in front of. With Whitney Houston, you said, 'Hello,' and stood on the other side of the room. I remember my nails were all chipped and I was sure she was thinking, What a tramp! She hasn't even painted her nails!

It was so different with Robbie. At the end, I hugged him and I didn't want to let him go. He probably thought, Get off me, you freak! But after we'd said goodbye, he said, 'Stacey's great. I want one. I think every home should have one.' I bet he'd swallow his words if that ever happened.

Robbie was very encouraging, but he was worried about my confidence levels. 'Do you believe that you can do it?' he asked me.

'I think so, but sometimes I get a bit scared,' I said.

'All you have to do is stand there and just give it to them on Saturday night,' he said.

'OK,' I said, but I was dreading it.

My clothes were chosen by Fay, our stylist, and I was really happy with them: high-waisted jeans; a Dolce & Gabbana Marilyn Monroe T-shirt that I just thought was the coolest thing in the world – and Fay let me take it home with me – and red shoes with gold studs. My hair was straightened and I had a fringe, so it was quite a different look for me. I had to pinch myself to remind myself it was me.

I was happy to be singing 'The Scientist' because Coldplay are one of my favourite bands, but I was really nervous before I went on. My mouth went completely dry and I kept coughing, as if I had something stuck in my throat. Everyone's going to be watching me, I thought, feeling completely panicked. It was a horrifying idea. I was terrified I wouldn't be able to remember the words and I started sweating and shaking. Every single bit of me was trembling. As the seconds ticked by, leading up to the moment I walked on stage, my heart was hammering against my chest.

All the time I kept thinking, Who am I? I'm no one. I'm just a girl from Dagenham. I don't know anything about this industry. I was clueless. I was walking into it blind.

I went out there and sang to the studio audience, who were wicked. Funnily enough, while I sang I wasn't conscious of all the millions of people at home, even though I was well aware of the audience figures. People kept saying, 'Millions of people will be watching,' but all you see is the hundred or so in the audience, and there are so many lights on your face that you can't really even see them. I did see my dad, though. How could I have missed him? He was wearing a T-shirt with my name on it and waving like a maniac. I had to look away, because I was worried he'd put me off.

Amazingly, it went well. I remembered the words, my voice didn't shake too much and the judges were all really nice to me. I got really, really good comments. They all said, 'It was such a good idea to choose that song. Well done.'

That was one of the best days of the whole competition. I was buzzing and I felt so good about myself. I felt even better when Coldplay sent me a plaque, which they'd all signed. 'To Stacey, we love watching you on telly. You've got a really good voice and we think you are lovely,' it said. It was so cool.

When I left the stage, I had that deflating feeling again, like I was a balloon losing all of its air. It was a huge sense of relief: Phew! I did it! And now I had to go through the whole thing again for the next show.

We rehearsed every day. First, you'd find out what you were going to be singing. If you didn't like it, you didn't have to sing it, though.

Next, you went into the studio and laid down a version of the song. They cut it down and edited it, then you'd start getting to know the edited version before you recorded it. After that, you'd practise it with Yvie Burnett, the singing coach, and you'd practise it for the rest of the week, with help from Yvie every couple of days.

We did choreography with Brian Friedman. Whether you were going to be standing still, walking across the stage or doing a dance routine, Brian would take you through it every step of the way. He was fantastic. Every week you did VTs, which were three-hour interviews where you sat there for what seemed like an eternity as they asked you question after question after question.

On Saturdays you were buzzing and on Sundays you just about kept buzzing with anticipation until the end of the results show. On Sunday night, after the announcements, you died. A part of you would completely collapse, even if you'd got through. It was the end of the week, the end of all the stress and anticipation of that live performance, and you turned into a walking zombie.

Some people complained about the busy schedule. 'I'm so tired,' they'd moan. Yes, it was busy, but it was so much fun. What's not fun about practising a song or a dance routine? What's not fun about filming? It's all fun, and having fun fills you with energy. So how can you not have energy when you're in one of the most privileged positions you could ever possibly be in? Get a grip!

I knew millions of people would have killed to be where I was. How could I not be having the time of my life? I just didn't get it when people complained and said, 'This is so tiring,' or, 'This is hard work.' Go away! I'll show you hard work! Hey, go and work in a mine or something. I couldn't understand it, because I loved every minute of it.

Well, almost every minute. I didn't enjoy actually going on stage. Well, not until the final. Up until then, I found it difficult to walk up to that microphone stand every week. It was really, really nerve-racking. Backstage, I would hear my name being called – 'Stacey Solomon!' – and reality would hit. Oh no, I've got to walk out there and sing.

Oh, my heart, my heart! It used to go like the clappers. I'd walk out on stage feeling horribly self-conscious, thinking, Everybody is watching; everyone is here. And every time I'd spot my dad in the audience, jumping up and down and cheering. Oh no! I'd think. There he is. Don't look over there. Don't look. I couldn't bear to look at my family. It put me off to see them standing there with those 'STACEY' T-shirts, waving at me and willing me on.

As the music started, I'd forget what I was about to sing. What's my first line? I'd think, panicking like a maniac. Then the first line would come to me – thank goodness! – but my voice shook every time. I just couldn't stop it. 'Get better!' I'd tell myself as I was singing. 'Be better than this, be better!'

I thought week two would be easier than week one, but it wasn't, it was worse. It was Diva Week and I was singing an old classic song called 'At Last', which came out in 1941. I'd heard it before, sung by Eva Cassidy, and I knew that Beyoncé had sung it for Obama at his inaugural ball, but I didn't really know it, because I hadn't listened to it that much.

It was new to me, even though I knew it, if that makes any sense. If you don't know the tune of something, you can't make it your own, and to make it your own, you have to learn the skeleton of the song, the bare melody, and know it inside out. Otherwise, you end up singing it just like some-one else and it doesn't complement you in any way.

I was still shaking when I finished singing and I waited anxiously for the judges' comments. Cheryl didn't say a lot, but Simon was quite critical. He said that I looked really uncomfortable during the performance. 'My advice to you is that you should just be doing your own thing,' he said. The audience booed his remarks and I just tried to keep smiling.

Then Dannii stuck up for me. 'Stacey, it was a beautiful performance,' she said. 'I know that you didn't know the song . . . but you got into it and you smashed it at the end of the song.'

The audience cheered. I was so thankful for Dannii's encouragement. She put her hand up for quiet. 'And you have to remember,' she went on, 'you've just turned twenty and you've come from literally singing in your bedroom to now performing on this stage. And it's what's uncomfortable about your performance which is your entire charm. I love it.' Thank you, Dannii.

We were each assigned a producer right from the start, and mine was Mark Wildesh and I loved him. He was like my bestest friend in the whole world. I called him Hammy, because he looked like the pet hamster I'd once had. Hammy kept me sane through the whole competition. 'How are we today?' he'd say as he set up my interview. 'What's going on? Got a bit of jeopardy for me, have you? Scared, are you?'

I had such a good time with Hammy. He was so kind to me whenever I got nervous. I was so lucky to have had him there, because some of the other contestants weren't all that nice. That wasn't because they weren't nice people; I think it was just a combination of being in a weird situation and under massive pressure. Some of them were older and they were worried that this might be their last chance for their careers to take off. They felt that their whole life depended on the contest and if they didn't do well, they'd be finished.

'Don't worry,' Hammy would say when people weren't nice to me. 'As long as you are nice, it doesn't matter.' He never let me get too down about it.

At the start, I had the feeling that no one liked me much. Lucie was always nice to me, but I felt she was overly nice, and she wouldn't ever spend time with me, even though we shared a room. She spoke pleasantly to the press about me, but seemed to avoid me behind the scenes. It was confusing, and it made things a bit uncomfortable at bedtime, because after Kandy Rain left the first week, it was just me and her. She was really pally with Rachel, so I didn't see a lot of them. Still, I thought they were both so talented, just really, really good at what they did.

As for the other contestants, some were likable and some weren't. I loved John and Edward Grimes, also known as Jedward. They had no airs and graces and didn't have a bad word to say about anyone. They weren't there to beat anyone; they were just really innocently doing their thing, so they were fun to be around, just nice, normal people.

Lloyd Daniels was just a little kid who didn't know what was coming to him. Too much happened to him too young and he ended up being a bit of a typical teenager and saying, 'I don't want to do it. See you later.' It was too much for Lloyd, I think. It was a bit too much for Rikki Loney as well. Rikki was sweet, but he was upset a lot of the time. He went quite early, though, so I didn't get to know him very well.

I didn't really get Jamie Archer. He wore sunglasses all the time, even indoors, which made me cringe a little bit.

It made me and Olly Murs giggle.

Danyl sometimes said things that upset me, especially when they seemed to be personally directed at me. Everyone saw it. I felt he had a bit of a problem with me, and he often said things like, 'It's not all about personality, you know. It's about voice,' or, 'It's not a personality contest. It's a singing contest and you've got to be a good singer.'

I think at first Danyl thought he was going to win. He was really nice then, but when he saw how much press everyone else was getting, he stopped being so friendly. He was really competitive with everybody; he'd walk into a room and say, 'So, have you seen who's supporting me this week? This celebrity wants me to win, that celebrity thinks I'm the best. Oh, and I'm the favourite to win this week, did you know?'

As much as you try not to let comments like that affect you, they're obviously going to make you think, Oh, he's going to win. I haven't got a chance. And that's depressing.

Danyl's not a horrible person, because he was completely different when we went on tour. I think it just bugged him that I wasn't technically the best singer, and yet people liked my personality so voted for me anyway.

'Hammy,' I used to say, 'he's making me sad. Why's he so mean? I don't say anything to him. I don't care how well he can sing. I just do my thing.'

Hammy kept me sane. He was constantly telling me not to worry; he was the nicest man. 'Come on, don't worry about it,' he'd say. 'Let's go and have a pizza. Don't worry. Let's have fun.' And we'd sneak off to the Italian restaurant round the corner.

I had a lot of great friends on the crew. There was Vinny the cameraman, who I nicknamed Vinny Jones. Then there were Justin and Eddie, who were on the ITV2 crew. They were brilliant. I called Eddie 'Slim' because he was just the skinniest man you ever saw; he and Justin would let me walk around with the camera saying, 'Action!' It was so much fun. My favourite researcher was Zoe. She was the person who interviewed me for my first audition and went back to the producers saying, 'I saw this girl . . .' She loved me. She was the best.

Dannii was definitely the best judge and I was so glad to be in her group. She was so kind and generous to me. For my birthday, she came round to the *X Factor* house, bringing me glittery cup cakes, a beautiful jumper and a bag that said, 'Love Dannii XXX' on it. And every week that the girls in her group got through, she gave us a lucky charm bracelet. I've still got all of mine. They're really cool and posh: one has Swarovski crystals all around the outside, another has little Chinese symbols and another has my birthstone embedded in it.

Dannii was always very friendly. 'Come into my room,' she'd say. 'Come and show me your outfits.'

She let me look through her wardrobe and gasp at her clothes. And she had the nicest PA, who I nicknamed Peppa Pig, because he had rosy red cheeks and a pink nose. Whenever we saw each other, we'd grunt. 'Come on, darling, let's have lunch,' he'd say. He really looked after me. And Dannii was my saviour loads of times, in different ways.

Week three was Big Band Week and I was singing 'When You Wish Upon A Star'. It's a song I really love, from the Disney film *Pinocchio*, but was it right for me? I was having a crisis of confidence.

I think I sometimes seemed uncomfortable when I was performing because I didn't know who I was, which direction I wanted to go in or what I wanted to sing. Some of the others had been singing for a long time and they'd established themselves in terms of style and direction: Lucie had trained to do musical theatre, Danyl and Jamie had both been singing in bands for years, but I didn't really know what kind of music I was into or what would suit my voice, so I let the professionals decide for me when it came to each category. I enjoyed the songs they picked, but I don't think I managed to establish a style that people would associate me with, and I think it frustrated the judges that I found it all a bit confusing and was a bit directionless.

I felt really alone, like I didn't know what I was doing, and I was unhappy and bewildered. It didn't help that a couple of people in the house had made cutting comments about my abilities during the week, either, so I was feeling very sensitive and didn't have anyone to talk to. I was really missing Zach as well.

Dannii helped me out so much at that time. During the week three rehearsals, she took me into her room and locked the door. 'I can see that you're not happy. What's happened?' she asked, with real concern in her voice.

I burst into floods of tears and told her all the little things that had got me down during the week, including the nasty put-downs people had been making and my anxiety about not really having a direction. She was so understanding and she let me pour my heart out and calmed me down.

It was just a build-up of everything, I think. You're in such a bubble in that competition, and you lose touch with the real world. I kept questioning everything. Is this real? I kept thinking. Is it really happening?

Dannii inspired me to go back on stage and do my best. She was always so encouraging, and I couldn't feel down for long, because Michael Bublé came to mentor us that week. He was so nice and friendly. I liked him a lot. I was already a fan, of course – everyone likes Michael Bublé, especially the ladies. 'I can't believe I'm meeting you,' I said, and he smiled in that gorgeous way of his.

The mentors all said the same thing, really, 'You've really got to feel it and believe it.' And it's true, I suppose.

If I was asked to mentor the contestants on the next *X Factor*, I think I'd probably say, 'Enjoy every second of it, because it will be over before you know it. Don't take it too seriously. I know it's your life. I know how much it means to you, but don't take anything anyone says to heart, because everything you do in this show is tongue-in-cheek.'

I wore the tightest, sparkliest silver sequined dress for my performance of 'When You Wish Upon A Star'. It was so beautiful, a fairy tale princess dress, and I felt like Cinderella in it, although I couldn't breathe because it was so tight. Still, there was no way I was giving up that dress. I wanted to wear it so badly that I didn't care if I suffocated in it.

It probably didn't do my singing any good to be constricted like that, though, because both Cheryl and Simon said they'd heard me sing better. Simon also said he was sick of seeing me just standing there in the centre of the stage, not moving, but believe me, no one could have moved very far in that dress. It was hard enough walking out on stage. Louis was very flattering about my performance, and Dannii stuck up for me again, and then the public voted me through, so I was safe for another week.

Whilst Dannii was my favourite judge, all the judges were really nice behind the scenes. I spoke to Simon all the time and we got on well, while Louis would come up to me and say things like, 'Let me tell you something. I need to tell you. Don't sing that song.' He is one of those crazy men you just laugh at. Cheryl always used to say hello and she was always really nice and kind and polite. She and Dannii are both stunning in the flesh, even with no make-up. They have perfect faces, with curved eyebrows, high cheekbones and beautiful eyes.

The live crew were all very supportive. When I was backstage just before going on to perform, they would all be saying, 'Go on, girl! Good luck!' For a few moments I could have a laugh with them and forget why I was there. Well, sort of. Every week I was more nervous than the last, because every performance meant more than the one before. I'd never thought I could get to the final or win, but the nearer I got, the more enticing it was. I've just got to get through, I kept thinking.

Once it was all over for another week, I'd unwind again and go back to my normal self, running around giving people nicknames and having fun with the crew. I give people nicknames because I don't remember names very well, so I did it to everyone. I even used to call one of the bosses Papa Smurf, because he had a grey beard, grey hair and he was really short. I don't know how I got away with it. If he had a white hat and blue body, he would be Papa Smurf to a tee, I thought, so I'd say to him, 'Go on, tell me, Papa Smurf, am I through?'

'Ho ho ho,' he'd reply, laughing at me like Santa.

I even used to have a joke with Simon. He was always drinking this water called Oxygen Water and I'd say, 'Do you drink that because you smoke? To get some oxygen in your lungs?'

'Oh, shush,' he'd say good-humouredly. Sometimes I used to sit in his chair, then when he came along I'd jump out of it into the next chair. He often patted me or rubbed my head, as if to say, 'Poor little Stacey.' He must have thought I was such a geek, but he was nice to me all the same.

One day, a group of children from a children's hospital came in. They were seated at the front, as if they were judging the show. 'You can be the judges this week,' he joked with them.

'They'll do a better job than you,' I chipped in.

'Just remember whose show it is, Miss Solomon,' he said.

'Oh no, please don't kick me off the show,' I cried, and we both ended up laughing.

Another time, we were all called into Simon's room as he

was getting annoyed because he thought nobody was being themselves in the VTs. He thought we were all putting on an act. 'I just want you to show me a bit of yourselves,' he said. 'Show me who you are. Don't just sit there and say, "Yes, sir, no, sir, three bags full, sir." Be yourselves.'

Just then I caught his eye. 'No, no,' he said, shaking his head. 'Not you.' He turned his attention back to the others. 'You see, Stacey never has to make anything up. She is completely herself.' I was really pleased.

Afterwards, Olly took the mick out of me. 'Who's Simon favourite then?' he teased.

'Oh shut up,' I said.

'Simon loves you. Simon thinks you're the best,' he went on.

'No, he doesn't. He thinks I'm really silly.'

I looked at Olly and laughed, and he grinned back at me. Suddenly I felt really happy. At last I was making a friend.

Chapter 10

As the weeks passed, I grew really close to Olly. He's one of the nicest boys you could ever hope to meet and he became my best friend in the world, along with Hammy. I just loved him to pieces and I was so proud to be his friend. It's funny how it happened, because I wrote him off as an Essex boy when I first met him. He was a bit cocky and, like, 'All right,' and I just thought, Go away! I know a million of you. You're in my life everyday.

But when I started talking to him, I realized we had a lot in common. It was such a relief to find that out. We were two nice people in a house where everybody else wasn't necessarily all that lovely. Olly's really genuine – and sweet and soppy and cheeky and funny. We were alike in many ways, although I'm not soppy like he is.

I had the time of my life with Olly. Everything we did together ended up being the best thing, and being his friend meant that I could forget about what the others were saying and doing. He really stuck up for me when Danyl had a go, too, and he was very protective of me. He wouldn't let anybody near me.

Soon we were together all the time. It was me and him everywhere we went. I never wanted it to be me and anyone else; I just wanted to be with Olly. I couldn't get enough of him. If they sent me off with someone else for the day I'd think, Huff! and I couldn't wait to see him when I got back to the house. One day, the boys went to Reebok and I went to My Wardrobe with Joe McElderry. It was the best place I've ever been and I walked away with a Mulberry bag and Vivienne Westwood shoes, but even so, all the time I was there, I was thinking, Why isn't Olly here? He should have been with me. It should have been us. At least Justin and Slim were there, filming it for ITV2 – they were so cool and lovely – but I wanted Olly there, too.

I couldn't bear being away from him and he was the same. If I was in a room talking to someone else, he'd come and find me. 'What's happening? Why aren't you with me?' We became a bit obsessed; we couldn't get enough of each other.

I didn't have a crush on him; we were just really good friends. I think people wanted us to go out. The thing was, I didn't fancy him. I absolutely loved him, but I couldn't imagine kissing him, even though he's really gorgeous. I loved everything about his personality, though, and being in his company was the best thing ever. I even loved his family. His nan knitted a hat for me! How sweet is that?

Every week, we did a piece to camera for the internet. It was something like, 'Hi, thanks for voting. It's week five now and we're having such a good time. Today we've been here, and this week we did such-and-such, and I can't wait for blah-blah.' One week, me and Olly decided to do each other's piece to camera. So he put on a wig and stuffed cushions down his top. 'Hello, I'm Stacey,' he said in a high voice. 'I'm well good and I'm fit. I'm proper fit.'

On Wednesdays we did a cooking challenge with Sainsbury's, and me and Olly often ended up having a food fight. One time I smashed a pie in his face, and another time he caught me out while we were making Halloween biscuits. I was concentrating so hard on making my biscuits good that I was completely unaware of Olly behind me, picking up a big bag of black icing and creeping up on me like a panto baddie. The next thing I knew, bang! I had icing all over my face and in my hair. It was so funny. We had such a laugh. He had the same energy as me and we just bounced off each other.

Olly used to get naked all the time. He loved running around in his pants. It made me cringe! I couldn't stand it. He'd chase me around the house in his underwear and run upstairs, swinging his hips in my face. Oh, it was so gross! 'Stace!' he'd call.

'Argh, get away from me!' I'd shout.

We went to so many cool things. It was just amazing to see the Back Street Boys at the O2 Arena. We had a box and everything. Can you imagine? We also went to the premiere of Jim Carrey's *A Christmas Carol* and we all walked down the red carpet together. Everything we did was just the best. Me and Olly were experiencing these things for the first time, together, and we were so genuinely excited, whereas some of the others didn't seem to share our delight. I don't know why. I think that some of them had been in the game so long they just expected it all to happen, while others, like Lucie, had been classically trained by Charlotte Church's voice coach and such like, so I suppose it didn't blow her away like it did me and Olly. We'd come from nowhere and now we were on the red carpet at a film premiere! We were just so happy.

When I think *X Factor*, I think Olly. He was the biggest chunk of my *X Factor* experience. Almost every memory I have of the show relates back to him in some way, because we lived in the same house for three months and did the most unbelievable things together, day in, day out. He was always in my room, since I had this massive space all to myself. We used to lie around making each other laugh. We never once got bored of each other's company.

Every single week, as soon as I knew I'd made it through, I'd be the happiest girl in the world as I ran off stage to find Olly. 'We did it!' I'd yell, throwing my arms around him. I was never in the bottom two, but I comforted him when he was in the bottom two. He cried his eyes out and poured his heart out to me.

On the Sunday show, we all sang and danced together in a group number. The producers always sandwiched me and Olly together, because they knew we were close and liked to play on the fact that everybody suspected we were going out. So it was always me and him singing together, which was great, because we got to practise together.

Nobody else got to see their families once a week, but I was given special permission, because of Zach. It wasn't enough to have our one-sided chats on the phone, I needed to pick him up and blow raspberries into his neck as I said, 'Miss you, miss you, really want to kiss you.' Although I missed him, I knew I had to make the most of the amazing opportunity I'd been given, for his sake more than anyone's. And I knew he was fine, because he had my mum, so I didn't have any worries. I had it cushy – and so did he, because Mum absolutely dotes on him.

Still, I loved going home and having a whole day of normality every week. It was usually a Wednesday or a Thursday. Everyone in the family would do their best to have some of the day off work or university and they'd all pile into Mum's house, where they'd keep me up to date with what was happening in the family and I'd tell them everything that was happening behind the scenes at *The X Factor*. I enjoyed those days off so much. They kept me grounded and reminded me how lucky I was to have such a great family. As long as I had them, especially Zach, nothing else mattered. I spent most of the day cuddling Zach – I just couldn't stop kissing him. Then, at the end of the day, I'd rush back to Olly, desperate to carry out my latest cunning plan to sneak up on him while he was cleaning his teeth and squirt mouthwash in his hair.

We cooked for ourselves in the house. We didn't have a rota; everyone just cooked what they wanted whenever they wanted, or went out and got Nando's with our Nando's free card. Sometimes I cooked for Jedward or Olly – once I made them a wicked mango mess with mango, meringue and cream – but most of the time we were too tired or lazy to cook, so it was sweetcorn in the microwave. We took it in turns to clear up the kitchen, usually leaving it until it got in such a state that we had to clean it or die of contamination!

We didn't have a lot of spare time to just hang around the house, but we still managed to play Guitar Hero quite a lot after I got it for my birthday. Dannii even played it with me. When we got back on a Saturday and Sunday, most people would watch the shows on TV in the lounge. I couldn't watch, though, because it made me cringe to see myself. If I'd been on my own, I might have been able to watch it and criticize myself constructively, but I hated the thought of seeing my performance with everyone else watching, too. It gave me a really weird feeling. Oh no, I'd rather not, I thought. Instead, I'd go and eat something or paint my nails or straighten my hair in my room, or watch *Shameless* in my bathroom. I'm addicted to *Shameless*. I hate to miss it.

My favourite songs in the competition were 'The Scientist' and the Keane song 'Somewhere Only We Know', which I sang in week four, Rock Week. Louis thought it was a boring choice of song, but Cheryl loved it. I was really happy with what I was wearing: a sleeveless leather top covered in tassles, black leggings and boots. There was room to inhale and exhale, at least!

Bearing in mind Simon's criticisms from the week before, I was determined to use more of the stage this time, so I started the performance sitting on a box and then walked across the stage and back again as I sang. Of course, Simon had to comment on it. 'It was extraordinary. It was like an *X Factor* miracle tonight. You walked,' he said. Funny man!

I'd never said I didn't want to move around the stage. It didn't bother me either way, because it wasn't a dancing competition. I wasn't worried about my dancing, what mattered was my singing, so I was happy to move if that's what they wanted me to do. I never understood why it was so important, though. The biggest star to have come out of *The X Factor* is Leona Lewis and I've never seen her dance in my life.

I opened the next show with the Dusty Springfield song 'Son Of A Preacher Man.' It's one of my favourite songs as it's happy and dancey and everyone knows it. I wore leggings and a top, so I was really comfortable, and I got to dance around a little bit. I was told to make it sexy, but I said, 'I don't want to be sexy. I'm not that sort of girl.' So I just enjoyed it instead of being sexy.

I thought it went well and I did everything right. The audience cheered and cheered, but Simon said it was a bit 'cabaret'. I wasn't that bothered when he said that. 'Well, I enjoyed it; it doesn't matter.' He also said he thought I was vulnerable for the first time. I think he meant that I might be voted out, but I wasn't.

By this point, I was the last girl in the competition. Would that count for me or against me? I didn't have a clue. I sang 'Who Wants To Live Forever' by Queen and luckily it went really well. I felt a lot more confident this week, for some reason. I think the song just suited my voice really well.

'You totally sang your socks off and that was beautiful,' Cheryl said. She wasn't usually very enthusiastic about my singing, so that meant a lot.

Next was Simon. Oh God, what would he say? I wasn't expecting praise. You never expect praise from Simon. 'Well, Stacey, you know I will always, always be honest with you, because I think that it's important.'

Oh no, I thought. Here it comes!

'And that was, by a mile, the best performance of the night so far,' he added. I was so surprised, and the audience went crazy. They roared and then they started clapping and chanting my name. Dannii stood up and high-fived me from a distance. It couldn't have been better, it really couldn't.

The next week was George Michael week and Dannii chose 'I Can't Make You Love Me' for me. I'd never heard it before, but I fell in love with it. I thought it was beautiful and so sad. I actually liked most of the songs I was given, but I wish I'd had the chance to make them my own. If I could go back and do the show again, I'd ask for different musical arrangements for the songs, to give me a definite style and theme. I'd sing in a more natural way and I wouldn't walk around or pretend I could dance. Instead I'd sit at the microphone, wearing floaty, relaxed clothes, just singing.

Cheryl enjoyed my performance of 'I Can't Make You Love Me' and she was very encouraging. 'You need to start believing you're the winner,' she said when it was time for the judges to comment. 'Because you could do it.'

As for the other judges' comments, week after week Louis said I was progressing and maturing as a performer. I wasn't sure, though. Until I could get over my nerves, dry mouth and shaking, I knew I wouldn't feel at home on stage. If I'm honest, I think I became a better singer once the show had finished.

In the semi-finals I sang the Take That song 'Rule The Word'. I loved the song so much, but I was a bit worried about some of the low notes. Would I be able to get down that deep? The song was written for four men, after all. I'd been singing boys' songs for the last six weeks and I really wanted a girl's song now. I mean, I don't mind singing boys' songs if it's moved up to a girls' range, but we couldn't transpose 'Rule The Word' to a higher key because we didn't have any rights to the song.

Fortunately, Louis was really enthusiastic about my version and Simon said he thought it was the perfect choice for me, so that was a relief. 'You're the only girl left in the competition,' Cheryl said. 'Represent!' Then Dannii said she thought I'd really developed over the weeks and was emerging as a star. Wow! I went back to the house on cloud nine that night.

There were only four of us left now: me, Danyl, Olly and Joe. One night, a couple of researchers took us bowling at Shoreditch House, a cool members' club in the East End of London. I whooped the boys at bowling! I beat them all and they all remember it.

After we finished bowling, I offered to get Olly a drink. 'OK, then,' he said. So I got him a Jack Daniels and Coke and a Coke for myself. As he drank his JD and coke, he started to get louder.

'Why don't we go upstairs?' I suggested.

'Yeah,' he said.

There were loads of famous people upstairs in the bar, like Matt Horne and James Cordon. Me and Olly had another drink and he became louder by the second, then he started spilling drinks everywhere. Whoops! The researchers were going mental.

'Tell him to be quiet,' they kept saying. Meanwhile, Olly was wetting himself with laughter and so was I. It was such a funny night.

In the end we were taken home because we were being too loud. People kept asking, 'What's wrong with Olly?'

Back at the house, me and Olly sat up all night talking. He'd clearly had a few. 'Aren't you drunk?' he kept asking me.

'No,' I said. I didn't tell him that I'd only drunk Coke all night.

'I feel smashed. Why don't you?'

'I don't know,' I said, giggling.

In the morning, Olly's first words to me were, 'I hate you!' I think he was on to me – oh dear. We had a laugh about it when his head had stopped aching, though.

I was more nervous than ever before the week nine show. I think we all were, because there was a massive difference between being in the last four acts and being in the last three. If you got to the final and you were 'an *X Factor* finalist', you'd made it to a credible point.

I sang 'Somewhere', a song from the musical *West Side Story*. Louis loved it and called me 'The Diva from Dagenham', which made me laugh. Cheryl said I'd given her goose bumps, Simon said I was 'back in the game' and Dannii said it was a perfect performance. I was through to the final. I couldn't believe it. My dream had come true!

In the final, I was going to be singing three songs: 'Feeling Good', 'Who Wants To Live Forever' and 'What A

Wonderful World.' So obviously I needed three outfits! The show stylist, Fay, was just the loveliest lady and she took me to Selfridges to choose my clothes. 'You can wear whatever you want for the final,' she told me. She was so cool. She let me pick out whatever I fancied. Oh my God! I felt like I was in heaven.

I chose a sequined Dolce & Gabbana dress for 'Feeling Good', and some black snakeskin Christian Louboutin shoes for my 'Who Wants To Live Forever' performance. Yes, I'm talking about the red-soled shoes that everybody craves. I think I nearly died. Luckiest girl in the world! I had a dress made to go with the shoes, a black Swarovski corseted minidress with a great big skirt that you tied around the waist so that it flowed behind, all the way to the floor. That dress was so beautiful. And so was the blue Temperley off-the-shoulder dress I wore for 'What A Wonderful World', which Fay teamed with a gorgeous Gucci belt.

Fay was so lovely to me. She used to give me all the cast-off show clothes that no one else wanted, and when companies sent clothes in, she'd give them to me. Since I was the last girl left in the competition, there were loads of dresses for me to dive into. I wore a pair of pink Lacoste wellies once on *The Xtra Factor* on ITV2, and afterwards Lacoste sent me some free pairs!

I gave loads of the clothes away to the children's charity my sister supports. Everything was brand new and some of it was really lovely, like Lipsy tracksuits and Dolce & Gabbana T-shirts. It was so cool to be able to give them away. I couldn't have imagined someone giving me a Dolce & Gabbana T-shirt when I was little.

So now I had my three outfits, along with a white Temperley dress and Gucci belt for the final. Then I heard that

I was going to be singing a duet with Michael Bublé. I was in the studio and my tummy just dropped to the floor. Michael Bublé is going to sing with me! It was so special.

One of the reasons you're desperate to get into the final is that you know you'll get the opportunity to sing with somebody unbelievable. You dream about it and I just couldn't wait. Being paired with Michael Bublé was an absolute honour. His voice is flawless. But he's not just a good singer, he's a proper musician who really knows what he's talking about and devotes his life to music. As I've said, I was already a massive fan, so I was thrilled to get the chance to sing with him.

The last time I'd met him was when I sang 'When You Wish Upon A Star' in week three. He was so lovely to me then and he was even lovelier this time. He's so small and cool and he really knows how to make you feel good. Joe and Olly didn't have much rehearsal time with their singing partners, but Michael was happy to rehearse loads.

He came in to hair and make-up while I was getting my hair done and tapped me on the shoulder. 'Hey, kid, you want to rehearse?' he asked.

'OK.'

It was so cool. He took me into his dressing room, where loads of his family and friends were sitting around, and we rehearsed in there. I couldn't believe it. I was in Michael Bublé's dressing room and he was giving me a singing lesson. 'A little bit higher here; a little bit lower there,' he said. 'Are you comfortable? Are you happy? We've got to enjoy this.' He's a really nice man, and so talented. He can work out harmonies in seconds, so he would sing a line and say, 'You sing this,' and it would be a harmony. 'Or maybe do this,' he'd say, suggesting an ad-lib. It was so clever.

166

For the final on 12 December, I felt I'd done well enough and come far enough to relax a bit. At last! This is the end anyway, and I'm here for it, I thought. So they were my best performances, by far. I hadn't been able to unwind before that. I just felt incredibly grateful to be there, just so happy and excited.

As usual, my whole family was there to support me. It was good of everyone to come and cheer me on every week. It meant they couldn't do anything else for ten weekends in a row, because not only were they there every Saturday to see me perform, they had to be at the Sunday results show as well. I'm so lucky to have such a loyal, dedicated family. Even better, Zach was allowed to come to the Sunday shows, which gave me an extra chance to see him.

Aaron also came to every single show, even though I hardly ever had the chance to speak to him, let alone have a proper conversation with him. I was aware of him being there and being supportive, but so much was happening that I couldn't really take it in at the time. I was distracted by everything and I was having the time of my life, so I kind of ignored him a little bit. Then, when I went home to see my family, it was so mad and busy that I was like, 'Hello, good-bye!' Poor Aaron. He never, ever, let me down; he stuck by me and took everything in his stride.

I was in another world. Ever since I got through that first *X Factor* audition at the O2, my life had felt strangely dream-like. Even now, when I'm singing at an awards ceremony or being photographed for a magazine, I have to consciously register that I'm actually there. It's so strange. I have to remind myself that it's real. So imagine being on stage with Michael Bublé and singing with him. It was just the coolest feeling I've ever had! That definitely felt like a dream.

We all had to sing the first song we'd performed in front of the judges, which in my case was 'What A Wonderful World', and they then gave their comments. Cheryl said it was nice to see me so much more relaxed and Simon agreed.

'You were turning into a nervous wreck over the last few weeks,' he said.

'Oh, thank you,' I said, a bit offended, even though I knew it was true.

'But now you're like a calm nervous wreck and you're singing beautifully,' he continued.

'Thanks,' I said, and I meant it.

'I'm so happy that you sang that song again, because it takes me back to the very first time we met you,' he said. 'You surprised me then and you continue to surprise me. You thoroughly, thoroughly deserve your place here tonight.'

'Stacey, it's just been the most emotional week ever,' said Dannii, wiping tears from her eyes. 'I'm very, very proud of you.'

I was so proud of myself, too. Standing in the middle of the *X Factor* stage as the results came through, clutching hands with Dannii, I felt so happy, even though I was frowning like crazy.

'The public have voted,' said Dermot. 'I'm about to reveal which two acts have received the most votes and are through to the next stage of the *X Factor* final tomorrow and, of course, which act has received the fewest votes and has finished in third place. That act will be heading home.

'In no particular order, the first act heading through to the next stage of the *X Factor* final is . . . Olly!'

I smiled as I saw Olly jump into the air and shout, 'Yes!'

'Stacey and Joe, that means one of you is through to the next stage of the final tomorrow night,' Dermot continued, 'and one of you has received the fewest votes from the public and is out of the competition. So here it is: in no particular order, the second act through to tomorrow night's final is . . . Joe! Congratulations, Joe, you are through to tomorrow night. Thanks so much, Joe.'

Dermot took my hand and said, 'All right?'

'Yeah, fine,' I said. 'I came third! That's really good. I'm really proud.'

'It's been an incredible journey,' Dannii told Dermot. 'I've made an amazing friend and thank you everybody who supported her from day one. She's an absolute talent and a star.' Wow!

I wasn't at all disappointed that I hadn't won. I was the happiest girl in the world. What an achievement! I'd done it all. I was there through the whole thing: beginning, middle and end. And when I came out of it, everybody had a good opinion of me. Not one person had anything horrible to say, so that was just perfect. I'd had the time of my life. I couldn't have asked for more. I don't even know if I'd have wanted to win; it didn't matter anyway, because I felt so thankful to have been there for the final.

It was my dream to win *The X Factor*, but my life and soul didn't depend on it. I've got many dreams that I haven't fulfilled, but it doesn't mean that I'm unhappy. I don't want to feel I have to win everything and then be miserable if I don't. I'd rather just go in and enjoy something. You get what you get and you make the most of it.

During the competition, I never once looked to see how many votes I'd got. There was no point, in my eyes, because the voting went up and down all the time. Olly told me that he never won a vote, but he still came second. I was never in the bottom two, like Olly was, but I came third. The polls don't mean anything. You can be really popular for the whole show, then make one mistake in the final and lose.

The X Factor is a mainstream pop show, so if one week you sang something that wasn't totally commercial, it could easily affect your vote. You tended to get the most votes when you sang a power ballad. A boy singing a current hit by a girl is always popular as well, partly because it's a current song and partly because a boy singing a girl's song is intriguing and appeals to that kind of audience.

Now it was down to the final two, I really wanted Olly to win, even though we both knew that he wouldn't. I was crying as I watched the final backstage. 'Why are you crying?' someone from the hair team asked me.

'Because I know Olly's not going to win.'

'Hmmm,' they said. They obviously sensed it, too.

Then we all got our phones out and voted for Olly. I love Joe, don't get me wrong, but I felt upset for Olly. When he didn't win and everyone ran over to Joe to congratulate him, I thought, What about Olly? He lost. Go over to Olly. Joe's fine; he won.

I ran on stage to hug them both, wearing the white Temperley dress I'd saved for the final, in case I got there. I was allowed to keep it afterwards, but not the Gucci belt. That had to go back, unfortunately. I felt sorry for Olly so I gave him a cuddle. 'You're in the final, so you're a winner,' I said.

'Yeah,' he agreed, looking downhearted.

As soon as the show was over, me, Olly, Joe, my sister, my brother and my dad went back to the *X Factor* house in Hampstead and started gathering up our stuff. My room was such a mess. It was full of all the clothes and girly stuff I'd collected over the ten weeks. We had to stuff everything into black sacks and squeeze them into my dad's car. We

Me, Mummy and a very little Zachary bum at Symonds Yat in the Forest of Dean, Wye Valley.

Zach, love of my life.

Karen (left) and Mummy – great friends.

First audition for the *X Factor*, eek!!
Feeling nervous.

Me and Dannii, BFF!
Love her!

X Factor tour fun times.

X Factor finals, wahoo, I'm singing 'What A Wonderful World'.

Dannii was brilliant with Zach, he completely fell in love with her.

Dannii comes to Dagenham. I'm sure she'd never set foot there before!

My Aaron!

Me on the road,
uh oh!!

Best brother and sis ever.

Me and Mum two.

At Soccer 6, with Zach
by my side.

Soccer 6 competitive!

Fun with my
gorgeous baby.

I'm a Celebrity gang – love 'em all.

Me and Gillers.

A long-awaited kiss.
Poor Aaron, I really
stank!

Surprise, OMG! Jemma had organized it all brilliantly.

Jemma's cake for me. See that cute little model of me.

From warring sisters to best friends – I ❤ you, Jemma!

My little prince, at the Palazzo
Versace hotel in Australia.

Cuddles on the carpet.

On the panel of *Loose Women* – what great girls! We had a laugh.

could hardly get them all in because there was so much, but I wouldn't leave anything behind. All these massage oil companies and nail varnish brands had sent in samples of their goods and I had to keep them all. They were just too good to leave behind.

Finally the house was clear and we were tidying up. 'What about the jukeboxes and the Xboxes and the Wii?' someone said.

Olly and Joe decided they didn't want anything, but I was allowed to take the Xboxes and the Wii. It was wicked. I love a good game. I'm a real Xbox, Wii and PlayStation fan. Mario is my favourite. I love everything Mario and I still play it now. It's really sad.

So that was it, the end of an era. Mad! I wasn't upset about leaving the house and *The X Factor* behind, but on my way home I started to miss Olly. There was suddenly a huge gap in my life. Where is he? I thought. It was horrible. I hated it. I wanted to be near him all the time, because I truly loved our friendship.

When I got home, Zach was lying in his little bed, sleeping like an angel. Although I knew I was going to miss Olly and the highs and lows of *The X Factor*, it was so lovely to be back with my little munchkin that I didn't care about anything else. I shouldn't have woken him up, but I couldn't help myself. 'Missed you, missed you, really want to kiss you!' I said, kissing him all over. That night, I went to sleep with him in my arms for the first time in ten weeks. It was absolute heaven.

Chapter 11

When I woke up, it was as if a spell had been broken and I was back in the outside world again. The only difference was there were paparazzi outside my house and my tour manager was ringing me to go through my schedule. I had been automatically signed to a management agency, along with the other *X Factor* finalists, so thankfully there was someone to organize and manage my bookings. I started doing interviews and photo shoots immediately and was on the covers of *New!* and *Heat* magazines. There were also gigs lined up all over the UK, in England, Scotland, Wales and Northern Ireland. It was all really fun stuff. My job was singing now – how amazing!

Even though there was a lot to do, it was really refreshing to be home and feel normal again. *The X Factor* is a hard, strange struggle, and being back with my family felt really good, whether we were cooking, chatting, acting like idiots, peeping out of the window at the photographers outside or doing absolutely nothing. It was lovely to be with my little man, too, and I wanted to spend every minute with him. I relished everything I did with him, even the everyday things, like bathing and feeding him.

Back with my family, I could relax and be normal. We didn't talk much about *The X Factor* or my career prospects. My mum and dad are so proud of me and they would do anything to support me, but we didn't get too excited about it all, because we knew that the kind of success I was having doesn't necessarily last long. Nothing lasts, really, so it's not a good idea to get used to a lifestyle unless you know for certain that you can keep it going. There's no point getting used to something unless you're set up and know that you're going to be where you are for the next ten years. Otherwise, six months later, you could be back where you started after getting everybody excited about something that never happens. I'm not saying my life wasn't changing; it was, but the important things stayed exactly the same: my son, my family, my friends. I saw a lot of Aaron again, too. We were closer friends than ever. He was definitely my best friend now.

In the run-up to Christmas, people kept asking me, 'How does it feel to be famous?' or 'Is it a shock to be famous suddenly?' But even to this day I don't think of myself as famous. I'm just not. I think you have to be established and around for a really long time before you can call yourself that. All right, some people know who I am, but that doesn't make me famous, not in my eyes. My dream of fame involves having a really prosperous career, maybe singing a string of hit songs or appearing on a really big TV show. Then I might think, Yeah, I'm famous.

People like Robbie Williams and Whitney Houston are famous; Holly Willoughby and Dermot O'Leary are big TV presenters, and Halle Berry is a movie star – I've just been on a reality TV show. Don't get me wrong, I loved it and I'm really grateful for the experience, but it doesn't make me famous.

A lot of people come out of those shows and get mobbed everywhere they go. When Lloyd Daniels went shopping after *X Factor*, he was surrounded wherever he went. I don't get mobbed. Instead, people tend to come up to me and say, 'Well done. We're really proud of you.' Or, 'I'm so happy you're doing good.'

'So am I, thank you,' I say.

Yes! I think. People like me. It's the best feeling. There's no downside to it, like there is to being mobbed or followed. It feels as if the people who like me are people like me: normal, down-to-earth, nice people.

Of course, it can be a little bit difficult walking through a packed train station, especially if someone says, 'Can I have a photo?' because that attracts a lot of attention. But just being in the street or a shopping centre is fine. I can go shopping and people might ask for a photo, but they won't crowd me. Generally they're not rude and they leave me alone, unless they see me being followed by photographers. Then they become curious and start following as well, whispering, 'Who is it? Who is it?'

About a month after *The X Factor* finished, me, my dad and Zach were driving into Romford when I realized we were being followed. I sensed it straight away. 'Dad, I'm being followed,' I said.

'Calm down and pull over,' my dad said.

I went to pull over, but the photographer must have thought we were turning off, so he sped up and went straight into the back of us, with Zach in the car. 'Oh my God, my baby!' I yelled. It was so scary.

It wasn't a big smash and everything was fine, but he had gone too far and he knew it. People say, 'You want it; you asked for it.' And I agree, to an extent, because I would have got out of the car and done photos – I wasn't trying to get away from it – but some photographers have got something wrong with them. I think you've got to be a bit nuts to do that job.

The photographer looked really shaken as he apologized. 'Look, you could have just stopped and asked for the photo,' I said. 'You didn't have to go mental.' He apologized again, swapped insurance details and then drove off without taking a single photo.

The photographers mostly wanted pictures of what I was wearing, I think. And it didn't matter what I wore; the paper would shape some rubbish story around it and say it was the best outfit ever. If I wore my jogging bottoms or my tracksuit, the caption would read, 'Look at Stacey's winter wonderland tracksuit!' It was always flattering, even though sometimes they must have thought, Oh God, that tracksuit again. We can't put that in there again.

The only person who sold a story on me was a boy from Ohio, who I'd met when I was out there on the theatre exchange programme with my college. He said that I'd kissed him. Big deal. Anyway, we had a really good laugh, but I didn't kiss him. I didn't kiss anybody on that trip. There was a picture of us in a hot tub, but everybody in that part of Ohio had a hot tub in their garden. Oh well, I thought when it came out. That's a good one!

My first photo shoot was for *New!*, and it was so good, because I did it with Zachary. It was me, Zach and a Christmas tree in a studio. I was in a red dress and Zach was dressed as a little elf. It was so much fun. Zach was blown away by the snow and the huge presents. 'Wow!' he said. 'Wow, Mummy!' He was really impressed, even though they were only empty boxes and bits of white paper. I loved it, too, because somebody did my hair and make-up and I got to choose the photos I liked. They weren't allowed to use the ones I didn't like. Yes!

It was so cool, with a proper set and good lighting. I was

really nervous. I remember thinking, I don't know what to do. I don't know how to look nice for photos. I just smiled the whole time. I wasn't very good at putting on those pretty, moody expressions that some people do so well. I think I'm better at it now, but in my first photo shoots I got my gums right out, because I didn't know what else to do.

My first gig was at G-A-Y on the Saturday after I left the house, and it was wicked. I sang, 'The Scientist', 'Somewhere Over The Rainbow', 'Son Of A Preacher Man', 'The Way You Make Me Feel' and 'Who Wants To Live Forever'. I love singing songs I can relate to. The lyrics have to mean something to me, then I can pretend to be in the song. I like it when I'm singing and I think, That's me. I'm singing about myself.

I love performing at G-A-Y, because there's always such a good atmosphere there. At a straight club, somebody always gets angry and wants a fight, but that never seems to happens at gay clubs. You couldn't get a less moody place. The clubbers all seem happy and lively, and everyone loves everyone. It's so much better. I love camp humour, too – it's clever and a little bit catty, but in a nice way.

It's funny, because the *Gay Times* always want to do pieces on me. They think I have a big gay following, but I don't know. If I do, I think it's because the way I talk is a little bit camp and I act a little bit gay, if that makes sense. I mean, gay from a boy's perspective, not from a girl's.

For my G-A-Y performance, I decided to wear the beautiful white Temperley dress I'd worn for two minutes on *The X Factor* when I was congratulating the winners. I was planning to wear it with some really high shoes. 'You should wear your pink Lacoste wellies instead!' Jeremy Joseph, the promoter, joked.

'I'll put them on again when I get back in the car,' I said.

'Have you got them with you, then?' he asked.

'Yes, they're my comfies,' I said.

'Then you've got to wear them on stage,' he urged. 'Go on!'

In the end he persuaded me to wear them on stage and I did the whole performance in my comfy old wellies! I wasn't nervous, I was excited. I knew the crowd had come to see me, so I felt supported. Everyone was cheering so loudly, it was amazing. I loved every minute of it. I was buzzing when I came off stage.

It was only after I left *The X Factor* that I remembered what it was like to sing for fun again. It so different when there's no pressure; it's another atmosphere altogether when you're not being told that you could be voted out of the competition at any minute. On the show, I found it hard to pretend that I was having a load of fun and everything was fine. But you can't help having a good time when you're singing to people who've come to see you and everyone's enjoying themselves. It all meant too much on the show, whereas now I could just have a laugh.

I was a better singer, too. No one can train you to sing, but they can help you with your technique. Being on *The X Factor* had taught me how to stand properly and how to breathe properly. It didn't change the way I sang, because everyone has their own style of singing and you can't do much about that, although you can imitate someone else's style, using your palate and oesophagus to adjust your voice. If you think about it, some people speak from the chest, others through their nose, so you can always change the way you speak and sing. But at the end of the day, you are what you are. On *The X Factor*, they don't want to change you too

177

much; they just teach you some techniques. So if you want to hold a note a little bit longer, or go higher or lower than you usually would without it affecting your voice and style, they show you how.

It's easy to sing if you're relaxed. If you're comfortable with your song and confident that you can sing it technically – if it's not too high or too low, too long or too short – then it's a piece of pie to lose yourself in the song and connect with the words. But if there's a part of it you can't get right, or a note you think is a bit too high, or too long, you will constantly be thinking about how long that note is, or how high you're going to have to go, and you'll never be properly in the song.

My Christmas break began a couple of days after the G-A-Y gig. I was so pleased to have a few weeks to devote to Zach and I wanted to spend lots of time at home over the holiday. Our Christmas was really nice and quiet, just the same as usual, except that Dannii Minogue gave me a massive silver bag – made by the same people who make Mulberry bags – full of make-up: Nars, Mac, Chanel, everything. It was the best Christmas present in the world.

I wrapped up some of the free stuff I'd come home with from the *X Factor* house to give to my friends and family as Christmas presents. It wasn't like I suddenly had loads of money to take everyone on holiday or buy expensive presents, because you don't get paid to go on *The X Factor*.

I knew what I wanted to do with my money when I did finally earn some, though: move out of my mum's house. If I didn't have Zach, I'd be happy to stay with my mum all my life, but ever since I'd had him, I've wanted him to have a house he could call his, not always be saying, 'Nana's house' or 'Grandad's house' or 'Aaron's house'.

I definitely didn't dream about buying a mansion. I didn't want a mortgage I wouldn't be able to pay five years down the line and I didn't need fifty rooms to dust every day! I don't see the point in living to excess. It's all right if you want to go on a fantastic holiday or buy something nice once in a while, but I think it's crazy and selfish to throw money around needlessly. I'd feel guilty if I did that. What about everyone else in the world? I'd think.

After Christmas, I did a really cool shoot for *Heat*. It had an *Alice in Wonderland* theme and I was photographed in a tiny, tiny house. Zach came along, but he wasn't supposed to be in the photos. Of course, he couldn't resist joining me in the little house, though. 'It's my house,' he kept saying, and I could understand why! In the end they included him in the photos and their cover shot featured me and Zach in the mini house.

Later, I did another shoot, for *Hello!* It was the Prince's issue – the one with the famous black and white photo of Prince William on the front. I was really privileged to be in that issue, which was the first *Hello!* to have a black and white cover.

What's funny is that the shoot showed me wearing the most amazing clothes and cool jewellery and pretending I was running around in this beautiful posh rented London pad I didn't own and would never have been able to afford. I know! Still, it was really fun and Zach was in his element. I tried to keep him off the set, but he insisted: 'No, I want a picture!'

I suppose it's not surprising that people started saying, 'You must be rich now!' Even random strangers in shops would make sly references to my new-found wealth. People honestly think that the minute you're on telly, you must be a millionaire. How wrong they are! It's not that you don't get paid well, it's just that, firstly, as I said before, you don't see the money for at least three months and, secondly, the minute you get paid, 20 per cent goes to your manager and 20 per cent to your booking agent. Then there's tax, and expenses like tour manager fees, rider and petrol fees. You're left with quite a small percentage at the end of it. If people saw only your gross earnings, they'd say, 'Yeah, she's rich!' But if they could see your net earnings, they'd say, 'OK, she earns a decent living.' It's really weird. I only see a fraction of my gross earnings.

I was determined to be cautious about money from the start. A couple of contestants left *The X Factor* and instantly rented smart apartments in London. How much is that going to cost a month? Thousands of pounds. And when it runs out, then what? Then there's nothing left. It's not even like they were putting down a deposit and paying off a mortgage. They were just giving that money away. I hate that idea; I can't think of anything worse. I'd rather put my money somewhere, and if in five years' time I can't pay my mortgage, at least I'll have a lump sum in my house.

I haven't had any financial advice; it's just common sense. For the first time in my entire life I had a bit of money, and the last thing I was going to do was spend it. I was determined to save until I could put a deposit down on a property. Then, I thought, I won't have to worry if nothing comes of my career, because I'll have a house. I'd be settled and secure on the property ladder at twenty-one years old. How fantastic!

That's what I just didn't get about the contestants who blew their money. You are so young, I thought. Go and invest in something that you will never have another chance to buy in a million years. But some people want to live for the moment, which is cool. Everyone's different. Some people are happy to live for now and have a great time and then go back to normal. 'I did that,' they can say afterwards. 'I had that lifestyle and I loved it.'

What separates them from me is Zach. When you have a kid, you can't be selfish. What about when he grows up? It's fine to have had the time of your life, but what about him? I decided it would be crazy to get a nice London pad, throw all my money away on enjoying myself and then have to start again for him. This way, I thought, we would both enjoy it.

'So where do you want to live?' Aaron asked me when I brought up my dream of owning my own house for the hundredth time.

'I don't know,' I said.

People kept saying, 'You're going to move out of Dagenham, aren't you?' And I'd think, Hey, I quite like Dagenham. In fact, I love where I've grown up. I walk out the door and I say hello to everyone, because they're like my family. If I were ever in trouble, there are a thousand people on these streets that would be there for me. Knowing that is such a nice feeling. You don't get that realness in a lot of neighbourhoods.

Take where my dad lives in Hornchurch, for instance. It's a little bit posh and they all size up each other's cars. Although my dad says hello to his neighbours every day, it's not the same hello that I have with my neighbours. They would never say, 'Come over and have a drink,' like the people across the road here would say. It's not the same. I don't care what anyone says, I know they genuinely want me in for a drink. They've always just been there as friends and I love it.

I'd been thinking about Grays, where Aaron lived, because

just a couple of miles away there's countryside and horses, which appeals to me. Still, before I could feel happy about moving there, I wanted to get to know some of the people in the area better and make friends with them. So I started going up there and hanging out in the pub where all Aaron's friends go and where he took me out. I was a bit worried about some of the girls, because they're mates with Aaron's last girlfriend, who isn't a fan of mine. But as it turned out, we clicked instantly. We quickly became close and now we're good friends.

As I've said, Aaron's mates remind me of my old Abbs Cross schoolfriends. Me and the girls had similar memories of what we'd got up to at school and the pop groups we'd liked and the TV shows we'd watched. It felt like we'd known each other for ever because we had so much in common.

No one was impressed that I'd been on *The X Factor*. It would have been different if they'd been primary school age, but a room full of twenty-one-year-olds just aren't that interested in *The X Factor*. It wasn't a big deal to them, so no one acted any differently towards me; they were all completely normal.

I know that people from zero to a hundred love the show, but it's different when you're in your twenties. You don't just walk up to someone and come over all giddy about it, especially when you're from an area like Grays. You wouldn't want to act that interested, because it would look silly. Even where I live, people just say, 'Well done,' and that's it. They don't rush up screeching, 'Oh my God!'

Someone who's been on a talent show is viewed differently to someone who's been successful in their own right. In many people's eyes, even if you've won *The X Factor*, you've just been on a telly programme. But if S Club 7 walked in they'd be impressed, because although they may think they're cheesy, they'd respect the fact that they'd had so many number ones. I don't mean to be rude, but being on a talent show is less credible. It's not cool and it didn't make me special.

Also, money isn't necessarily a driving force for some of my friends, who have different dreams in life. They aspire to take care of their families and have fun. Not everyone wants to be a singer, a lawyer or a doctor. They don't look at me and think, She's successful. They just think, Good for you, and they are very happy for me.

A lot of my friends are really family-oriented and have the best time being stay-at-home mums and devoting their lives to their children, which in my opinion is a full-time career in itself. They just want to get by and enjoy themselves.

When I'm asked to a premiere, I sometimes take a friend along. For instance, I took a friend and her daughter to the premiere of *Tangled*. She loved it, but I know some of my friends would be like, 'No thanks.' Aaron isn't interested in that kind of thing. It doesn't appeal to everyone. In fact, the lifestyle I've chosen doesn't appeal to as many people as you might think, because it's sometimes not real, or it doesn't seem real to an outsider looking in. There's a lot of networking involved and industry chit-chat that doesn't interest people outside of the business – and why should it?

It probably seems a bit false to people who don't want to be in the entertainment industry. I see it with Aaron. When I say, 'Do you want to come to these TV awards?' he'll say, 'Not really.' You could ask a thousand teenagers and they'd all want to go, but when you get to a certain age and that's not your chosen lifestyle, you just want to be normal.

Going to a premiere is different. It's so exciting to be around people I never thought I'd get to meet. There's often fancy food, cakes and drinks, and everything is sparkly and beautiful. You get to walk down the red carpet at the beginning and go home in a nice car at the end. It's often more like a dream than a social event – then the minute I get home, it's back to reality!

I love it, but I understand why Aaron doesn't want to come along. It's not his dream night out, because he's coming to work with me. It's like me following him when he goes off to render and paint a house. At the end of the day, it is part of my job.

A friend of mine saw me on *This Morning* and I was with Keith Lemon. She loves Keith Lemon – she thinks he's hilarious – so she said, 'I saw you with Keith Lemon. That was so funny.'

'He's lovely. We had a laugh,' I said, and that was it. I couldn't have gone on to say any more about it, or recount everything he said and how he said it. That would have made me cringe.

When I meet celebrities, they're at work, like I am, and they tend to be exactly how they are on the telly. They always will be that way unless I become really good friends with them and they start relaxing in front of me. So it's not like I can ever say, 'Oh, she's a right cow,' or, 'He's really horrible,' because I never see that side of people. I've never met anyone who isn't exactly how they are on the telly. They're just how you'd expect them to be, because that's their job. Their job is to keep up an appearance.

The best thing about Aaron's group of friends is that a lot of the girls have kids. Jade is the same age as me and she has a little girl called Lilly who is the same age as Zach. Lilly is now Zach's best friend; she's a day younger than he is and they're really close, like a boy and girl version of each other. It's so nice when your kid has friends to play with. You can go to the park and watch them in the playground while you sit on the grass with your mates and talk. It's perfect!

Some of my old schoolfriends have got kids now, too. Jade from Abbs Cross has a little girl and she's lovely. I think it's so nice when people leave school, fall in love with someone they went to school with and that's it. It sounds wrong and everyone goes on about young mums, but to me it seems just like the old days when people didn't have anything except each other. You fell in love and settled down and had kids, simple as that.

Most of my friends who have kids are with the fathers of their children and some have been with them since they were thirteen years old. It's really sweet and it's all they want. Their lives focus around their kids, their partner and their home.

They don't want to do what I'm doing. They just don't aspire to have a career. And although some girls want a job or a career first, or in between kids, I believe that ultimately 90 per cent of us want to have kids and a family and that's all we've ever wanted.

Chapter 12

Peeping at the audience from behind the stage, fluttering with nerves, I stared out at the massive sea of people. So this is what 10,000 people looks like, I thought. Oh my God, it's like a hundred times the size of the audience at *The X Factor* live shows! The noise was deafening. People were screaming their heads off and the atmosphere was reaching fever pitch.

My heart started thumping. 'Will I be any good?' I asked myself. I was terrified and totally out of my comfort zone.

It was time to take my position underneath the stage. We all started the show there, rising up in lifts and appearing on stage in the order we were voted out of the competition. I went to my place and waited for my cue. This is it, I thought. *This is it!* The sound of 10,000 people shouting and stamping their feet filled the building. Down in the depths of the auditorium, the vibrations went right through me.

Suddenly the lights went off above me. 'And now, what you've all been waiting for: your *X Factor* finalists!' boomed Jeff Brazier, the show's host.

Oh no, I thought, my skin prickling with anticipation. Here it comes.

There were five acts going up before me: Lucie, Lloyd, Jamie, John and Edward and Danyl. Soon it would be my turn and I couldn't mess it up. There was so much to remember. I was completely buzzing, but I was also worried about my dance routine to the brand-new song I was performing,

'Queen Of The Night' by Whitney Houston. Everything about that routine was making me nervous. One: I'd had to learn the song from scratch, so it didn't come as easily as my other songs; two: it had a faster rhythm than my other songs and I had to move and shake it and dance sexily around a pole with four dancers. I *so* didn't want to be doing that.

That morning, we'd done a dress rehearsal and sound check at ten o'clock. There was so much to remember in the 'Queen Of The Night' routine that I'd started to panic. Why have they done this to me? I thought. I'm never going to remember the choreography, let alone pull off the whole performance.

At the end of the rehearsal, everything was swirling around my head: lyrics, high notes, dance moves, the lot. Luckily, I wasn't the only one in a fluster. Everyone was thinking, How did we get here? When did it happen? When did this get so intense and scary?

The *X Factor* tour is always a massive sellout and this was the biggest, maddest *X Factor* tour ever. Our first show was on Monday, 15 February 2010, two months after I'd left the *X Factor* house. After two days' rehearsing in a little studio in London, we'd come to Liverpool seven days earlier to prepare for our first show at the Echo Arena, which is one of the biggest venues in the UK. Everyone was excited, but we all felt a bit daunted by the fact that we were at the start of a fifty-three-date tour, with only two days off over the next month and a half. What if I get a cold or a sore throat? I thought anxiously. What if I can't go on one night?

Tonight was the night that counted, though, and I had to give it my best. The audience was full of people who had voted for us over the ten-week TV series, so we owed them a fantastic show, especially as they'd paid a lot of money to come and see us live. We were all determined to make it a night to remember.

I thought back to the first concert I'd ever seen, the Spice Girls at Wembley Arena. Me and my sister were obsessed with the Spice Girls as kids. We begged and begged my dad to get us tickets to go, and in the end he gave in, despite the cost. I was ten years old and it was one of the most exciting experiences of my childhood – I also got to see them when they did their comeback tour ten years later, which was wicked. Three years on, and who would have thought that I'd be singing at the same venues the Spice Girls had performed at? It was unbelievable! I had to keep reminding myself that it was real.

From below the stage I could hear the intro starting. It began with a blast of Carmina Burana, the scary opera music they use for the *X Factor* judging part. One by one, each of us rose up onto the stage. It was the best feeling; I was so excited. The audience went crazy, cheering and cheering us. The noise was incredible. It just got louder and louder as I went up in the lift, and I felt more and more excited and ecstatic. I arrived on stage feeling overwhelmed. The noise of the crowd was like a massive wave of sound crashing all over the stage. It was amazing. I loved it.

Finally Joe rose up into the spotlight, the crowd screamed even louder, the music reached a crescendo and bang! It went dark again. After a short pause, the guitar intro to our first song, 'I Gotta Feeling', started up. It was a group song; the boys came out from behind the doors at the back of the stage and sang the first lines, then me and Lucie came out and sang, then John and Edward jumped out and did their bit. Everyone was running on adrenaline; you could just feel it. It was so brilliant. The whole audience started singing along, dancing and going mad. It was mind-blowing, just the biggest buzz ever.

When we left the stage at the end of the song, I thought, I want to do that again a million times over. Once you've been out there the first time, you realize there's nothing better. It's electric.

I sang 'The Scientist' as a taster quite near the beginning of the show, and then near the end, just before Olly and Joe, I sang another three songs: 'What A Wonderful World', 'Queen Of The Night' and 'Who Wants To Live Forever'. In the few first shows, I was out of time or out of tune a couple of times. We all were, because we were learning how to perform in a massive arena. Everything about it is different, from the way the backing music sounds to the size of the stage. Not all stages are the same. If the stage is in the middle of an auditorium, there can be a delay on the music, and it takes a little bit of time to get used to.

I wore different costumes for each of my songs and for the group songs, so I changed into six costumes over the course of the concert. They were all outfits from the show. I didn't really want to wear any of my show clothes – I would have preferred to wear short floaty dresses as it's a bit more me – but you have to maintain your image from the show. I was the one who sang the ballads and the slow songs, usually wearing a long ball gown, so they wanted to stick with that look for continuity. I loved it, but I also wanted to look young and be myself.

During *The X Factor* competition, I got blonder and blonder and more and more tanned, then when the show finished, I went even further. I wanted to be really blonde and really tanned. My aim was to be perfect, flawless and blonde. Later on, though, I started to feel like a tangerine. I need to get rid of the tan, I decided. But if I was going to get rid of the tan, I needed to get rid of the white hair as well, so I went back to my natural colour. Now I can imagine going blonde again, but not that blonde. Honey blonde, maybe, but I wasn't born to be peroxide.

On tour, we had a make-up artist called Lou, who taught me a few essential tricks. For instance: don't put black eyeliner right inside your eye, put it just underneath; don't use lip liner, because it'll make you look like a transvestite; and draw your eyebrows higher. She taught me which colours looked nice on me and advised me against anything too bright. As time went on, with her guidance I started to do my make-up a bit better. I'm not anywhere near as good as Lou, but I feel I can go out looking half decent now, rather than wearing caked-on foundation and big, thick lines of black eyeliner.

Lou taught me a lot. After all, I was an inexperienced girl from Essex, so it wasn't unusual for me to have a bit of a ring round my chin where I hadn't blended my foundation into my neck. Sometimes I'd draw my eyebrows really thick as well, so I'd have big dark eyebrows and too many eyelashes. It wasn't horrendous. It was never a case of, 'Oh no, look at her make-up!' But the way I wear my make-up now is more subtle.

It's not always lovely when someone does your make-up, though. The idea is nice, but there's something really personal about it, so the minute they do something you don't like, you think, I look hideous. I hate this! That happened a couple of times on *The X Factor*, but there was nothing I could say or do. You have to go on stage looking the way they want you to look. There's a brief and you can't get in the way of that, so I didn't feel I could object. When you come from somewhere with no opportunity to a place where you might have a chance to do something great, the last thing you want to do is jeopardize that, so I didn't say anything if I didn't like my make-up or outfit. I accepted it all.

I've learned now that you should definitely stand up for yourself, because you end up feeling better about the way you look and giving a better performance. Back then, though, I would have agreed to anything. I didn't want to risk going against the grain. You could have put me in a Pierrot mask with a white face, red cheeks and a big triangle hat and I wouldn't have complained. I was just so grateful to be there.

I had been secretly dreading my 'Queen Of The Night' dance routine, but suddenly I found myself (not very secretly) loving it. I don't know what happened; I just let go and went for it. 'Whooooo!' Once I'd relaxed, I enjoyed every second of it, and about halfway through the song it began to feel like I was at a party.

It's just the most overwhelming feeling to think, while you're performing, There are 10,000 people in this room, all having the night of their lives with me! It's like being under a waterfall of happiness. You feel so good about yourself. It gives you an amazing sense of achievement and a real sense of worth. You feel so proud, too. The only other thing that could ever make you so proud is your kids. So I often took a moment in the middle of a song to take in all the excitement and think, Yes, I'm singing and dancing and having the time of my life, and everyone around me is enjoying themselves. It doesn't get better than that.

I could easily have done that tour for a year. Every night you got this massive buzz, because you went from being really anxious and sick with nerves to feeling ecstatic as you got up on stage, where everyone was screaming at you. You went from one extreme to another and it felt fantastic. Then there was a huge sense of satisfaction at the end of the show, when you were saying your goodbyes to the audience from the stage. Applause is such a wonderful thing. I loved it as a kid and I still love it now.

After the performance, I often went straight to bed because we didn't get back to the hotel until 11p.m. or midnight. If we had a matinee the following day, then I really needed my sleep, but sometimes a few of us would watch a film in someone's room. We stayed in some nice hotels on the tour. The one in Brighton was really special. It had a cottagey feel to it and there were pop art pictures everywhere.

Our weekly highlight was spray-tanning night, when a lady came and topped up our fake tans. Everyone got sprayed, even Joe. Some of us loved it, especially me and Olly. It gave us a really good, natural tan – well, everyone except me, because I used to beg for extra layers, sometimes as many as three! I couldn't get enough of it. I felt I needed it, what with all those bright stage lights bleaching out my face. You always look pale under floodlights, no matter how many spray tans you've had. In daylight, though, I looked like an Oompa Loompa, but I didn't care. Aaron used to laugh at me when he came to visit, but I thought it looked nice with my bleached blonde hair. I liked the look: it's really fake, but pretty.

These days, I don't wear fake tan because I can't be bothered with all the palaver of getting it on my clothes and scrubbing it off my body. The sheets go orange and you go patchy and smell of biscuits. Don't even think about wearing white if you've just put fake tan on! Still, it's good for touring and I still like the look – I want to look like I've been on the beach and my hair has been dyed by the sun. Whenever I see really fake tanned girls I always feel a bit jealous.

One of the best things about being on the tour was being back with Olly again. It was good to see everyone else as well; we all had such a great time. We travelled around on a tour bus with the dancers, and me and Olly always sat together watching films. He was sometimes a bit soppy over me, but only in a jokey way. Anyway, as much as I really loved him, I knew I could never be attracted to him.

I much prefer a cooler approach from a guy. Aaron is the type to shrug and say, 'If you don't like me, you don't like me.' And that makes me think, Hold on a minute, I might have to put some effort into this one. If it's not a challenge, I don't think I'm interested.

'So, don't you love me?' Olly would ask with a grin.

'Of course I do, just not like that,' I'd reply. I loved him to pieces. He was my best friend.

Things were starting to happen with Aaron now. We'd liked each other for ages, but it just hadn't been there before, perhaps because we weren't spending enough time together. It's funny, I don't know what had changed, because we were still apart, but suddenly I got really excited when he said he was coming to see the show in Brighton. I was definitely starting to have feelings for him. Maybe it was because he was so down to earth and I knew he'd keep me grounded. Everything else in my life was up in the clouds and he was my normal.

My family weren't all that keen, though. They thought Aaron was a lad's lad as he's a painter and decorator who goes to the football and has a season ticket. He wasn't very affectionate or expressive in front of people, either, so he came across as a real bloke. I must be attracted to a certain type! But at the same time the guy I like has to show me a bit of love and attention for me to be interested, otherwise, it becomes a bit gross.

I think my parents thought, Oh no, not again! when they first met Aaron. But when they saw that he was committed and came to every *X Factor* show, their attitude slowly began to change.

He's coming to Brighton! He's coming to see me, I thought, as the tour bus headed east from Cardiff on 26 February. I couldn't wait to see him. But we had four shows in two days in Brighton – two matinees and two evening shows – so I wouldn't really get to see him properly until late in the evening.

When he rang to arrange meeting up after the show, my tummy turned over. I got to the hotel before him, and when I went out to meet him I suddenly felt a bit shy. 'What did you think of the show?' I said, looking at him sideways.

'Really good,' he replied, smiling.

Olly saw us walking into the hotel together, because he happened to be walking out right at that moment. He didn't say anything – he just looked at us and carried on walking – and I didn't register anything was wrong, because Olly was my best friend and I didn't think he'd mind about Aaron, especially as we weren't officially together. I was wrong, though. It upset Olly that I had a boyfriend and he got a bit funny after that, especially as Aaron came to see me quite a few times.

It probably wasn't so much that Olly fancied me, more that we were everything to each other at the time. We'd shared the biggest experience of our lives and the connection between us was really special. So I think he felt that our friendship was threatened. I understand it now, because it's normal for your best friend not to like it when you start going out with someone. It means you've got less time for them, because you're too busy thinking about your boyfriend, so of course your friend's going to feel left out in those circumstances. But I didn't get it at the time and it just made me angry. I couldn't understand why I had to choose between them, why it had to be one person or the other. Couldn't I be close to both of them, but in different ways?

Our friendship went rubbish after that, which made the end of the tour difficult. It was really sad for me. I'd be at the front of the bus and he'd be at the back, and I'd be lucky if I got a look off him. He wouldn't talk to me, either. It was horrible.

I was constantly telling Aaron, 'Olly doesn't want to talk to me.'

'Why the hell do you care so much about him?' Aaron said, getting annoyed. 'Why does it matter so much that he doesn't talk to you?'

'Because he's my best friend and I love him,' I'd reply, going on to explain how much Olly meant to me – or *trying* to explain. It wasn't that easy to justify how much I loved another guy to my new sort-of boyfriend! It just didn't make sense to him – unless I was in love with Olly. But it was Aaron I was in love with, not Olly. I wouldn't have slept with Olly because I didn't feel that way about him. I loved him to bits, but I *was in love with* Aaron and I was so happy to be with him.

Now I was getting it from both sides, so in the end I couldn't talk about Olly to Aaron and I couldn't talk about Aaron to Olly. I just had to go around thinking to myself, I've got nothing to say to anybody. It was so strange.

Olly started hanging out with the dancers a lot more after that. Obviously it did my head in a bit, because he was *my* friend on the tour. 'Why aren't you talking to me?' I asked him. 'Why aren't we having fun? Why aren't you spending time with me? Why are you with them all the time? Nobody else is allowed to be your friend except me.' We were both as bad as each other.

'Where's Aaron?' he'd say, cutting me short.

'What the heck?' Suddenly I'd feel embarrassed and think, What's happened? What have I done?

'I'm not even with Aaron properly,' I said. 'I like Aaron and Aaron looks after me and Aaron is there for me, but it's not like we've come out and said, "Right, we're going out!" so you can't get angry at me, you just can't.'

I don't get it when people say that a boy and girl can't be best friends. Why can't they? In my eyes, it's completely normal. What's the difference between us, apart from our genitals? Who is to say that we don't think in the same way? If there's no sexual attraction, it's just like we're the same sex. You're no more physically aware of them than you would be of your best girlfriend.

That's how it was for me and Olly, as far as I saw it. I never looked at him and thought, I'd love to walk down the aisle with you, but we loved each other and everything we did together was fun. I felt the same way about Dana and Lauren and some of my girlfriends from Grays: I always knew that if I rang them up and we went out, it was going to be the funniest night ever, even if we were just sitting in a McDonald's car park, drinking milkshakes and spitting bits of paper through a straw.

It's true that some relationships start off as friendships. That's what happened with me and Aaron in a way, although I think we always liked each other. But if you're only friends with someone and then they start going out with someone else, you can't really object. You can feel a bit moody about it, maybe, but you can't say, 'What are you doing with him? I like you.'

It can ruin a friendship if one person likes the other romantically, but the other person doesn't feel the same way. Or, at least, it can't stay the same. You have to step back slightly, keep your distance a bit, and that immediately changes the atmosphere. The problem is, you'll be having a laugh with a friend who fancies you and then halfway through you think, Am I flirting? Does it seem as if I'm flirting? Oh God, get me out of here! It's weird.

Fortunately, Lou, the make-up artist, and Jeff Brazier took me under their wings. I also hung out with John and Edward when I could. I thought they were brilliant. Nothing about them was contrived and they weren't in any way trying to be something, despite how it might have seemed, and they never upset anyone. But they weren't around much, because they were really busy doing other gigs and personal appearances.

There were always loads of groupies outside the hotels waiting for John and Edward. There was a group of ten or twelve people who followed them everywhere, screaming, 'Jedward! Jedward!' They were the craziest people in the world. They had Jedward hair and wore Jedward T-shirts; they had Jedward everything. They were just obsessed.

Somehow they always knew in advance which hotels we were going to be staying in and they would book themselves in before we arrived. They just wanted to be near John and Edward and be their friends. It amazed me that they had the money to do it. They went everywhere: I saw them in England, Ireland, Scotland and Wales. Where have you come from and how do you get the money to pay for the flights, hotels and travel? I'd think. They were obviously insanely rich and crazy.

John and Edward loved it, though. They loved their fans and used to spend lots of time with them. I didn't have fans like that, not groupies that followed me around. I signed a lot of autographs, though.

It was painful not being close friends with Olly any more, but I was still really enjoying the shows. As the routines became more repetitive, I started to have more fun on stage. I'd done the dances so often it ended up being built in, robotic. I didn't often go wrong, so I felt really relaxed. 'Thank you so much,' I kept saying to the audience, because without them I wouldn't have been there. You can't thank people enough when they've given you some of the best bits of your life. I was enjoying myself because of them and I was full of appreciation, especially as the tickets to the *X Factor* shows were so expensive. It's crazy. I don't know how people do it. Every single one of our audiences was really nice, and it was an honour to perform in front of such lovely crowds.

Every day before the show, we'd meet up with something like a hundred people in the hospitality rooms. Most of them were families with terminally ill children who were big *X Factor* fans. It felt great to be able to spread a bit of happiness, chatting to the children, signing autographs and taking pictures, and it made me feel so lucky and thankful to have a healthy kid. It was scary to think that the people I was meeting were just normal people like me, with normal lives and normal children, then one day they woke up and their child had a terminal illness. There's nothing you can do about it when it happens to you, except make your child's life as good as possible.

I have to do everything I can to make sure my baby has all he could ever possibly want, I thought. Because if life gets taken away from me or him, there's nothing you can do about it. That's just what happens.

It made me want to do more for all the charities that help children. I didn't care how many terminally ill people I had to meet if it made a difference. Meeting ill people can be tough, because you feel so upset for them, but that's nothing compared to going through it yourself. We were lucky to meet them and see things from their side of the fence, but they were the ones going through it with their families.

As the tour went on, though, I started to find it more and more difficult, just because it was every single day, and when you meet a hundred terminally ill people every day, you start thinking that everyone is terminally ill. It's the scariest thing. It gets out of proportion in your head and you get carried away by it – or I did, at least. It wasn't healthy for me. I started worrying that something awful was going to happen to me, and every day I'd pray, 'Please God, don't let anything happen to Zachary.' I didn't even want to think about it, but because I saw it every day, I couldn't avoid confronting it. Then I started to feel superstitious. If I carry on thinking about it, what's going to happen? I wondered. Will I bring it on myself? It was such a strange feeling.

Of course, when we came out of the *X Factor* bubble and back into reality, you realize that you only know of one child who is ill or dying, rather than hundreds. The statistics brought me back down to earth, but they didn't stop me wanting to help every children's charity in the UK.

As the tour drew to an end, I think we were all looking forward to going home. Don't get me wrong, it was the most amazing experience and I wouldn't have swapped it for the world, but it was a bit like Groundhog Day by the end: every day, the same people, the same songs, the same routines, the same costumes. We had very few nights off. I never complained, though. I knew that there were plenty of people out there struggling to make something of themselves, dreaming of an opportunity like ours, and we were so privileged to be there. I think everyone on the tour appreciated that.

Three days before the tour ended, we all went out to a random club for a drink. I had a wicked time; it was a great night out. Me and Jeff Brazier had a really big fight about who was better at dancing. 'You're rubbish,' I said, and we ended up having a dance-off on the floor, doing roly polies and headstands to see who could do the most outrageous moves. I did everything that he did, but he said he won and I was rubbish. To this day I still believe I won, though.

Even though it gave me a huge sense of achievement to have got through the tour without missing a show, after fifty-three dates I was ready for something new. I think we all were. OK, on to the next thing now. I've done that bit of my life, I thought. Our last concert was on 4 April in Aberdeen and everybody just went to bed afterwards. There were no emotional goodbyes, because we all knew we'd bump into each other on the circuit. It was really weird saying goodbye to Olly like we weren't friends any more, though. I think we both said, 'Bye, good luck!' The same as we'd say to anyone.

On 5 April, I flew back to London from Scotland with Jeff, on the earliest flight I could book at six o'clock in the morning. I wonder if I'll ever see Olly again, I thought as the plane took off and I left the *X Factor* tour behind. It upset me to think that we wouldn't be friends any more. I still loved him so much – he was my link to one of the most important episodes in my life.

I tried to shut out the hurt of what had gone wrong between us and focus on the future. After all, I couldn't wait to get home to my little mooch and kiss him from head to toe. I'd missed my munchkin so much. He was growing up and changing so fast; there was something different about him every week. I was really looking forward to spending more time with Aaron as well, now that we were officially going to be a couple. It was so wicked to be in love, right at that beginning stage, when you get butterflies in your tummy and you feel like you're walking on air. Every morning I woke up on a high.

Chapter 13

After the tour, I had about three days off before I went back to gigging and doing interviews. As usual, I was asked, 'Is there anyone special in your life? Have you got a boyfriend?'

Now, at last, I could give a direct answer. 'Yes, I'm with someone.'

It meant that I didn't have to think up replies to all the questions that went with having to admit I was single, like, 'What's your type? Are you looking for someone? What kind of guy do you want to be with? If you could be with anyone, who would it be?'

You can't really say, 'No comment,' to those kinds of questions, so you have to be ready with snappy answers and think up men you fancy on the telly, which I find really hard to do. 'Someone funny,' I'd say. 'Not too good looking so they love themselves.' I could never think of anyone. I mean, I love Lee Evans but I don't fancy him; I just think he's really funny. I think Keith Lemon is funny, too, and I definitely don't fancy him. Sorry, Keith.

Who do I fancy? If I could be with anyone? I don't know! I used to be quite attracted to the lead singer of the Libertines. I also liked Amy Winehouse's ex-husband, although I don't think what he does is attractive. My type is a man who looks normal and a bit rugged, but the only person on telly I could think of like that is the builder with a beard who Susan went out with on *Desperate Housewives*. Oh God, there isn't anyone, really.

Now that I was officially with Aaron, it was a relief not to have to go through all of that again. And if anyone asked probing questions about him, I was allowed to say, 'No comment.'

Of course, interviewers started asking questions about Aaron and Zach. 'How do they get on? Has it been easy to introduce Aaron into Zach's life?'

The great thing was that Zach had known Aaron for ages, so he was really used to him. I don't think anything changed for him when we got together as they'd always loved being with each other. Aaron made it clear from the start that he really cared about Zach and he spent loads of time with him. If they hadn't got on so well and I didn't know that Aaron loved Zach with all his heart – even more than he loved me – then I wouldn't even have thought about being with him. Zach was more important to me than anyone or anything. He was always my number one priority.

Zach loved playing with Aaron and running around his house. There was no jealousy there at all, except when Zach was tired and said something like, 'No, she's my mummy, not yours!' Silly stuff like that. Most of the time he loved us all being together. It helped that Aaron had a bulldog called Molly. Zach loved Molly so much that he called Aaron's house 'Molly's house'. Zach also spent time with his dad on a regular basis, which was really good.

The next question interviewers asked was, 'So what are you up to at the moment?'

I was doing gigs all over the country, at clubs, for Tesco and Asda corporate parties and at horse-racing events. The audiences were always wicked; everyone cheered really loudly and made lots of noise. I had about twelve songs in my repertoire, six of them from *The X Factor*. I usually sang four at every gig and I always sang 'Who Wants To Live Forever', because everyone seemed to want to hear that one. It wasn't my personal favourite, but you've got to give them what they want! My favourite songs were 'The Scientist', 'Somewhere Only We Know' and 'You Got The Love', the version by Florence + the Machine. Although it sometimes got a bit repetitive singing the same songs, I still really loved gigging and it was well paid, too.

In the early spring of 2010, the RAF Squadronaires contacted me about guesting on their new album, *In the Mood: The Glenn Miller Songbook*, a collection of brand-new recordings that was due out at the end of May. The Squadronaires were formed at the beginning of World War II to raise morale and entertain the troops. They still play military gigs to this day, and they do private gigs as well. I said yes immediately. My grandfather fought in the RAF in India during the war and I knew he'd be so proud of me if I featured on this album. In fact, everyone in the family would be proud of me, especially as one of my cousins is in the army and has been to Iraq and Afghanistan.

Recording with the Squadronaires was a lovely opportunity, especially as 2010 was the seventieth anniversary of the Blitz. One of our main focuses in history at school was World War II, and we learned about the music as well as what everyone went through, so the tunes of that era are very familiar to me and I find some of them very moving. Listening to them makes me think about how English ways stay the same, however advanced we become. It's funny that the answers to our problems never seem to change: 'Stay firm, be strong, keep positive and pull together.' Nothing can dampen our fighting spirit, no matter how many technological leaps forward we make.

The Squadronaires contacted me because they'd seen me perform 'At Last' on *The X Factor* and they wondered if I would sing it again with them. I couldn't refuse. If people have the guts to go out there to protect our country and fight for us, then why shouldn't we do our bit, if we can? No matter what, you should do what you believe in, and I believe in what our soldiers do, the support their families give them and everything they go through.

I know people with relatives who've fought in Iraq and Afghanistan and come back different people because of the terrible things that happened there. They can't sleep; they can't look at life in the same way; they can't do anything. The horrors of war have long-term effects, both physical and psychological. My grandad developed skin cancer seventy years after being in the harsh sun when he fought in India, which shows that the consequences of war can affect you at any time.

So if the Squadronaires and their music give pleasure to soldiers, ex-soldiers and their families, then why on earth wouldn't I want to contribute? Everyone deserves a little pleasure in life, and this cause was something close to my heart.

As soon as I said yes, we went straight into the studio. It was so nice to be recording again; I really felt good about it. I'm doing music again! This is so much fun! I knew the song well, so all I had to do was enjoy myself.

The band did their own arrangement of 'At Last' and we recorded it in the studio together, with the band leader conducting us. We had the freedom to do whatever we wanted, so we spent most of the day playing with all the buttons, messing around, changing things and saying what we did and didn't like. Everyone had a good time. It was a really lovely experience. I hadn't done anything like it since I'd been in the studio at *The X Factor* and it made me so happy. It ignited my desire to do my best and enjoy myself to the full.

The album was being released to commemorate the seventieth anniversary of the band and there was a reunion for any surviving original Squadronaire musicians, their relatives and friends. My grandad was too ill to come along and watch me, sadly, but he was thrilled that I was appearing on the album. My dad came, though, and my dad filmed the whole thing and sent a copy to my grandad, along with a big frame of photos showing me performing with the band in RAF uniform. For Grandad, it was amazing to see me in that uniform. 'Wow!' he said when he saw the pictures.

It was a real honour to wear the uniform, but I felt a bit of a cheat, because it was an original RAF uniform from the 1940s. Somebody did something really special in this, I thought – I wasn't sure I deserved to be wearing it. It was the best night, though. It was really, really good. I love that genre of music, especially when it's live; it sounds completely different to when you hear it on a CD. It always gives me a weird feeling, because I get a sensation of going back in time. It's like being in a scene from *Pearl Harbor* or something.

The Squadronaires decided to release 'At Last' as a single, so I did quite a few TV appearances around its release, including interviews with *GMTV*, *This Morning* and *Loose Women*. It was so much fun being on *Loose Women*; there's never a dull moment on that programme. Everyone has so much to say and they've all got different opinions. You're sitting there, in the middle of four women, and one person says, 'Oh yes!' and someone else says, 'Oh no!'

Oh my God! I thought. Luckily, I'm never stuck for something to say.

Everyone has a laugh on *Loose Women* because it's so laid back. It's such a cool show. They all have their cups of tea and they invite you to join in the conversation. 'Come on, just talk about whatever you like,' they said. 'You can say the most random things you want to.' When you leave, you get a little gift from the presenters, and I got a maxi dress and loads of cool moisturizers.

It was great, because it gave me the chance to talk about the Squadronaires and the important job our soldiers are doing. One of the best things about my work is that I'm able to help people and causes. I'm always being approached by charities and I can never say no. I'm such a softie. 'You can't always say yes to everyone,' my manager tells me, but how do you choose between them? Who's more deserving? Personally I can't make that decision. I think it's mean to choose, so I prefer to do a bit for everyone and that's what I try to do.

If I'm asked to do two charity events on the same day, I go back and ask them to find me another slot so I can do both. 'Right, one of you on one day and the other on another day.' If they want you and it's going to help their charity, they'll find you a different slot.

It can be a lot of fun raising money for charity and it gives you the most amazing feeling to go out there and do something to help. I've done the Barnardo's children's charity walk, which was lovely; I did an event for Great Ormond Street Hospital and I went to London Zoo for another children's charity, Cancer Research Little Stars. How can you not enjoy going for a walk with kids on a nice sunny day? Or going to the zoo? It's the best fun.

Children's charities are my favourite, even though it can be quite heart-rending. Most of them are aware of what's going on, so you want to distract them for a few hours. You'll do anything to make them laugh, whether that means sitting with them, swapping jokes, having a photo taken with them or going for a walk in the park. How could you deny someone that? I'm so lucky to be able to help; I couldn't possibly say no.

The other cause that's close to my heart is breast cancer research, partly because I'm a girl, I suppose. I want to know about it and I want to make sure I've contributed. I loved doing a photo shoot for Tickled Pink, the Asda campaign for breast cancer, when I spent the day dressed head to toe in pink flowers. I really got involved in that campaign and went to all the fundraising fashion shows they held, where I met a lot of people affected by breast cancer, some who'd got over it and some who still had it.

I also threw a party for the Living TV show *Party Wars*, which follows a similar format to *Four Weddings*. The prize for whoever won was £5,000, to donate to two charities of their choice. There were four of us in the competition, and we all went to each other's party and judged them, giving points out of ten.

Although the parties were held in May, the show was scheduled to be aired in the autumn, so it made sense to make mine my twenty-first birthday party because it was coming up in October. The big twenty-one! It was only a simple party – nothing really extravagant. I was given a small budget by Living TV and I had to call in favours when I went over budget. I actually managed to sort out a free bar all night because it was going to be on telly!

It was so good. I was lucky enough to hold it in a marquee in the garden of a big manor house in Oxfordshire. How perfect. I'd never had a party like it in my life. It had a Winter

Wonderland theme and all the guests had to wear white. There were ice sculptures everywhere and icicles hanging from the ceiling, and even though it was summer, they didn't melt. Everything was white. There was white flooring, white furniture and big white drapes swung back to reveal the dance floor, which was starlit.

Only my friends were invited, because it had to be a real party, so there weren't any famous people, apart from Jeff Brazier and model and TV personality Bianca Gascoigne, who I get on really well with. I'd be embarrassed if I didn't invite Jeff to my parties. He'd get the right hump. I would have liked Jedward to come, but they were off doing gigs, and I hadn't spoken to Olly in ages. A lot of my friends from King Solomon High School were there, though, as well as my new friends from Grays and even a few old Abbs Cross mates, including Joely.

There were about 150 people in total. It was so cool. Everyone had the best time because it was a free bar, and I went for it. The Living TV cameras didn't stop me. It was my twenty-first, after all, so there was no way I wasn't going to drink. A couple of days later, there was a newspaper report saying, 'Stacey Solomon has birthday bash, gets drunk and swears like a trooper.' Well, I never swear except when I'm drunk, so you knew I was drunk that night! Leave me alone, I thought. I didn't get to celebrate my eighteenth, and now someone was begrudging me a few drinks on my twenty-first? Surely I was allowed to drink for one day in a year. But no, I had to be told off: 'Oh, isn't she terrible?'

I had such a great time and so, I think, did everyone else, because we ended up winning the competition, getting ten out of ten for the party in the final vote. Who needs an eighteenth when your twenty-first is so good? I gave half the prize money to Barnardo's and half to Asda's Tickled Pink campaign.

On my actual twenty-first, we went to Quasar, where me, Natalie, Frank, Jade, Jordan and Chelsea chased each other around with laser guns. It was so much fun. Quasar is one of my favourite games, especially as it doesn't hurt like paintballing does. I love creeping around with my laser gun, hunting down my targets. It feels like I'm on a secret mission. My main tactic is to hide in the corner, thinking, I'll just bide my time. I get so into it that I get really scared and feel like I'm actually going to die.

Conscious that time was ticking by, I became more concerned about my future. My dream was to get a record contract, but it wasn't happening and I couldn't help wondering what I would do next. It was nerve-racking, but I tried not to think about it too much. I felt like I had to make the most of what I had now and do whatever I could. 'Work really hard and see what happens,' I told myself. 'If it doesn't happen, it doesn't happen.'

I wasn't going to give up without a fight, but I knew I could also be happy doing something else altogether. I could never forget the lesson I'd learned when I'd had Zach. I'd thought my life was over then, that there was nothing for me to look forward to, but I was so wrong. Zach was the start of everything, not the end. He was the best thing to ever happen to me. I just didn't realize it at the time.

I'd learned that even when life doesn't go according to plan, when you don't get what you want and it feels like your heart is breaking, there's always something new around the corner. And you never know, what's round the corner might be much better than what you have now, so it's important not to be scared of the future. You have to have faith that things will work out for you. I was so lucky to have had the opportunities I'd had. I just needed to wait and see what happened next.

I could always go to uni, I thought. I could do English literature or law if I wanted to. I could do almost any course now that I had a national diploma, apart from a science degree or medicine obviously. But until I knew what the future held, I would work as hard as I could. Working hard is the key to success, even when you're already successful. When you get a number one album, you haven't won. That's not the end. You can't sit back and say, 'I've done it now.' You have to carry on working hard to make the next thing happen.

Then, out of the blue, I bumped into Olly at a gig in the summer. We'd both been booked to sing at the same venue without knowing it. It was brilliant, because the moment we saw each other, all the bad feelings melted away and we were really good friends again. Neither of us brought up the past; we just didn't think about it. That night we had such a laugh again, just like we always used to. I was so happy; I had my friend back. We started phoning each other all the time again, which was really nice. We'd been through so much together; it was brilliant to be back in touch.

It seems to me that it's hard to get radio play on Radio 1 if you're from *The X Factor*, as they want to play artists who've come up through the ranks; coming *The X Factor* route is perhaps looked upon as easy and cheap. Since Radio 1 is the biggest station, if you want your records to sell, you have to get good air play with them. Fortunately, Olly and Joe had number ones, and because their singles were so popular Radio 1 had to play them, but it was perhaps harder for them than it would have been for someone who hadn't been on *The X Factor*.

That's what stopped me from getting too excited when I heard that I was being considered as a possible contestant for *I'm a Celebrity . . . Get Me Out of Here!* My heart leapt, but I didn't think there was any way I'd actually get on the show because I'd never seen an *X Factor* contestant in the jungle. It just hadn't happened before. I knew I really wanted to do it, though. In my family, *I'm a Celebrity* and *The X Factor* are our two favourite shows, the ones we always watch every year.

They're complete opposites, but they're both so entertaining. Whereas *The X Factor* is a really emotional programme, and you watch it on the edge of your seat, willing your favourite contestant on, thinking, Please do well! *I'm a Celebrity* is more lighthearted entertainment that you can happily laugh at, without thinking too hard about it.

I was asked to an interview with the executive producers of the show. 'You do know that if you go into the jungle, you're going to be covered in bugs and maybe even eating bugs, don't you?' they said. 'There are a lot of bugs.'

'Yes, but don't you get to jump out of a plane and things like that, too?' I asked.

'Yes, there is an element of that, but there are also a lot of bugs –'

'You get to live outdoors in a real camp?' I said.

'Yes, but you must remember the bugs –'

'That sounds so cool,' I said. 'I'd love to do it!' It sounded amazing to me, like the ultimate camping adventure.

They must have thought, Blimey, she actually wants to be on this show. She must be a freak!

The interview lasted about an hour and a half and I babbled on for most of it, chatting away like they were my friends. I told them all about how I'd loved camping as a kid when we went all over the country with the whole family. 'It's the best. It's cheap and you have the most fun because you have to make do with what you've got,' I said.

Then I told them how, as an adult, I'd camped at V Festival and Glastonbury. 'That's got to be just as grim as the jungle,' I said. 'Trust me, I love it.'

I also talked about how I'd relish the extreme physical and mental challenges of doing *I'm a Celebrity*. I wanted to challenge myself and see how I coped with the bushtucker trials and living in the jungle. 'People just wouldn't expect it of me,' I said. 'But that's what it's all about, isn't it? You'd be bored if you just sat there camping and drinking hot chocolate for three weeks.'

I talked non-stop. By the end of it, they probably thought, Oh, go away!

If they thought I talked a lot, they should hear Zach when he really gets going. He can talk for England; I think he takes after his mum! It was so wonderful when he first learned to speak. It changes your relationship with your kid when you can talk to them, and it means the world when they first look into your eyes and say, 'Mummy, I love you.' Honestly, it's the most amazing feeling! Now we chatter away continuously. Those *I'm a Celebrity* producers would have their hands over their ears in no time if they had to listen to us for more than five minutes.

I went home from the meeting thinking, I really hope they pick me. I didn't care if people said that you were only meant to do the show if you were at the end of your career, or looking for a comeback because you weren't doing well. It didn't matter to me what anyone said; I just wanted to do it. I kept my fingers crossed every day after that.

I didn't tell anyone about the interview, though, just in case I didn't get it. I hate getting people's hopes up and then dashing them, so I never tell anyone about anything until it's definite – not Aaron, not even my mum. I guessed they would be interviewing a fair number of people, so the odds were against me, especially as I'd only just come off *The X Factor*. Still, I didn't stop hoping.

In September, Aaron and I went on our first holiday together. We were supposed to be going to Thailand; in fact, I'd booked two weeks in Thailand and couldn't wait to go, until I looked at the weather reports a week before we went and saw that they were having a monsoon out there. 'I don't want to have a holiday in the pouring rain!' I wailed at the travel agent, 'I couldn't bear that. It's our first holiday in two years. Is there any way you can change the booking to somewhere hot?'

Thankfully they managed to change it to Egypt. I wasn't that excited, because I'd been to Egypt before. On the other hand, I *had* to go somewhere hot where I could do nothing for two weeks, and Sharm El Sheikh was the perfect place. We wanted to take Zach, but Mum felt I needed a proper rest. I think she secretly wanted him all to herself!

We had such a lovely time. We hardly did anything for two weeks. It was so quiet. Well, except when we did dive bombs in the swimming pool. We were staying in the posh-est hotel and we really got in trouble for our dive bombs. I felt like a five-year-old. Oh, but it was so beautiful there. The gardens were full of flowers and there were flamingoes and storks wandering around.

We had such a good time when we went out in the evening, too. It was a bit like when we first met on holiday in Kos, but better because it was just the two of us and this time we actually spoke to each other. I was so happy, because everyone was foreign and no one recognized me, so we could just have fun. We went to Pacha at Naama Bay and I had the time of my life.

Our room faced the sea and we could walk straight out onto the beach. It was paradise. We did loads of snorkelling, but I didn't fancy learning to scuba dive because I'm a bit claustrophobic. I'm happy to be on the surface with my little snorkel, but I feel a bit funny when it comes to going down into the depths and having to breathe. If I make it onto *I'm a Celebrity*, I hope they don't give me any cave trials, I thought as I swam around looking at the fish down below. I have a real thing about caves. They trigger my claustrophobia really badly. I couldn't even begin to think about my phobia about spiders. I just had to block it out of my mind!

Me and Aaron used to lie around on the bed in our room for hours with the balcony doors open, doing nothing, being lazy. One day, about halfway through the holiday, we were lying on the bed when my phone rang. It was Ben from my management agency. 'Guess what?' he said.

'What?' I asked, not daring to believe that he could be calling to say that I was going on *I'm a Celebrity*.

'You're going into the jungle,' he said. 'Whoo-hoo!'

I couldn't believe it. I felt like jumping up and down on the bed. *I'm a Celebrity* was such a cool programme to be part of. I'd loved *The X Factor*, and I knew this would be just as much fun. It was an amazing thing to do and I would be around some really interesting people.

I turned to Aaron and smiled. 'What?' he asked.

'I'm going on *I'm a Celebrity*!' I yelled.

'Shut up!' he said, throwing a pillow at me. *I'm a Celebrity* is his favourite programme. He's too cool for *The X Factor*, but he admits to liking *I'm a Celebrity*.

'I am, I am! I didn't tell you, but they want me.'

'That's the best one of the lot,' he said when he realized I was being serious. 'That's going to be much easier to watch than sitting through *The X Factor*.'

'I know, I'm really excited,' I said. After I'd danced around the room for a few minutes, we went back to lying there in the warmth of the afternoon, doing nothing, being lazy, listening to the sound of the sea. It was time to make the most of living in luxury, because I was going to be roughing it big time in Australia!

Chapter 14

Night after night I sat glued to reruns of *I'm a Celebrity*, watching Katie Price crawling through a tunnel in a dark, dark cave, with huge frogs clinging to her back, having bugs poured all over her as she tried to find stars for the bush-tucker trial. Each star was a meal for one of the other contestants back at camp and she was determined to get as many as possible. Suddenly, heavy jets of water were sprayed on her, pushing her down through the tunnel into a water hole. Oh my God! For me, this was terrifying because of my fear of enclosed spaces, but for her it was horrendous because she has a phobia about water. 'Get me out of here!' she shouted. She was trembling from head to toe and gasping for breath when they lifted her out of the hole.

I dreaded the hole. Give me bugs in any normal scenario and I think I can get over it, but I don't think I could go deep down in a cave and deal with the bugs as well. It just seemed too difficult. I shuddered at the thought. I have to be brave, I kept thinking, convinced I would be made to do a trial in a cave. I have to complete every trial. I can't ever say, 'I'm a celebrity, get me out of here.' That's not good enough. That's losing.

In the two weeks before I flew out to Australia, I spent every night sitting at my computer YouTubing every single trial that had ever been set on the show. I wanted to know exactly what I was letting myself in for. 'I'm going to have to do that,' I kept telling myself. 'And I *will* do it.' I kept reminding myself that I would be doing it for Zach, to help improve our lives and build a better future for him. I'd be paid to be surrounded by bugs for three weeks, so it meant a lot for me and Zach.

I was certain I'd be nominated for every trial, so I decided there was no point in thinking I wouldn't. I studied them all so that I could get my head round what I would be going through. 'I'm not going in there like an idiot and saying, "Oh no, I can't do it!" I have to do it,' I repeated to myself. I properly talked myself into doing each trial.

I thought everything through as calmly and logically as I could. It was all well and good someone throwing bugs on you, I decided, because it's something you have no choice about. It just happens to you; it's physically forced upon you, so in a way it's not too bad. There's nothing you can do if you're standing underneath a bucket and they say, 'Right, answer this question,' and you get it wrong and they pour bugs on you. Once they're on you, they're on you. You might as well invite the rest of them to crawl all over you, too.

What scared me was the idea of having to make a conscious decision to pick up a piece of disgusting food and put it in my mouth, then chew it and swallow it. Making yourself do something like that against your will feels so wrong, but you have to sit there and force yourself. 'I'm going to eat that,' you tell yourself. 'It's going to be moving around in my mouth and I'm going to have to kill it in my mouth, but I'm still going to eat it.' I struggled to convince myself I could do it. I knew it would be a lot harder than having a bucket of bugs tipped on me, because I'd have a choice.

The only way I could deal with my fear was to remind myself constantly of what I was facing. I had some really strange dreams about eating carcasses. One night I was eating

218

the middle of a cow, and another time I was feasting on a kill, like a lion. I had loads of falling dreams, too, mostly falling into water, and I also dreamt my teeth were falling out. My mum says she has the same dream all the time, so maybe it's hereditary. In my dream I was thinking, Help, I've got no teeth! Nobody is going to vote for me because I'm toothless. I suppose I was so anxious that my mind kept turning things over night and day.

The only other bit of preparation I did was to get bio sculptures on my nails. After all, I didn't want a repeat of that terrible moment when I met Whitney Houston and realized my nail varnish was all chipped! Bio sculptures are layers of really thick nail varnish and they last for weeks, so I could be sure that they'd stay on until I made it out of the jungle.

I had to be really, really secretive about the fact that I was appearing on *I'm a Celebrity*. It's even worse than *The X Factor*, because there's more publicity surrounding who goes into the jungle than who's made it onto the *X Factor* finals. When I came back from Egypt, I had to do my initial interview in total secret at home. That was the one where I said, 'Yes, I'm really excited about going to Australia, but I don't know how I'll get on.'

I made sure not to mention that I suffered from claustrophobia and was scared of caves. No way would I have said anything about that, because you could be sure then that I would have been put in a cave! I didn't tell them about my lifelong fear of spiders, either, but then my mum blurted it out.

'She's petrified of spiders,' she said.

'Mum, you are an idiot!' I yelled, slapping my head in frustration.

Next I had to do the famous jungle photo shoot, where

the photos are given to the press once the contestants are announced. It's all well and good doing a photo shoot, but this was really cheesy and embarrassing. I had to turn to the camera, smile and wink. Oh God, I so didn't want to wink! 'Don't make me wink, please,' I begged the photographer jokily. For one set-up I wore a black glittery top, then I changed into a couple of different dresses for another, and finally I was photographed wearing jungle gear.

The photo shoot was in London and there were paps outside, so we all had to be sneaked out undercover. It was like an MI5 operation. Someone must have seen me or got wind that I was there, though, because my name was leaked to the papers the next day. That then meant that at every gig I went to, people asked, 'So are you going on *I'm a Celebrity*? What are you doing next?'

I wasn't allowed to say anything, even though I wanted to be open about it and tell everyone, 'No, sorry. I'm not going on it,' I had to lie. 'Wish I was. I'd love to, but I'm not.'

It was really hard. I kept worrying about what they would think when they found out the truth. 'She's a good liar, the cow!' I was concerned that I could lose friends over it.

People were constantly asking about it, so in the end I had to slow down my work and lead a quiet life. I couldn't go anywhere without a reporter coming after me, so I stayed at home for a bit, which suited me to a tee. Since I was going to be without Zach, Aaron and my family for the next four weeks, it was a good excuse to spend all my time with them now. I was actually glad that things went a bit mad so I could stay in. I spent the next couple of weeks really enjoying Zach and trying not to think too much about how hard it would be to be parted from him.

*

Finally the day came for me to fly to Australia. I had no idea who I was going to spend my time in the jungle with, because you don't meet any of the other contestants until you go in. I'd read all the speculation in the papers, but the only one they got right was Linford Christie.

I flew to Australia with my buddy Kieran, the ITV exec who'd be looking after me. I love that man. We got on so well. We spent the whole twenty-four-hour flight watching films and being silly. It was my first ever business-class flight and we lay back in our reclining chairs and ordered as much food as we could eat.

When we got to the hotel in Brisbane, we weren't allowed out because our identities were still a secret, so I was stuck in my room for a few days, doing nothing, getting over my jet lag. There were paps outside the hotel, so we weren't allowed in the swimming pool or anything. We couldn't even step outside.

I just stayed in my room and watched loads of films and ordered more and more food. I just ate and ate. I'm going to stock up before I go in there, I thought, so I stuffed myself with every sweet you can think of, every flavour M&M, crisps, chocolates, chips, fried breakfasts, spaghetti bolognese, pasta, pizza, salads, puddings and cakes. I wanted to eat everything I wouldn't have access to in the jungle. My favourite food is curry, but apparently in Australia it's not the best, so I didn't risk that. I didn't want to ruin my love of curry!

On the fourth day, Kieran woke me up and said, 'Wear something nice. You're going to meet everyone today.' I got dressed and put on flat shoes. 'No, wear the heels,' he said.

'Heels? I want to wear flats,' I replied, surprised.

'Go on, dress up,' he urged.

Fine, I thought. If everyone else is going to be dressed up, I'd prefer to be in heels.

At eight o'clock that morning, we got into a massive posh car and drove to a really smart estate. It was a big new-build on a lake, with all these beautiful houses around the water. It was a stunning setting, but I couldn't appreciate it as much as I would have liked to, because while everything was being organized and some of the other contestants were taken inside, I sat and waited in the back of the limousine for ages, getting more and more nervous.

After an hour, there was a tap on the car window, 'Come on, quickly. They're ready.'

Oh no, I thought, my heart pounding. Actually, I don't want to go in there and meet everyone. I walked along a red carpet lined with paps and into a room where there were two men. 'Hello,' I said nervously. I recognized one of them immediately. 'I know you're off *Coronation Street* but I can't remember your name,' I told him.

'Hello, I'm Nigel,' he said.

'Hiya, Nige,' I said, smiling stupidly.

The other man was looking at the floor, looking really embarrassed. 'Hello,' he said. I realized immediately that he wasn't being unfriendly or rude; he was just 100 per cent uncomfortable. It seemed like he didn't want to be there at all. It was Shaun Ryder. I didn't recognize him because he was famous before I was born. He made his music in the 1980s and I was born in 1989.

Soon everyone else started coming in: first Kayla Collins, the Playboy model, then Sheryl Gascoigne, Paul Gascoigne's ex-wife. I was always seeing Sheryl at kids' film premieres with her little boy and she'd always been really lovely to me when we'd met. 'Oh, a friendly face,' I said, with relief.

I saw TV presenter Gillian McKeith, who I recognized, but wasn't sure why. Then I met rapper Aggro Santos, former Bond girl Britt Ekland and ex-MP Lembit Opik. I knew who Linford Christie was, of course – the Olympic gold medal-winning sprinter – I was really excited about meeting him.

We all started talking and there was loads of banter. We were having a good time straight away. I remember saying to Linford, 'I want to race you one day,' and I think they put that on the telly. Really embarrassing! 'Yeah, I'll give you a race.'

'OK,' he said. He was probably thinking, What an idiot.

Me and Linford clicked straight away. I thought he was wicked, such a lovely guy, a really genuine bloke. He was so funny as well. I called him Linny and he didn't even care. 'You know what, I like you,' he said. I was so happy. 'You're nice. You're funny,' he went on.

He took the mick out of me a bit, but he was really nice. I thought, You're brilliant. I love you.

When Ant and Dec were helicoptered in, alarm bells went off in everybody's heads. Hang on, they're not meant to come unless there's a trial, we all thought. In past years, the contestants went to their camps on the first day and that was it.

'Maybe they're going to introduce us to the show and show us to our camps,' we hoped.

Ant and Dec walked into the villa and immediately divided us up into girls and boys: girls on one side, boys on the other. 'OK, the challenges start from today,' they announced.

We all looked at each other in horror. Oh no!

'It's Camp Bruce versus Camp Sheila.'

Even worse, I thought. That means we're up against Linford Christie and the gang.

It can't be that bad, we were thinking. They're not going to throw us in at the deep end and give us the worst trials. It'll probably be some assault course race or something like that.

They told us that the winning team would get to stay the night in the posh villa, instead of going straight to camp, while the losers would be staying in a makeshift camp – a really bad camp, in other words.

'We have to win this,' we said, but at the same time we'd mentally prepared ourselves to go into the jungle that day, so it didn't matter all that much if we didn't win. Anyway with Britt and Kayla on our team, you can guess what we were thinking, We don't have a chance in hell!

Ant and Dec flew away and the rest of us got into separate helicopters, pink for the girls and blue for the boys. When we arrived at the site, we couldn't see a thing. We were put in separate tents far away from each other, thinking, Uh-oh. What's going to happen?

After all my preparation, I still didn't know if I'd be able to go through with the trials. What if I can't? I kept thinking. Would I be able to do the things I'd been telling myself I could? I'd got myself into a bit of a frenzy in the weeks leading up to the show and I was definitely quite anxious. I was looking forward to it, too, though, because I'd wanted to meet everyone. The trials would come later, or so I'd thought, and I'd cross that bridge when I got there. But now here I was on the other side of the bridge before we'd even started!

Ant and Dec appeared again and invited us out of our tents and sat us on a long bench.

'Hello,' they said.

I recognized their tone of voice. It was their 'Welcome to

your trial' voice. Oh no, they've already begun, I thought. It was all very sudden, coming almost directly from the hotel to a trial, and it was a trial involving every single one of us. No one was getting out of it.

'We've called this trial Terror Vision,' they said.

All kinds of things went through my head. Wonderful, I thought. Does that mean we're going to have to answer questions about television shows? I was worried, because I didn't know anything. I don't even know the name of the character Nigel plays in *Coronation Street*, I thought. Oh no, it's going to be awful.

The girls were looking at each other as if to apologize in advance. 'Sorry, girls, sorry,' we kept saying.

The boys were looking at us as if to say, 'Ha ha, you're going to lose. Look out. We're not scared of anything.'

Now we had to put ourselves in order for the trial: one, two, three, four and five. I put myself at number four. I didn't want to be last, but I didn't think it was fair to put myself first, because I guessed that it would start easy and get harder, which it did.

The trial was held inside a big, TV-shaped box. Kayla and Lembit went in first. They had to put their hands in three holes, one at a time, and pull out a star. They couldn't see what was in the holes, so it was a test about overcoming nasty sensations. The first hole had crickets in it, the second had rats and the third had snakes. I didn't think they were very scary animals. For me, a cockroach is worse than a rat or a mouse. A cockroach can crawl inside your clothes, whereas rats can look furry and cute and you can flick them away.

Kayla barely put her hand in the first hole. The moment she touched something, she pulled it away. She just couldn't

225

do it. Why do we even bother putting ourselves through all this? I thought.

Next up was Gillian McKeith versus Shaun Ryder. 'This is our second chance. We can do this, girls,' we told each other. We were trying to be optimistic about it. This section was called, 'Not the 10 O'Clock News' because they had to read out some headlines and say if they were true or false.

'Is something going to land on my head?' Gillian asked.

Ant laughed. 'You're ahead of me,' he joked. 'This is a bushtucker trial, so expect some surprises along the way, whether you get the questions right or wrong.'

You could see Shaun thinking, Whatever, while Gillian looked really worried.

'Go on, Gillian,' we shouted, cheering her on.

Shaun was asked a question and gave the right answer, while Gillian started yelping before anything had even happened. She jumped out of her seat and was told to sit down again. Then a load of slime fell on her. 'Ah! Help me!' she screamed.

She got her question wrong and was showered in bugs – mealworms or cockroaches, I think. She ran to Shaun for help and begged him to brush them off her, then she started crying and saying, 'I'm sorry, I can't do this.' She just freaked out.

'Gillian, you can stop the trial at any time by saying, "I'm a celebrity, get me out of here",' Dec said.

'I'm a celebrity, get me out of here,' she said, sobbing softly. She insisted on being hosed down immediately.

'Gillian, are you OK?' Dec asked.

'No, I'm not really, no,' she said, wiping away the tears. 'I have a serious phobia about insects.'

Right, two down, three to go. It's not looking good, we

thought. If the boys won the next trial, we would have lost.

Next it was Sheryl versus Nigel in a karaoke competition where they had to sing 'Summer Lovin''. There were six words missing and the winner was whoever got the most missing words right. Meanwhile gunk and bugs kept falling on them throughout the trial.

I wasn't sure how Sheryl would do, but she seemed like a strong character to me and I was confident that she would be resilient. Nigel looked a bit like he didn't want to be there, but he had a laugh anyway and they both got through it. Sheryl won, so we were in with a chance again. It's not over yet!

Next it was my turn. I walked into the box, which was seething with cockroaches and mealworms from the three previous trials, so I was surrounded by bugs before I'd even started and they were crunching and squidging under my feet.

It was me against Aggro. I was shaking all over. 'It's only Aggro,' I told myself. 'Come on. You can do it. You can beat Aggro.'

Oh no, it was an eating trial! I knew it the moment I saw a plate with a big silver cover over the top. What's it going to be? Don't reveal it to me, I thought.

I lifted the cover. 'In front of you are two kangaroo penises,' Dec said. 'This round is a straightforward race. The first person to eat an entire kangaroo penis is the winner.'

'His penis looks smaller than mine!' I shouted. Everyone just laughed, but from where I was I was being faced with something huge, raw and disgusting. Oh my God, I don't want to eat a willy, I thought. I really don't want to do it. But there was no way out and no time to think about it. I drilled it into myself that I could not lose. I had to do it.

The minute the clock went I reached for the willy and stuffed it in my mouth. I chewed it about three times and tried to swallow, but gagged because it was still too big to get it down. Then I chewed and crunched like I've never chewed or crunched before. It was so gross, so chewy and gristly. Finally, I gulped it down and opened my mouth to show it was empty. 'I swallowed that willy!' I yelled. It was all over in about twenty seconds.

The aborigines of north-eastern Australia actually eat kangaroo willies as part of their diet, I was later told. Mine seemed indigestible, though, with all that gristle. That willy's probably still digesting inside me now.

I turned to look at Aggro. 'Has he done it?' I asked. No, he'd spat his willy out. I suppose it was worse for him, because of being a boy. He didn't mind the taste so much; he just hated the idea of it.

I hated the taste and the idea, but I just had to win. I wasn't putting that thing in my mouth and then not winning. There was nothing in my head that would have allowed me to do that. There was nothing saying, 'Yes, just chew it for a little while and then lose.' No, no, no! It was, 'If that thing is going anywhere near my mouth, I'm winning this round.'

Now the score was two all. The girls were really in with a chance! But, oh dear, it was Linford Christie against Britt Ekland. Oh, why? I thought. Then again, there's an aura about Britt that projects strength and goodness, so I couldn't help looking at her and thinking, She can do anything, this lady. If she was willing to go into the jungle at sixty years old, I reckoned she was super strong.

She walked calmly into the box and sat on a chair. This round was called 'Disastermind', and Linford and Britt had to answer general knowledge questions with a box on their head. I guessed that they'd have something poured into the box while they were being asked the questions. Thank goodness I didn't get this round, because the next minute Britt had giant spiders all over her face. They were climbing up her cheeks and in her hair, but she didn't flinch. She answered two questions correctly and the box was taken off her head.

Linford was obviously so scared that he only managed to answer one of the questions, so Britt beat him! 'Yes! We did it!' we screamed. Gillian McKeith or no Gillian McKeith, we'd won!

It was such a great feeling knowing that we didn't have to go straight into hell. Instead we were taken back to the massive villa where we'd met, and there we had a huge dinner of curried fish and peppers in a beautiful tomato sauce, with spinach and rice. You know what, it was the best meal I've ever had. It was so worth the willy.

The best thing about doing the trial was that we all did it together. What scares you most before you go into the jungle is the thought that you might be first up for a trial. You think that nobody will understand what you've been through and then you'll have to explain why you didn't get enough stars for everyone's dinner. The fact that we all had to go through our first trial together was reassuring. Right, everyone knows how it feels, I thought. We all know our limits and what we can and can't do. It made me feel on a level with everyone who'd done the trial, and after it was over, I thought, I can do anything here.

For breakfast the next morning we had croissants, cereal, toast, salmon, cheese – everything! We just scoffed it down. Meanwhile, the poor boys had to sleep on a mattress on the floor in the jungle on their own. I couldn't help feeling a little bit sorry for them.

Eventually, though, it was time to make our way to Camp Sheila, wondering what horrors would be in store for us there.

Chapter 15

Me and Shaun were crammed into a tiny helicopter high in the sky. I couldn't see the ground when I looked down, just endless clouds. We'd been rising through the air for more than an hour, and the higher we went, the more nervous I felt. I was shaking with nerves. I wasn't dressed for the occasion in my vest and shorts, either. No one had told me that I'd be skydiving that day.

I really wanted to do it, but it was such a scary prospect, so Shaun went first. His dive partner shifted him to the edge of the exit and gave him a practice run by hanging him out and bringing him back in. Then out he went, with his partner strapped to his back.

It's me in a minute! I thought. We circled and circled for ten whole minutes, waiting for the airspace to clear, then it was my turn. My partner strapped himself to the back of me and sat me on the edge. It was freezing cold and the air was rushing around my ears. My feet were dangling out of the helicopter. Right, here comes my practice run, I thought.

Then my partner started edging me out. 'Aren't we doing a practice run?' I asked, clinging to the sides of the helicopter.

'No, we've already done that with Shaun,' he said.

'But I'm not ready!' I insisted. 'I'm not prepared. I'm definitely not ready.'

'Let go of the side,' he ordered.

'I don't think I want to. I don't think I want to let go of the side,' I said. So he just pushed me out.

Then I was free-falling, fifty seconds without a parachute. Believe me, fifty seconds feels like a long time when you're falling out of the sky, dropping like a stone. It was the maddest feeling, like being on a flyover that never ends. The first ten seconds were really scary, but after that, I kept thinking, This is the most unbelievable thing I've ever done! I can't tell you how good that feeling was. I would recommend free-falling to absolutely everyone. You can't live without doing it. It is the most overwhelming, fantastic experience.

Eventually my partner released the parachute and we floated down to the ground, which was even more amazing. It was like having wings. I was gliding through the sky and I felt like a feather. I felt so lucky. Look what I get to do, I thought to myself. I'm so incredibly lucky. I made sure that I enjoyed every single moment of it, because I knew I was having one of the best experiences of my life.

I landed on my feet, not my bum, and walked away after my partner detached me. 'How on earth did you land like that?' Shaun asked, amazed.

'I really don't know,' I said with a smile. I was so happy. My first solo trial was over and it had turned into a wonderful adventure.

'Enjoy every second of this, because three weeks will fly by,' I told myself. Recalling how quickly my time on *The X Factor* had passed, I was determined to make the most of it.

It's such an extreme situation to be in. One minute I was doing a trial and wishing I was somewhere else, the next minute I was flying through the sky. It was crazy, really crazy. Let's be honest, it's not normal to fall out of the sky. But the great thing about doing something like that on a show like *I'm a Celebrity* is that you feel safe in the hands of experts.

Me, Shaun, Kayla and Linford were in the skydiving

group, and after we'd all landed we were sent on our way to our camps, so me and Kayla set off for Camp Sheila, leaving Shaun and Linford to head for Camp Bruce. It was sad for me because I felt really close to Linny.

I really came to respect Kayla as well, as she's a really nice girl. I know everyone has their opinions about her being a playmate, but I thought she was intelligent and genuine. I think the outside world just thought, Oh, another glamour model. Getting to know her, I realized, You're a clever girl and there is nothing wrong with you. By the end, the general perception of her seemed to be that she wasn't an idiot and she stuck up for herself. She was quite needy, but lovely with it.

Back at the camp, we met up with all the other girls. They'd been canoeing and potholing and they'd really enjoyed it, because they'd paddled down beautiful rivers and potholed without any bugs! They were very excited to hear that we'd been skydiving. Kayla and I were on a real high, but were careful not to rub their faces in it. None of the others would have been able to do it anyway, though, because they were excluded for medical reasons.

We all had a decent dinner that night of kangaroo and veg, with rice and beans, which we cooked ourselves. The kangaroo tasted a bit like chicken, which was fine with me as I love my Nando's! We had some fruit for afterwards and then we went to bed.

Sleeping outside was one of the big challenges I had to overcome. We were each given a swag, which is a mattress and sleeping bag combined, with a hood that goes over your head, so that someone else has to do you up and seal you in. It felt like a coffin, in my eyes, and I knew there was no way I could sleep like that, all zipped up with no way out.

It reminded me of that dream you have when some-body's sitting on your chest, or the one where you can't breathe. It must be a claustrophobia thing with me. Not in a million years would I be able to fall asleep after I'd been zipped up in a swag. Apart from my fear of being shut in, if one little spider got in there with me and I couldn't unzip myself to get out, I would have panicked.

Everyone else was fine with it, but I just couldn't do it. I don't like locking my front door because I worry that I won't be able to get out quickly if there's a fire. I don't like locking my windows, either. I have to know that there are easy exits. I'm such a space person. I have a real thing about it. Lifts don't bother me, though, so it's not too extreme – unless I get stuck in one, of course. But no one would like that. I think it's more of a problem when I'm lying down than at any other time. I feel all right if I'm standing up.

In the end I slept on top of my swag, inside my sleeping bag, which left my head exposed. Then I was terrified that something was going to drop on my face while I was sleep-ing, so I did up the neck of the sleeping bag really tight, turned the hood around and put it over my face. For the first couple of nights it took me a really long time to relax into sleep. I tried sleeping with both arms tucked into the sleeping bag, but that was impossible. I had to have one arm out in case a bug came along and I needed my hand to brush it away. So I slept with my sleeping bag up to my neck, the hood over my face and my arm underneath the flap of my swag. Each night, I lay there for hours with my eyes wide open until I was so tired I fell asleep.

That was how it was for the first two days, but after that I was so physically knackered that I ended up falling asleep as soon as it got dark. I was just flat out on top of my swag and I got over my anxiety and insomnia. I soon learned to switch off at night and spring into action when I woke up.

One of the things I really enjoyed about being in the jungle was not having a phone. Life was nice and simple. It got dark and I was ready for bed; I woke up when it was light; I cooked at dinner time and I didn't eat between meals. I snack so much when I'm at home, but I didn't have the chance to do any of that. I couldn't. It was a really refreshing change. The only real problem was missing Zach. It was a long time to be away from him, totally out of contact. But I was doing this for him, I reminded myself, so it was worth it.

The next day it was the Sheilas versus the Bruces, with the public voting for who would do the trials. The first person they voted for was Gillian, of course, against Shaun. To cut a long story short, we didn't eat in Camp Sheila for the first three days, because Gillian didn't do well in any of the trials.

Unfortunately, there was an eating challenge and, because Gillian's a vegan, she couldn't eat any animals. She barely ate the things she could eat, though. There was a fruit called a vomit fruit because it makes you throw up and she ate it all and brought us home one meal, which was great. Anyway, I'd never judge her for saying no. We didn't see the other trials, so we assumed they were horrendous. Poor Gillian, it was always going to be difficult to win.

Me and Kayla were given the next challenge, against Shaun and Aggro. We turned up thinking it would be really fun, but when we got there we were faced with a massive pool of stinking green gunk. Oh no! we thought.

Two of us would be going in there while two stayed dry on the side. Me and Kayla looked at each other. 'I don't mind. I'll do it,' I said.

The challenge was for me and Aggro to put on frog suits and splash across the pond to Kayla and Shaun, who had to squirt green slimy 'frogspawn' into our frogs' mouths while we sat on rotating lily pads. When the pouches in our mouths were full, we had to splash back across the pool and tip the slime into a tube.

You can imagine what I was thinking: Great, I'm against Aggro in a physical challenge, and I'm dressed up in a frog outfit! I didn't let it get me down, though. 'You signed yourself up for this,' I told myself. 'You can't pull out of it now. Just do it and beat Aggro. You can do it!'

It was really difficult, because there were logs all the way across this gunky pool and you had to climb over them to get to either side. I raced hard against Aggro and I wasn't that far behind him, but he was faster and stronger than me. 'Quick, keep going. Come on, we'll get there,' I kept saying to myself. I tried so hard, but we still lost.

When I pulled myself up onto the rocks at the end, I was panting hard and my whole body was shaking. Argh! I was covered in frogspawn.

Kayla burst into tears. 'That was so horrible!' she said. 'I didn't want to squirt frogspawn in your mouth. It was going all over your face. You couldn't breathe. I can't believe you had to do that!'

She was crying her eyes out. 'Why aren't you sad?' she asked me. 'That was horrible. They made me squirt things in your face.'

'It's OK,' I said. It wasn't nice, but she was from America, where I've been told that *I'm a Celebrity* is a lot tamer than the UK version. They're cushioned over there, apparently, because people just won't tolerate the kinds of trials you see in England.

'I'm so sorry,' she kept saying. 'You guys are just horrible.' She was genuinely upset and felt really guilty. It was so sweet.

If I'd been in her position, I probably would have felt the same, so from that perspective I was glad I'd done it, because I didn't feel guilty. Before I went on the show, I told myself I wouldn't say no to anything. I promised myself I'd do everything. If I'd been voted out the first week and I hadn't done anything difficult, I would have been really disappointed in myself. If you set yourself a challenge and then don't bother with it, what's the point?

The girls' camp didn't win any meals for three days, so I didn't eat. There were rice and beans, but after a while I just couldn't eat them any more. The beans were like baked beans without the sauce and they tasted of fart – so gross and disgusting! The rice was wholegrain, plain and chewy. It was so stodgy that you'd start gagging while you were chewing it. You were trying to swallow it because you were hungry, but you ended up choking on disgusting, stodgy food.

After Gillian ate the vomit fruit, we were given a couple of possum sausages. No one else liked them, but I loved them. They were really good. 'Yes, I'm going to eat them all,' I said when the others turned them down.

The next day, Camp Sheila joined Camp Bruce. Great, finally we're going to get some food, I thought. We hadn't seen the boys for three days and I was really happy to see them all. They were fed and content and had been having fun, and the whole day revolved around us meeting each other. There wasn't a challenge or a trial because the football was on in the UK and *I'm a Celebrity* wasn't going to be on that night.

The best moment of every day came at sundown, when we saw the rope in the trees above us moving. It meant that someone was attaching our food to the rope to lower it down to us; dinner was coming. We became like vultures, staring at the rope at the same time every day, waiting for it to twitch. Then a bag would come floating through the sky towards the camp. 'Our food's here!' we'd cry.

The food came in a furry skin bag. There was never anything particularly nice, except for those possum sausages and the one time we had shrimps. Often there would be a whole slab of meat in there – kangaroo or crocodile or whatever. You had to hack at it to divide it up and cook it. It was gross.

Linford was the best when it came to preparing the meat. Nobody else wanted to deal with it, because they didn't know what to do. How would I know which is the good bit of the meat and what to get rid of and what to keep? Linny really knew what he was doing, so we left him to do his magic. I got to cut and prepare all the vegetables, which I enjoyed. It was something to do at least. After eating rice and beans for days, it was so yummy to have a bit of flavour at last. When there were garlic cloves in the bag, we were in heaven.

I thought about food all the time. There must have been so much footage of us saying, 'Oh, M&Ms! Oh, Walkers Crisps! Oh, I could really hack some white chocolate!' It was our main topic of conversation throughout the day.

I guess that's because, the moment you're deprived of something, it's all you can think of. After ten days we were saying stupid things like, 'Do you remember Coke? Do you remember peanuts?' Like we'd been away for years. 'What about chocolate?' It was just ridiculous and a little bit pathetic. We were obsessed. We were constantly asking for stuff: 'A bit of tea or coffee? A bit of sugar? Please can we have a tiny bit of sugar or jam? Then we could make rice pudding.'

When we weren't talking about food, we sometimes had debates sitting on logs around the fire. They'd start with someone expressing an opinion and somebody else saying, 'Wait a minute!' Then other people would join in. 'I agree with him,' or, 'I agree with her.' Most of the time, it was really interesting to listen to everyone's opinions.

One night, Linford and I had a real disagreement. It didn't make any difference to how much I loved him, though, views or no views. He seemed to think that although it's fine for men to sleep around, it's not acceptable for women. He said that society allows men to behave like that, because that's just how they are, whereas a woman who sleeps around is branded a slag.

I didn't agree with him in any way, shape or form. I think if a man is doing it, he should be branded just as much as a woman is – if anyone's going to get branded that is.

'It's a male society, unfortunately. Women can't expect to do what men do,' he said.

'What the hell?' I said. 'Don't you dare!' I laughed and pushed him sideways.

'Women are meant to be more decent than men,' he said a bit later on. Oh my God!

I don't believe there should be any stigma surrounding it. You are who you are. If you want to sleep with loads of people, it's your life and your prerogative. Man or woman, it shouldn't make a difference. We all come from the same place and we all go to the same place, so there's no difference in my eyes. Everybody is equal, whether you're a man or a woman.

Linford began to elaborate on his argument, which got me even more frustrated. He said that the problems had all started with the women's liberation movement and women campaigning for equal rights. He seemed to be implying that there should be one rule for men and another for women.

'Hang on a minute,' I said, 'this is even worse than what you just said to me. If you're saying that you would tell your daughter she's only allowed to do certain things, but to your son you'll say he can do whatever he wants, then I think you're wrong and a bad person for doing that. I think that's awful.'

There is nothing I feel stronger about than everyone being treated the same. If I had a boy and a girl, I would tell them both, 'You do whatever you want to do and be happy. You've got ninety years maximum. Enjoy it. Do what you can in the time you've got.'

It really bugs me that men still get paid more than women, and that a man often gets offered a job over a woman. Why is that? Women are just as clever and just as capable. I'm not a women's rights activist, but I don't believe in opinions like the ones Linford expressed and I find it really difficult to hear them. He kept saying that it was just society's view and that he wasn't being sexist, but he also said that you can't separate yourself from the way society looks at things.

If I'm set a challenge against a man, I'll do my utmost to be just as good, if not better, than he is. There are too many people sitting there saying, 'But a man can do it better.' Men are at the top, so it's easy for them to sit there and hire other men. When they hire women, it's because women are loyal and less likely to try to take over their business. If I take on women, I can control them, they think. Not all men are like that, of course. My dad is the complete opposite. He would rather have Karen go back to work while he does the cooking and cleaning. There are men out there like my dad, but they're the minority.

It annoys me that women are fed the idea that they're physically and mentally weaker than men. I would never sit by silently while someone said that. I'll put my views across strongly, because I really believe in them.

'I don't believe that men dominate and you get more rights than me. I choose to believe I rule my own world,' I told Linford.

'No you don't, men rule the world,' he said. 'It's your life, but men rule the world.'

It was incredible to me that there were other women listening to him who didn't argue. How can a woman sit there and hear all that without saying anything? How could they let him say, 'Women shouldn't, women mustn't, they can't'?

No, no, no! To that I say, 'I will and I have! I'll do anything I want to do, thank you.' We've all got a brain. Why can't we do whatever we want to do?

Jenny Eclair, who'd joined the camp later, told him off a few times: 'I'm getting quite cross with you, Linford. That's the kind of male opinion I hate.' I think she was too angry to get into a proper debate about it.

I said, 'As a friend, I'm going to tell you that you need to stop right there. What you are saying totally goes against the way society is currently moving. I don't think you should think like that and I don't think you should force those views on your kids, either. That's going backwards socially and back in time. We're all trying to move forward and progress and get somewhere, but you're talking about going back to the bad old ways. That's crazy.'

Whereas Jenny was getting pretty annoyed, I don't get angry or swear when I'm having a debate. I get emotional and loud about things, but I'm not angry. 'We're going to just have to agree to disagree,' Linford said, and we did.

'If that's your opinion, I don't agree and I don't ever want to hear it,' I told him. 'But I'm telling you now that it's the wrong way to think. I won't tell anyone how to be, but that is so wrong. I feel I'm just as good as you, woman or man. You could have won a million gold medals, but I feel I'm just as good as you. End of story.'

I can't understand why women accept these kinds of views from men and don't say or do anything. If every woman said, 'Hang on, don't take me for an idiot, I'm just as good as him,' then we'd move forward a lot quicker. We need to get people to take us seriously so that we can really get somewhere. We need to speak out so we can get better jobs and be paid as much as men are. If I didn't get a job because of sexism, I would never, ever take it lying down. I would take my case to court and fight. Unfortunately, there are too many people who can't be bothered. I wish they'd stand up and say something.

The fact is that there are just as many women as there are men, so we really can change things if we want to. We have the bargaining power as men need us to reproduce. What are they going to do without us? Have babies by themselves?

It's strange how people think it's weird for a woman to be a feminist, when all it means is that she believes in equal rights for men and women. When people hear someone's a feminist, they talk about them like it's a disease or as if they're mentally ill, and a lot of girls seem to think that it means someone's a lesbian or something. That's rubbish. It's simply someone who believes she's every bit as good as a man.

At school I learned about the FTSE 100 and how men have most of the top jobs. We weren't learning about women's rights; it was just general knowledge. I remember looking at the figures and thinking they were ridiculous. Why is it like that? I wondered. I couldn't understand it.

To me, women's rights are no different to civil rights. Everyone should be treated the same. We saw what happened when a whole country started to believe in the superiority of one race, before and during World War II, with the Holocaust. What would have happened if the Nazis had succeeded? We'd have one race of narrow-minded people who would all be the same. It would be so hideous!

Things have changed for women, but they could get even better if people were more open and less worried about having an opinion. People seem to be too concerned about expressing their views these days, in case they say the wrong thing or haven't got enough hard information to back themselves up. But I think that if you genuinely believe in something, then nobody will beat you in an argument.

Of course, Linny genuinely believed his argument and thought he was right, so I was never ever going to change his mind. That's why we had to agree to disagree. By the end of it, though, he was saying that it wasn't necessarily his view, just the way society looked at things, which I don't agree with.

At the end of the day, me and Linford are from different worlds. He's fifty and his views are old school – the product of his background and religion. Mine is a more modern opinion, which conflicts with everything he says. I understand that it's quite hard for someone like him to hear what I have to say, just as it's hard for me to hear his old-fashioned views. It's a clash of opinions.

I'm so far removed from his generation. I know a lot of girls who are doing their own thing now, going out and getting what they want and working to build their chosen careers. These are girls from poor backgrounds, with no money, not rich kids with connections. They say, 'I'm going to do what I want to do and I'm going to make a success of it.' It makes me so happy to hear them say it, because that's the way I believe we should live our lives.

Chapter 16

'Where's Bob?' I asked.

'Medic Bob' is the man who comes over before every trial on *I'm a Celebrity* and says, 'Hello, I'm Bob. G'day. Today you are going to encounter a lot of animals, but don't worry, none of them will hurt you, but they may bite you.'

You think, Oh my God! Why are you even here, Bob? You're just making it worse.

What I feared the most were spiders, but Bob explained to me that because spiders are arachnids, they can't be used in trials as much as cockroaches and mealworms, which are a lot more common. Did you know that a female cockroach that gives birth on 1 January will have six million direct descendants by 31 December a year later? So that's why there are so many of them!

Oh, the things I learned. I used to question the rangers all the time, so you can imagine how bored I was. Still, it was good to hear that arachnids only came out in certain trials. Surely that meant I wouldn't come face to face with spiders every time? That's what I was hoping anyway.

At the start, Gillian did a trial every day. Then it came to a harness activity, which Gillian was excluded from participating in, so I was picked instead. I was hoping it wouldn't be too bad. Either way, though, I was determined to come back with all the stars I could. We hadn't eaten much in days and we were hungry!

I tried to prepare myself for the worst and started going

through the drill in my head again. 'You've got to get through this. You've got to do it,' I told myself over and over again.

In case of bugs, I covered up as much of my body as I could. I wore a vest, a T-shirt and a shirt, with the buttons done up to the top to stop anything getting inside, and I pulled my socks up over my trousers. I felt more and more uneasy as I waited for the trial to begin. I guessed they were sorting out the jungle creatures at the last minute, so they wouldn't all crawl away. The anticipation was terrible.

The longer I waited, the worse it got. I had no idea what was ahead of me and my imagination was running wild. 'Stop thinking!' I said to myself. 'You're going to be fine.' I was in a right jittery state.

I already knew that the trial was called 'The Australian Job'. Because of the name, I was hoping I'd be driving cars, or jumping from car to car with my harness on – with no creepy crawlies involved. 'Don't worry, there won't be any bugs,' everyone said as I waved goodbye to them at the camp.

Maybe there won't be, I thought, trying desperately to be optimistic. Maybe it will just be a fun trial?

Finally, I was told to walk up a nearby hill, where Ant and Dec would describe what the challenge was. 'Don't turn around,' the director said. So the trial was behind me, then. I really wanted to turn around as I trudged up the hill to my doom, but I did as I was told.

Ant and Dec were smiling when I arrived at the top. 'How are you?' Dec asked. **TOP**

'Oh, wonderful,' I said.

'Are you being sarcastic?'

'Oh no,' I said. 'I wouldn't hug me, I stink in every way,' I said, hugging them both.

246

'How are you feeling?' they asked.

'I'm smiling, but I'm not happy.'

'Do you want to know what the trial is?'

'No, but go on, tell me anyway.'

'OK, this is the Australian Job,' Ant said. 'Behind us you can see a bus, which is teetering over the edge of a quarry.' I turned to look. There was a big bus hanging off the edge of a cliff. It looked like the Scooby Doo bus. My heart leapt to my throat. Was I going on that bus? It could topple at any minute. But I knew that wasn't all. What else? I thought.

'Inside the box are ten stars. Some of them are fixed in lockers; some of them are hanging free. It's your job to go in there and unleash all ten stars. Now, you've got to get them and bring them back to the front of the bus and put them in the ticket box.'

'Every star in the ticket box at the end will count as a meal for camp, Dec went on. 'You've got ten minutes to do it.' I nodded uncertainly. 'And this is a bushtucker trial, so . . .'

'. . . I'll be joined by . . . ?' I asked.

'You know my script,' he said. 'You'll be joined by some jungle nasties.'

'Cool,' I whispered. I was practically gasping with anxiety.

A harness was attached to me and I went on my way, shaking like a leaf. I still couldn't breathe properly. I didn't even feel like my head was on my body. My mind was somewhere else, but I kept silently chanting, 'You can do it. Everything is going to be fine. Don't worry.'

The moment I stepped onto the bus I could see giant spiders crawling across the floor. The hairs on my arms and on the back of my neck stood on end. I looked away, then the timer started. There were wooden bathroom cabinets all around the bus in the luggage rack area. I had to slide the cabinet doors open, see if there was a star inside among whatever else was in there – bugs and spiders! – and untie it.

My biggest fear was that I would slide open a cabinet door and a load of spiders would jump in my face and on my clothes. It was horrendous. I just hated it. I made myself open the first box. Oh my God, it was bristling with huge, brown huntsmen spiders. They were wandering all over the walls of the box. I felt sick. It was my worst nightmare come true, but I willed myself on. 'You can do it. Just put your hand in and get the star,' I said to myself. 'They're only spiders.'

Just then, a spider landed on my shoulder. I yelped and flicked it away. 'Brrr! Don't worry, it's just a spider,' I said, my voice trembling with horror. I shook my arms again and tried to steady my quivering hands. 'Just carry on. Just get the star out.' I went on fiddling with the knots, trying to work the star free. But there were three knots, and they were all tied tightly, so it took me ages to get it loose.

Please just let me get the star off, I thought. Please! I'm in here surrounded by bugs, isn't that enough? Why are there so many knots, on top of everything? Finally, I slid the star off the rope, and put it in the ticket box.

I moved on to the next cabinet, which was infested with cockroaches. Cockroaches are so horrible! They crawl up your sleeves, all up your arm and in your hair. I wasn't sure if I could put my hand into the locker and touch them. It was well gross. I kept flicking them off me as I tried desperately to untie the star from the wall. There were cockroaches scuttling all over my hands and arms. Then – bang! – there was a massive explosion and the back doors of the bus blew off.

'Whoah!' I yelled. 'What the hell?' The bus started tilting scarily.

'Try and relax, Stacey,' Dec called from outside the bus.

'OK,' I said. I kept on working at the star in the locker full of cockroaches. At last, I untied it and pulled it out.

'You've got five minutes left. You're halfway through the trial.'

'Thank you,' I said.

I was constantly being given directions and all I could say was, 'OK,' and, 'Thank you.' I've always got something to say, but now I could only whisper the odd polite word or two. They'd never had anyone as polite on the show before, they said. I remember I did the same thing when I was in labour. I kept saying, 'Sorry' and 'Thank you'. It must be the way I react when I'm really, really nervous. I just want to make sure everyone around me is happy, so that nothing bad happens.

The next box was stuffed with fish guts, which spilled out all over the floor when I opened the door. I put my hand into the slimy mess and grabbed hold of a star. At this point, the bus was leaning at a sharp angle, facing downwards, and it was really hard to keep my balance. As the bus tipped further, more fish guts fell on the floor and there were spiders and cockroaches falling all over me. 'Oh, crumbs!' I said ever so politely. Fortunately, because the string was slimy with fish guts, the knots were easier to untie and I soon pulled the star free.

There were more cockroaches in the next box. 'Come on, Stacey!' I kept saying as I untied the star. 'Come on!' I'd been assured beforehand that nothing would harm or poison me, so I wasn't scared about that. It wasn't that they could kill or hurt me; it was just them and the fact that they were bugs. I didn't want them in my clothes, hair or pants.

I put the fourth star in the ticket box. I could see three stars dangling from the ceiling at the end of the bus, so I moved towards them, but as soon as I stepped forward, I slipped on fish guts and fell down. I tried to get up, but slipped again. The bus tipped and everything on the floor and in the open lockers spilled on top of me. It was so horrible. Spiders, cockroaches, crickets, mealworms and fish guts fell on me from all angles. Nothing could have been more disgusting.

Finally, I grabbed for one of the stars, thinking I could pull myself up. But it was attached to the ceiling with Velcro, so it instantly came away and I slipped clean out of the back of the bus. 'Aaaaaah!'

'Wheeee!' I found myself flying through the air, attached to a rope. 'Oh no!' I cried, thinking of the stars I'd left behind. Still, I was extremely relieved, even though I was dangling precariously over the quarry, covered in fish guts and bugs. The trial was over.

I was lowered to the ground and Ant and Dec came over to speak to me. I didn't want to talk to them, though, I just wanted to go somewhere and cry. 'How did that go?' they asked. 'Are you pleased?'

'No, I only got four,' I said. I was really disappointed. I tried to keep a smile on my face as they counted up the stars and we said goodbye.

'Can I go to the toilet?' I asked one of the crew, trying not to show how close to tears I was. He pointed to a portaloo and I went inside, locked the door and sobbed silently for a few minutes, tears pouring out of my eyes. I missed my mum, Zach and Aaron so much in those few minutes! I just needed someone to cuddle. When I came out, the cameraman gave me a drink of his clean water, which made me want to cry again. He's so kind, I thought. I was so emotional. He ended up becoming one of my really good friends.

I was crying because I'd just been through the scariest and most horrible experience of my life. You wouldn't want to be faced with that situation in a million years. I found it hellish to be stuck in a bus on top of a cliff with bugs all over me, trying to undo knots. But, I reminded myself, I'd put myself up for it by agreeing to go into the jungle. It was my decision, so it was no one's responsibility but mine.

I was there to challenge myself and because I wanted to find out what I could and couldn't do. Was I really scared of spiders, or was it just psychological? As it happened, I found out that, yes, I am very scared of them, but I still managed to be in a room with them without freaking out. You have to test yourself in life. If you don't, you're no one.

I felt proud I'd gone in there. I'm not joking when I say that before I went into the jungle, I couldn't even pick up a house spider in a glass and throw it away. Now I'd had enormous hairy spiders crawling all over me. I don't think I totally overcame my fear, but I did something I never thought I could do. I still don't like spiders, but I'm not that bothered about them any more.

Although I was proud of myself, I was also experiencing the lowest, weirdest feeling. I was pleased I'd got through the trial, but at the same time I felt humiliated and traumatized. It was awful. I'd had to talk to Ant and Dec when I just wanted to cry. I'd had to pretend I was fine, when instead I wanted to break down. I think I was crashing mentally, after getting all psyched up for the trial. I'd suppressed one of my greatest fears for a few minutes, but I hadn't done as well as I'd wanted to. I was going to have to go back to camp and tell everyone I only got four stars. I felt like a failure. I wish I could have shown them just how bad the task was.

They're all going to be really disappointed in me, I thought. They'll think, She could have done better than that.

On my way back to camp, I decided it had definitely helped me to watch all the YouTube videos from previous episodes of *I'm a Celebrity* beforehand. Gillian and Jenny had come back from their first trial saying, 'That was horrendous. I didn't realize it would be like that.' But I went to every trial knowing it was going to be appalling. I didn't think that it would be anything less than shocking and horrifying. I would recommend that everyone who goes on *I'm a Celebrity* tries to prepare themselves psychologically. Think hard about what you are going to be faced with over the next few weeks and try to find a way to deal with it mentally, because it isn't easy.

Bad as it was, I've never had nightmares about that trial. I forgot about it the moment it was over. I just didn't want to think about it any more. That's done and I'm probably going to have to do another one soon, so get over it, I thought.

Back at camp, I managed to tell everyone that I'd only got four stars without bursting into tears. They were all really sweet about it. 'It's fine, absolutely fine,' they said.

Then I got into my bikini and jumped into the freezing cold pool to have a wash. You're not allowed in the shower when you've been covered in bugs, because the shower water is recycled and the dirty cockroaches would contaminate it. So when you've been on a trial, you have to go in the pool. Now I have to go into the pool, on top of everything, I thought resentfully.

But although the pool was freezing cold, you always felt refreshed when you got out. And somehow it helped you put your bad experience behind you. Right, that's over. All finished. That's it, I thought once I was clean. It wasn't nice, but it was good, in a funny way. I felt really proud to have done it.

Most of the time I couldn't bear to get in the freezing cold pool, so I only had about three baths and four showers the whole time I was in the jungle. Unless I had a trial or got really dirty in a challenge, I stayed away from water. It rained the whole time we were there, so our clothes were damp and our towels were soaking wet and they stank. The idea of getting out of the freezing water and wrapping myself in a stinky, wet towel just wasn't appealing, and I couldn't bring myself to do it very often. I'd rather be dirty. But hey, at least my nail varnish wasn't chipped!

Next it was time for dinner and bed. The meal was really good. I can't remember now what it was, but it was something decent, so I didn't feel so bad about only getting four stars.

The next trial was another Gillian McKeith exemption for medical reasons. She couldn't do much, really. I felt sorry for her, poor woman, and for her children watching her. For days she'd been crying and saying she was miserable. We'd seen her faint in the live trials, she'd lost loads of weight and she really wasn't feeling well. She was obviously very unhappy, because she was in tears every day and seemed to have a lot of issues.

By now Nigel Havers had left; he just walked off. I thought, Fair enough. At the end of the day, there's nothing wrong with going if you're brave enough to say, 'No I'm not enjoying it and I'm leaving.'

I respected Nigel. He's what I'd call old school. He's one of those men who holds the door open for you and pulls your seat out. He's a film star and a gentleman, so for him to stick his head in a load of bugs was embarrassing and humiliating in my opinion!

It struck me that Nigel wasn't there for the money. Most of the people who moan are only there because they want the money, I reckon, but Nigel put himself up for the experience, didn't enjoy it and went. He was put in a prison costume at one point and he didn't want to wear it, because he didn't want his wife to see him dressed like that. 'It'll upset my wife and me,' he said. 'I can't do it.' So he left.

Good on him, I thought. If it's not for you, it's not for you. You don't know until you get there. I think it is a little bit crazy to stay if all you're going to do is go on about how much you hate it and how miserable you are.

In the end I went up to talk to Gillian while she was in the 'jungle jail'. 'You're fainting in front of your children. No amount of money is worth that,' I said to her through the bamboo bars. If you're so afraid and have so many phobias, you should go. There's nothing keeping you here. You said it's unbearable.'

'It would be stupid for me to leave,' she snapped. 'I have a television career and if I walk out on my contract I won't work in television again. That's the way it works.'

A couple of minutes later, I said, 'Gillian, ever since you've been here, you've said that you don't want to face your fears –'

'You're the classic person who doesn't understand what a fear is versus a phobia,' she said angrily. 'You don't understand phobia.'

She was being quite aggressive and, being the emotional wreck I am, I started to get upset. I tried one last time to get her to listen, though. 'Honestly, Gill, if your phobia is that intense and that bad and you're having to get up and deal with it every day . . . it's hard for us to hear as well.'

'Then don't listen. Just go back over there,' she retorted.

'OK,' I said, stung by her words.

I went over to the river and peered into the water, trying to hide the fact that tears had sprung to my eyes. I thought that if I leaned over the river, the tears would fall in and no one would notice. Then Linford and Sheryl got annoyed with Gillian for upsetting me, when really it was just me being over emotional.

'It's my fault, I shouldn't have said anything,' I told Linford. 'It's none of my business. I don't understand.'

'No, you have a right. She's not sick,' he reassured me, putting a comforting arm around me. 'You're an honest person, so you told her. Don't let it upset you.'

I was asked to do the next trial in Gillian's place, because she was exempt, and this time I got to do it with Aggro. Yes, I'm not alone! Thank God, I thought. I knew he would be a strong ally.

We made our way to a jungle clearing, where we were given Mario brothers costumes to put on. I was Mario, in red, and Aggro was Luigi, in yellow, and we each had blue braces and a moustache. It was so cool, because we actually looked like the Mario brothers. Any normal girl would say, 'Oh my God, get this off me,' but I was very excited to be dressed as one of my favourite games characters.

Despite that, I still couldn't relax, because I kept thinking, Please don't let there be bugs.

Ant and Dec revealed the trial, which was going to take place on an assault course about 40 feet above the ground. You wouldn't have wanted to do it if you suffered from vertigo, that's for sure. There were ten balloons tied to the assault course – each one counted as a star – and we had to untie them and let them go.

I hardly heard any of the instructions. I was just thinking, Bugs? Bugs?

'And who are we going to be joined by?' I asked.

'Yes, and you'll be joined by . . .'

Oh no! I thought, panicking. But then it dawned on me that 'Medic Bob' hadn't come to see us. Hold on a minute, I thought. Where's my Bob? Where's my bug brief? Where's the man who says, 'You'll be fine. There are a few things that bite, but don't worry.'?

Ha! There was no 'Medic Bob'. That meant there were no bugs. What a relief. Now I could concentrate on what me and Aggro had to do.

We were harnessed up and hooked onto a zip wire, then a member of the crew put a magnet on me and a magnet on Aggro and attached us to each other. We had to go from right to left along the assault course without our magnets coming apart. Every time our magnets came away, we would lose a star.

We got up onto the assault course and started walking at about one mile an hour because we were attached. It was, 'Left, left, left; right, right, right; a little bit left; a little bit right.' We were going so slowly, it was hilarious.

We inched our way along, releasing balloons as we went. 'Don't look down!' Dec kept shouting, because we were really high up and looking down made you feel dizzy. I felt safe with my harness on, though.

Finally, after a few scary moments, we reached the end of the course. To win our last star, we had to jump through a huge circle of paper, still attached by the magnets. This was called the 'Leap of Faith' and it was really exciting. 'One, two, three – jump!' we shouted.

I screamed at the top of my voice as we smashed through

the paper and fell 20 feet. Soon we were hanging from our harnesses, swinging through the air over the jungle. It was so cool. Even better, we ended up winning all the stars, which was amazing. We could go back to camp and say, 'Yes! We got all the stars.' It was the only trial without bugs and we really enjoyed it. Best of all, there was loads of food for everyone that night.

Chapter 17

Two weeks in and I was really enjoying myself. The simple rhythms of everyday life in the jungle are very relaxing. It was a proper break from the outside world. You went to bed when the sun went down and got up when it was light. There was nobody on the other end of a phone telling you what to do or hassling you. When you weren't doing trials, you did your own thing, which was a lovely feeling.

Even the trials weren't so bad after a while, because you got used to them. OK, another bug, you'd think. What are they going to do this time? The same as last time: wriggle, crawl and scuttle around as usual. In one trial, I was wheeled around in a giant pie case and covered in stinking fish guts and raw meat. At the 'Rank Banquet', I had to eat pig's brain. It was disgusting, but I went for it.

'This will really help my intelligence,' I joked as I spooned it into my mouth. 'I hate you!' I told Ant and Dec.

'I've got no idea what that would taste like,' Dec said. 'What does it taste like?'

'Mushy chips?' I said, trying to think of a matching flavour. 'Intelligence?'

Next, I had to drink a cup of cockroach mead. 'That's a beer, isn't it?' I asked.

'Yup.'

'Here we go.' I downed it in one.

'Well done,' Ant said. 'You're very speedy!'

'Well, I don't want it to last, do I? For God's sake.'

Finally, I had to eat what Dec described as 'lady kangaroo bits'.

'No!' I protested, picking up the plate. 'That is gross!' I laughed nervously as I chewed it. I hated the idea of what it was and became almost hysterical. 'That's disgusting!' I said.

'What's it's like?' Dec asked.

'Furry,' I said, taking it out of my mouth. 'What the hell!' Could I really carry on chewing it? I was shaking my head as I put it back in my mouth, then finally I managed to swallow it.

'Well done, Stacey, that's your three main courses,' Ant said. 'Was that the worst?'

'Yes,' I said, fishing around my mouth for stray hairs.

I always had a right laugh with Ant and Dec after the trials, and I enjoyed the group challenges, except the ones where I had to put my hand in a jar of spiders and things like that. Actually, I couldn't do that one. I still couldn't bear the idea of spiders crawling on me, so I was happy to go to jail instead.

Every day we did something different. One day we had karaoke, and another time we made our own bedside cabinets, which was fun. We had to cook our own food and we didn't have any recipe books, so we had to make it up on the spot and enjoy ourselves preparing it. I really liked being around everyone, even though there were occasional personality clashes.

I loved it when Dom Joly and Jenny Eclair arrived, followed by Alison Hammond, the TV presenter. Some of the others were a bit fed up at first — 'Why are there new people?' they grumbled — but I was happy about it. 'Ah, more people!' I'd been a massive fan of Dom Joly's *Trigger*

Happy when I was little, so when he joined us I thought, He's going to be so funny. And he was. He's a really nice, genuinely funny man. Dom was in his element in the jungle. He loves a challenge and doing new things, and he loves finding new animals. It was good to have someone else there who was enjoying himself.

Dom and I had a running joke about our massively different backgrounds. He lives in a posh village in the Cotswolds, where Liz Hurley and loads of other celebrities live, and I'm from Dagenham. He has a Canadian wife who does art, and I'm with a painter from Grays.

He was always saying, 'God, that wouldn't happen in the Cotswolds,' or, 'They wouldn't do that in the Cotswolds.'

'No one even cares,' I'd hit back. 'No one wants to live in the Cotswolds. It's rubbish; it's for boring old people. That's where people go when they want to be boring. You want to come to Dagenham.'

Our lives are so different, but our morals and sense of humour are the same. We laughed at all the same things and we shared the same thoughts and opinions, so it didn't matter at all where we came from. I thought it was brilliant.

Jenny Eclair is one of those ladies who seems to me to have a really depressing outlook on life, but in reality she's actually very happy. She's so pessimistic about women and age, but she makes money from telling jokes about topics like that and I suppose the inspiration must come from somewhere. She jokes about periods, menopause and how men are the worst thing in the world. Oh, and how we're all going to die!

I found her really funny, but my sense of humour is stupid funny, whereas hers is dry and cynical. 'Yes, I'm cynical, and you will be, too, one day,' she used to say to me. 'It will happen, don't you worry. You won't be this happy for the rest of your life.'

'I really don't want to grow up,' I'd say. 'I don't want to be cynical. I don't want what has happened to you to ever happen to me.'

'Oh it will happen,' she said, nodding her head. 'It happens to everyone.'

Jenny was kind, though. One night, when Alison and Britt weren't feeling well, she stayed with them all night and kept getting them water and taking them to the toilet, which was really lovely of her.

I think Shaun enjoyed himself. I was always asking him questions. 'What do you do? Where do you live? Where do your kids go to school?' He told me loads about himself, but we didn't talk about his wild past. I like Shaun and thought he was really funny and nice, so I didn't want to hear anything that would make me think differently about him.

I'm really scared of things like drugs. Just talking about them makes me shudder and cringe. I'd rather not know if someone has taken them, because then my opinion of them would change. Even though it's in the distant past, I really don't like it. I'm so strongly against drugs that if Aaron told me he'd done drugs, I don't know if I could be with him. The whole idea makes me feel physically sick. I don't know why, but I can't stand it.

What connected me to Shaun was that I felt we were alike. He had his normal wife and all his kids at home, he wasn't worried about what he was doing in there and he didn't care what anyone thought of him. He was just him. I'm really drawn to natural people, people who are themselves all the time and who tell the truth. He reminded me of my old school mates; he could easily have been one of them.

Britt was very nice, too. Every day she went to bed and woke up perky. What a beautiful film star lady. 'Goodnight, darling. I love you, darling,' she'd say. But there were times when I'd look at her and think, This isn't good for you. She's sixty years old and she was sleeping outdoors. She wasn't well half the time; she was always getting a cold and different infections. If you want to get ill, the jungle is the place to go. The nights were cold and damp, and our bed and clothes were wet so we were soaking all the time. It had been really hot in all the previous years, but north-eastern Australia was having the worst rain it had ever had that year. Then, of course, a couple of months later, there were the most terrible floods.

I love you so much, I thought, looking at Britt. I think you can do anything. You're a strong woman. But I didn't think she should be out there at night and I felt really bad for her.

Lembit was a funny old man. He's one of those people who sits there talking to you for ages and ages and forgets what he's actually talking about. 'I don't even know where I was there,' he'd say. He's got such a good heart. He really wanted to do well and be good and make people happy.

In the third week, the evictions started. And it wasn't like *The X Factor*, when you lost someone once a week; these evictions happened every day, completely shaking up our routine. People were dropping like flies, one after the other – gone, gone, gone. Sheryl, Lembit, Britt and Alison left before we knew it.

The moment people started to go, I had one thing on my mind, and that was Zach. I was hoping he was nearby, because I was longing to see my mooch. It was agony waiting to see him, Mum and Aaron again.

All I could think about was seeing him again. Even though I was enjoying the peace and simplicity of life in the jungle, I missed him desperately. So every time someone left, I felt a stab of envy, because it meant they'd be getting together with their family again. Sometimes I felt like running out there with them, just so I could see Zach.

I wouldn't say I was glad when Gillian went, but the camp was more relaxed after her departure. We could mix the meat and veg spoons for starters! Because she's a strict vegan, we had to make sure the pots for meat and vegetables were kept separate; now we could use them for anything. Other than that, though, it didn't make much of a difference when she left. I'd enjoyed her company most of the time and I didn't see all that much of her anyway because one of us was usually off doing trials.

When there were eight of us left, we did a girls versus boys challenge. It was me against Linford Christie. Oh dear! We got dressed up as kangaroos and we had to squash fruit until we'd filled up a tube with juice. I soon worked out that it wasn't about how many fruit you squashed, it was about moving the pulped fruit out of the way to allow the juice to get down the tube.

I won! The prize was a luxury night for two of the girls in a room. I didn't want it, so I gave it away, but the other girls refused to go if I didn't, so I went and took Jenny with me, because she'd also done a trial that day.

We walked up to the heights, where a cosy sleepover awaited us. There were loads of sweets, too! Of course, I instantly jumped into Jenny's bed, because my idea of a sleepover is everybody jumping into one bed. I poured all the sweets onto her bed and said, 'Right, what are we doing?'

'Your bed's over there,' she said, pointing to the other side of the room.

We had a really good time. Jenny gave me all the sweets and let me sleep with the lights on, even though it made all the bugs come out. That was really kind of her. She just wants everyone to be happy.

I'm a Celebrity feels a lot less competitive as a show than *The X Factor*. In my opinion, it hardly seemed competitive at all. When you go, you go. As far as I could tell, no one appeared all that bothered about winning. We were all too tired and hungry to worry about that – and you have to be good to each other, or life would be very difficult. You have to look out for each other and be sensitive to other people's wants and needs.

At the end of the day you've got to survive for three weeks without going insane, which is hard enough in itself. So you can't start being too competitive, or that's the way I felt anyway. All I thought about was getting up, doing whatever I had to do, making the best of things and drying my clothes. I didn't have time to plan a strategy for winning, or even to really think about it. I just had to get on with it.

Towards the end, I started thinking I'd like to win, but only because it's nice to win. I wasn't bothered. Not in a million years did I think I'd be the favourite; it just didn't occur to me. It wasn't announced that I was the favourite to win until we were in Australia, by which time I was locked away in the hotel and knew nothing about it.

By the time there were five of us left, the atmosphere was quite different. At night time, when the camp was full, everyone would be shouting goodnight to each other and we'd take ages to settle down. Now that there were only a few of us and we were all really far apart, we'd just call out, 'Goodnight!' from our distant swags.

Where is everyone? I thought. As the last day came closer, I couldn't wait to get out and see Zach. Sometimes I thought I might just make a run for it and go and find him. The minutes and hours until I saw him seemed to go on for longer and longer. I wasn't the only one feeling jealous of the person leaving each day; we all were. If anything, I reckon the competition was to see who could get out first! Everyone was craving some wine or a bit of chocolate, and we all wanted to see our families.

Two days before I left the jungle, I had a video link call with Zach, Aaron and my mum, who were all sitting on a sofa in their hotel room. It was so great to see they were all OK. Zach just talked and talked. 'I've seen the dolphins and I've been to the zoo and seen the koalas . . .' As he told me all the great things he'd done, I realized how much he'd changed in just four short weeks. He was talking so well that it seemed like he'd grown up about ten years.

I was so happy to hear that he'd been having such an amazing time. He'd been to the Steve Irwin zoo and a dolphin show, and he'd played with all the other celebrities' children. He and my mum and Aaron had been in Australia for a week, having the holiday of a lifetime, while I was having the holiday from hell!

Then Zach said something that almost broke my heart. 'Are you going to come home with me?' he asked.

I took a sharp intake of breath. 'Yes, of course I am, darling,' I said, my voice cracking with emotion. I couldn't bear him to think that I'd abandoned him. 'I'm coming back to you in a day or two and then we'll be together again.' At that moment, I just wanted to run and find him and hug him, to reassure him that I was there for him. My poor little boy.

After a little while I said to Aaron, 'Are you all right?'

'All right,' he said. He hates being on camera because he gets embarrassed.

'I miss you,' I said. I couldn't help myself.

Oh dear, he was so uncomfortable at that. He turned to Zach and said, 'Er, have you told Mummy about the koala bears?' He didn't want to say anything soppy on TV in front of millions of people.

I made a joke to lighten the atmosphere. 'I thought I didn't have a boyfriend no more,' I said. 'I thought the penis thing threw you off.'

He laughed. 'I let that one go for once,' he said.

It was so hard to say goodbye. I wanted to talk to them for the rest of the day. 'Bye, Zach,' I said, waving. 'I'm going to see you very, very soon.'

The days just got weirder as more people left. Now we were down to three: me, Shaun and Dom. Two more nights and it would be the end.

Dom left the next day and then it was just Shaun and me. One more sleep until it was all over. I didn't care about winning any more. I've never come better than third in all my life, I thought. So this is going to be good. Whatever happens, I'm going to feel great.

Shaun and I spent the day together. 'What would you like to do today?' we were asked.

'Can we have biscuits and hot chocolate and watch a film?' we said.

We were told that we could have anything we wanted for our meal that night, but only if we agreed to do a live trial for the final. 'OK,' we said. We were craving our favourite foods so much that we were prepared to make that bargain. 'Let's eat today and worry about the live trial tomorrow,' we decided. I think we both came to regret it, but not until the next day!

We wrote a list of everything we wanted and had our final meal at 4p.m.: saveloy, chips, chicken chow mein, wan ton soup, shredded beef, pork salt and pepper ribs, ice cream, a Terry's chocolate orange, pancakes, meringue, Coke, Sprite and beers for Shaun. We also got to watch *Toy Story*. It was paradise.

The next day, Medic Bob appeared as we were getting into our shorts and vests for the trial. 'Why did I have to eat that food?' I asked myself. 'I could have just gone home, nice and easy.' But no. We really, really wanted that food and now we had to pay for it.

The last trial was a lot worse than I thought it would be. It was called 'Bush Spa' and everyone came back to sit and watch it. I went before Shaun. First, it was a hair wash. I lay on a plastic lounger with my head back and they poured mealworms all over my hair. Instead of shampoo, I had maggots! Fine. I could bear that, although it made me whimper quite a lot.

Next I had a green ant 'manicure' and a crayfish 'pedicure'. This was horrible, because green ants bite and squirt acid into you and the bites last for ages. I had to put my hands in a box of green ants and my feet into a box of pinching crayfish. 'Oh my God, get them off,' I pleaded. 'That frightens me. They are proper biting me.'

Finally, I had to face my worst fear. They pulled back a blanket to reveal a plastic box full of massive spiders and told me to put my head in it for thirty seconds. My whole body started shaking; my limbs were like jelly, my stomach was churning and I couldn't move. Just do it! I thought, willing myself to step forward. 'It's only for thirty seconds.'

I closed my eyes and put my head in the box. Great big spiders started crawling up my face as more were being poured onto me. They didn't step on me; they felt their way around, testing out where they could walk, cautiously exploring the territory. I kept making these little noises, I don't know why. 'Mmm, mmm, mmm.' It was to stop myself screaming, I suppose. At least they're only on my face, I thought, to comfort myself. They can't get down past my neck. But then I started to worry that when I pulled my head out of the box, I might squash a spider as I squeezed through the rubber opening. The thought of squashing a spider on my face was just horrific. It made me feel sick and faint.

It was the longest thirty seconds of my life, but when it was finished I didn't have the guts to pull my head out of the box, even though I was desperate to get away. What if a spider comes out with me? I thought. I want to leave my head in here. They love me now. Leave me alone. It's weird the stuff that goes through your mind.

Eventually, about two seconds later, I whisked my head out. 'Please get anything off me now,' I begged Ant and Dec.

'Well done,' they said, giving me a cuddle. 'You did so well.'

'Thank you,' I said, still shaking like a leaf. Again I had that weird low feeling and I just wanted to go off and cry on my own, but I couldn't.

At last it was time for the results of the public vote. Me, Shaun, Ant, Dec and the other contestants gathered on the wooden platform next to the bridge leading out of the camp.

'The votes have now been counted,' said Ant.

'Stacey, Shaun, you've entertained millions of viewers for three memorable weeks,' Dec went on. 'They've watched you night after night and loved every minute of it.'

'This is it. The public have had their say. It's time to reveal the results we've all been waiting for. The winner of *I'm a Celebrity . . . Get Me Out of Here!* 2010 . . . and the new Queen of the Jungle is Stacey Solomon!'

It took a few moments for it to sink in. I remember Shaun hugging me, then I hugged him. Then I hugged Ant and Dec, who sat me on my 'throne'.

'Stacey, how do you feel? You're the new queen of the jungle.'

'Thank you so much,' I said, completely overwhelmed by it all. 'I don't know what to say.'

They gave me a jungle crown and sceptre, and I was told I had to walk over the bridge. 'Where's Zach?' I asked.

'On the other side of the bridge.'

I was directed to walk across the bridge and stop and pose for all the photographers on the other side, but there was no way I wasn't going straight to Zach, knowing that he was only a few feet away. I couldn't stay away from him. The minute I knew he was on the other side of the bridge, I was like, 'That's it! I've got to go!' I had to be with him. People are so mad if they don't run straight to their children. You've got to be crazy. I hadn't seen him for four weeks! Since he wasn't allowed on the bridge, I ran past the flashing cameras and rushed to find him. The photographers went mad because I was supposed to be doing photos, but I had to ignore them to get to Zach. 'I need to see Zach first,' I said. 'Then I'll do the photos.'

It was so amazing seeing my son and holding him again.

Those first few moments of being with him filled me with the most overwhelming sense of exhilaration. I felt intoxicated with joy. We clung to each other and neither of us wanted to let go. It was such a special feeling. I was really happy to see my mum and Aaron, too, although I was worried about hugging Aaron because I stank so much. I just wanted us all to go back to the hotel and spend some proper time together. It was such a relief being out of the jungle and back with the people I loved most in the world.

That night, the wrap party was held in some club in Brisbane. I went in and headed straight for the pool table! As I was standing there with my pool cue in my hand, a wave of exhaustion swept over me. I was happy, but I was also really tired – I didn't even register that I was out of the jungle. One man came over and said, 'Hi, you won't know me, but I know you. I'm the man with a camera in the rock, and I've been filming you from nine until two every day.' It was so funny.

Every single crew member was so nice to me it made me want to cry. They all came up and said, 'Hello, I think you're wonderful.' What a lovely thing to say!

We flew home the next day at eight in the morning, and my dad, sister, brother and stepsister met us at the airport. I didn't expect them to be there for one second, so it was a really fantastic surprise. My dad, bless him, feels like he's never in the picture, because I always take my mum everywhere, so he felt like he'd missed out. I'd missed him so much while I was in the jungle, and all I wanted to do was see him and talk about it all. Oh, Dad, I really needed you! I thought as we hugged each other. It was so great to be home with all the family.

Chapter 18

'Hey, where are you going?' I asked my tour manager and manager. 'This isn't the way to my house!'

'The road's closed, so we have to go this way,' they said.

'What do you mean? It can't be closed. We came on that road.' I was really puzzled.

'They're doing night road works,' they said.

I knew they were lying, but why? It didn't make any sense to me. I started having a meltdown. What if they were kidnapping me? It was a ridiculous idea, but what was going on? I looked out of the window. 'We're heading for Loughton! Why are we going there?' I asked frantically. 'We're nowhere near my house!'

'It's a really long diversion,' they said. They were laughing now, but I was close to tears.

Things just hadn't seemed right since they'd hustled me out of the gig I'd just done in Chelmsford. I hate rushing at the end of a gig. I think that when people pay you to come and sing for them, it's right to spend some time talking to them afterwards, saying thanks and that you hope they had a good time. But my managers were insistent about leaving, and there was nothing I could do.

Then my friend rang me. 'Are you coming down the pub?' she asked.

'Yeah,' I said. 'I'll make it just in time for last orders.'

But on our way back, we'd taken a turning that took us in the opposite direction to Dagenham and now we were heading for Loughton.

My phone rang again. It was my sister. 'Will you pick me up from work?' she asked. She works nights at a country club in Loughton to help pay her way through university.

I was crying now. 'Well I might as well, because I'm half-way to Loughton now,' I said.

The guys seemed quite happy to pick up Jemma. I told them where to go and we drew up outside the country club. As we sat in the car, waiting for her to come out, I looked at my watch and realized I'd never make it to the pub for last orders. It was so frustrating. Then Jemma's bar manager came out to the car. 'Sorry, she's not finished yet,' she said.

'Are you joking?' I said. I was close to boiling point now. 'I didn't come all the way down here to wait for her to finish work. I've missed last orders at the pub already; I've missed going out with all my friends. I don't want to be here!'

'Well, go in and get her, then,' she said.

'No, I'm not going in there. I'm not getting out of the car.'

'Go on,' she said. 'She ain't going to come otherwise.'

I got out of the car in a right strop. I don't want to go in there, I thought. I was really annoyed. Eventually, though, I went inside, where I was directed to one of the function rooms.

'She's just through there,' a waiter told me, pointing to a pair of double doors.

I pushed through the doors at top speed. I was going to find her and drag her to the car. But then I stopped in my tracks. I couldn't believe my eyes. The room was packed with people I knew. I did a double take. I'm not joking; every single member of my family, Aaron's friends and every one of my friends, from my first school to the last, was in this massive room. Suddenly everyone cheered. 'Here she is! At last!'

It was a huge surprise. I had no idea, not the slightest hint or clue that it was coming. I was genuinely annoyed with Jemma as I stomped through the country club looking for her. But my frustration melted away as soon as I saw what she'd done for me. She'd organized the whole thing single-handedly and it was the best party I've ever been to.

Jemma did a press interview on my behalf while I was in the jungle, and she spent the little bit of money she was paid for it on my welcome-home party. It was so good of her. I couldn't believe what she'd done. The party even had a jungle theme: there were jungle cupcakes covered in green glitter and a chocolate fountain with lion- and tiger-shaped sweets and biscuits to dip in it. Jemma set up a bushtucker trial and pulled five of the guests up to eat fish eyes and guts and other disgusting stuff she'd bought from the butcher and fishmonger. 'If Stacey can do it, everyone can do it!' she said. And they all did. My friends Jordan, Frank and Dana, and Aaron's mum and his sister all ate fish eyes.

I was overwhelmed that Jemma had arranged the whole party herself. She's so special, my sister, the best sister in the world, and I love her with all my heart. It's so funny to think of how much we used to argue. We literally hated each other as children, but now we'd do anything for each other and I just think she's amazing.

Thankfully, she gave me enough time to get over my jet lag and exhaustion before she threw the party. When I arrived home from Australia on 7 December, I needed a bit of a rest. I did a photo shoot for *Heat* magazine, then had the rest of the month off, thank God.

I wanted to spend lots of time with Zach after being away so long. He was a little bit clingy with me when we first got home. Every time I went out, even if it was just to get a pint of milk, he'd say, 'Are you coming back?'

He'd never worried about that sort of thing before. I used to say, 'See ya,' and he'd yell, 'Yeah, bye, Mum! Go away!' But after four weeks apart, he didn't want to let me out of his sight. It made me feel a bit tearful when I walked out the door. I'd sniffle a bit and tears would prick my eyes, because I felt guilty that I'd left him for a month. On the other hand, it made me feel wanted, which I quite liked. It didn't take him long to get used to having me around again, though.

I had been thinking long and hard about my future. I couldn't be absolutely certain, but I was fairly sure that I would have been dropped by my management company if I hadn't been asked to appear on *I'm a Celebrity*. Maybe it's time to move on, anyway, I thought. Perhaps a change would be good for me.

On Christmas Eve, I decided to look around and see what my options were. I was made aware of Max Clifford and knew of his success with people like Simon Cowell. I contacted Max's office and made an appointment to see him. I spoke at length to Max and Denise Palmer-Davies from his office, both of whom I instantly liked and found they understood my thoughts and feelings for the future.

I threw myself into Christmas after that. It was the first year that Zach properly understood what it was all about, so we had the best fun leaving carrots out for the reindeer and mince pies for Santa. Zach had already met Santa five times at all the different grottos I'd taken him to, so he was incredibly excited when it came to Christmas Eve. Like children all over the country, he tried to keep himself awake for Santa's visit, but in the end he fell asleep and missed him! When he woke up to find a stocking at the end of his bed, he was beside himself with delight. It was so sweet. I loved it so much. We both did.

Unlike the year before, this Christmas I had some money, so I could splash out and make it really special. I bought my mum a laptop; I got my dad tickets to see Arsenal; I bought Jemma a new nurse's watch; I put money into an account for Zach and I paid for my brother to do a crash course in driving.

I also said that I'd take the whole family to Israel in September. Well, you only live once, don't you? Me, Zach, my mum, my dad, my stepmum, my sister and her boyfriend Lee, my brother, my stepbrother and sisters, my little brother Josh and Aaron are all going to Israel. I can't wait for that holiday!

Best of all, on Christmas Day I gave Zach a stegosaurus robot the size of a Labrador. He can sit on it! It moves around and roars and he can feed it leaves.

He wasn't quite sure about it at first. When he opened it and we turned it on, he ran away. 'No! It's scary!' he cried. It took him a little while to get used to it, but once he'd seen us all having a go, he started to edge closer and finally said, 'I want a go.' Now he won't leave it alone.

I had some lovely texts on Christmas Day. My phone was beeping with messages from friends all day, including my *X Factor* and *I'm a Celebrity* mates. Even Jedward texted me to say, 'Merry Christmas, love you!' They're so nice. I wish I could see more of them, but they're always off doing stuff in Ireland.

I had a long think over Christmas, spoke to the top people at my management company and decided to make the move to Max Clifford. Now it feels like everything is happening how I want it to happen. I can be hands-on when it comes to making decisions about my career. Since then, a lot of things have been happening to me very quickly with regards to TV, music and promotional activities, and the good thing is I'm right in the middle of it and know exactly what's going on. Max Clifford Associates is a very friendly agency and I feel really relaxed there, so I'm totally happy.

Brilliantly, I've been going into the studio to write my own music, the way I want to do it. I've always wanted to write and sing songs based on my own experiences. I'm a big fan of Lily Allen and Kate Nash, as well as loads of other random artists that no one would ever associate me with because it never came across on *The X Factor*. Back in 2009, I didn't know what I wanted, what I was into or who I wanted to be as an artist. Now I know I'd like to make a nice, chilled-out record about my life. I want to sing in my own style, and speak honestly about my experiences and everything I've been through. I love the way Kate Nash and Lily Allen write about the things that every girl goes through. When I listen to them, I think, I know what that feels like! I've felt like that before.

I want to write songs that make people go, 'Oh yeah! I know what it's like to feel that way,' and 'I love that feeling' and 'I hate that feeling'.

When I look back at all the things that have happened to me in my short twenty-one-year life, I think, Wow, how have I done all of that? I've given birth, been on *The X Factor*, toured the country, done *I'm a Celebrity* and met a fantastic boyfriend. It's amazing! I've only been on the earth for ten minutes; I don't know how I've done it all.

I have so much to write about! I have so many experiences and feelings to put down into my songs. The words really flow when I'm in the studio and I'm having the best time ever, being creative and working on my album. It's the most exciting thing! These days, I'm always writing down my thoughts in a notebook and on scraps of paper. I've always been interested in hidden meanings within poems and songs, and how you can write about things without making them explicit. Now I'm playing around and experimenting for myself.

I'd like a career in TV as well as in music and I'm in talks about a presenting contract at the moment, so we'll see what happens. There's so much I want to do, but I guess I'll try to take things one at a time, even though I know it won't be possible, because I like doing lots of things all at once. I love being busy.

It was great winning *I'm a Celebrity*, because I realized that people like me, which is a really good feeling. Knowing that people are behind you, supporting you, is the nicest feeling in the world. It's overwhelming to think that people want me to do well. It gives me a real sense of security.

I can't believe how lucky I am. Everything has gone so well for me and I'm so fortunate. I've got the best family and friends and network of people around me – and I never want to die. I want it to last for ever! When I look back and think about the ups and downs I've been through, it's hard to believe I've got to where I am today. I never thought everything would work out for me the way it has.

It hasn't always been a smooth ride, of course. Unfortunately, things didn't work out between me and Zach's dad, probably because we were so young. I'm sad about that, because it means Zach hasn't got the nuclear family everyone dreams of, but Zach has a mum and a dad and that's all he needs. We both love him very much.

Dean gave me half of what is the best thing that's ever happened to me, so I'll always care about him and I'll always thank him for that. Dean will always be Zach's dad and he's an amazing father. He loves Zach with all his heart and sees a lot of him, which is fantastic. It makes me so happy that Zach has a good relationship with his father. I wouldn't want it any other way.

To think there was a time when I thought that life had nothing to offer me, when I was at the very lowest I could have been, feeling hopeless and full of despair. And now I feel like the luckiest girl in the world. It just shows you how you must never lose hope, because your life can turn around at any time. There's a light at the end of every tunnel and you must never stop believing.

All I know is that if you're positive and you work really, really hard and believe in everything you do, you can't go wrong. Whether you get what you want at twenty-one or 101, you can't go wrong if you work hard and stay positive, because you'll always be happy. And if you have dreams, remember that no one can stop you from fulfilling them, apart from you.

I always wanted my life to be a fairy tale, ever since I was really young. 'I'm going to be a princess,' I used to tell my mum. 'I'm going to be a singer.' That's all I've ever wanted. I still believe in fairy tales and I watch them to this day. I'm the biggest kid you'll ever meet in the whole wide world. Of course, not everything has worked out exactly like a Disney movie and I wouldn't expect it to, but I want my life to be as close to a fairy tale as possible and I'll do all I can to make it that way.

In January 2011, I was driving along in Grays when I passed a house with a 'For Sale' sign outside. I stopped the car and took another look. It was a big white detached nineteenth-century house with a vine hanging over the porch. That's such a pretty house, I thought. I really want to go in and see.

So I knocked on the door and the owners let me in to have a look.

I fell in love with it the moment I stepped inside. There's plenty of room for all of us; Zach can have a bedroom and a playroom and there's a big garden for him to play in. It's everything I've ever wanted for him. Zach can be happy and settled here, I thought. He can have his friends round and have his birthday parties here. He can have a paddling pool in the garden.

My dream is to make a loving, welcoming home, always full of people, with delicious smells coming out of the kitchen. I really enjoy cooking and I want to learn how to do it well. At the moment, I only cook stuff like spaghetti bolognese and shepherd's pie, nice easy things that I know everyone eats. But since my favourite dish is curry, I'm going to get going on the curry front, too, now that I've got my own kitchen. I can't wait, to be honest.

I hope I'll end up having a massive family in my lovely home. I want my mum to live with me, too. I need my mum. I don't know what I'd do without her. She's the one person I can rely on every single day. She's my rock. I know it sounds cheesy, but she's always there when I need her. If I get scared, I still have to come home and sleep in my mum's bed. She's my safe place. As long as she's near me, I feel protected and out of harm's way. I love her so much.

My dad is the best dad, too. He's incredibly supportive of me, and he's taught me so much. His enthusiasm and love for life have always inspired me. I haven't always been the best daughter, but he has never stopped loving me and I've always known that I could rely on him 100 per cent. What more could I ask for?

I sometimes wonder if it's hard for Aaron, because he's

moving into my house, with my kid. When I think about how young he was when I met him, I realize what a big thing it is for him to be lumbered with me and Zach. He wasn't even a little bit into the idea of having a child when I met him and he's only twenty-two now, but he never moans and he dotes on Zach, so he must be happy about it. He's very content doing what he does; he's fulfilled in his job and in his life, so he doesn't need to be Mr Sole Breadwinner. We're happy, me, Aaron and Zach, and now we're moving in together, like a proper family. What a long way we've come.

I'll never forget that I'm only who I am and where I am because of where I come from, because of Mum, Dad, Jemma, Matthew, Zachary, Joshua, Karen and the extended family. I'm talking about my dad's family, my mum's family and all my friends who have been there for me since the very beginning: I wouldn't be the person I am without them.

Thank Yous

Zachary – for being the centrepiece of my life, the core of my world of which only good can come. For making me realize the meaning of life. For stopping me from becoming wrapped up in myself and my needs. For saying 'See ya, wouldn't wanna be ya,' every time I leave for work. For loving me all the way around the world and to the stars and back! For being the only living thing on this earth that makes me fill up every time I look at you and try to comprehend just how unbelievable you are, and how lucky I am. For being my most prized possession and most admirable creation. For being my Zachary. I am and always will be in total and utter awe of you.

Dad – for being the backbone of my personality and giving me unconditional love no matter how unloveable I behaved! For telling me I can do and be anything I want to be and for believing in me since the day I was born.

Mum – for being the mother that most people dream about, taking the good times and the bad and smiling at the end of them all. For never being able to celebrate a single birthday until I was sixteen because I was always such a nuisance. For being My Rock, My Voice, My Life, My Mum.

Karen – for meeting my dad and making him a happy man. For taking us all in and adding us to your family. For being my second mum and my only listener throughout everything.

For giving me a beautiful, intelligent, gorgeous little brother who makes me and my son very happy.

Jemma – my lovely sister who I have spent three-quarters of my life in petty squabbles with and stealing clothes from. You are the most extraordinary person I've ever known, and without you I would not be as grounded and appreciative as I am today. You are an angel.

Matt – my little brother, even though you are six-foot tall and tower over me, you are still my little brother!! You work so hard running my website, constantly nagging me to go on Twitter and Facebook too, that it's thanks to you the support I have following me and the people who have stuck by my side! You and your dreams make me so proud. I know you are going to be so successful and have such a prosperous life like you deserve!

Nana – my Jewish Bubba who kept me filled to the brim with chicken soup and kneidlach. Who also told me I was the luckiest girl in the world as I had my family – thank you Nana for teaching me the only important thing in life. I still believe it to this day and I miss you with all my heart and soul, and can't wait to see you again one day.

Granddad – a man who devoted his life to others, called me his shnoggle woggle and always greeted me with a lovely smile and cuddle. The man who taught me respect and discipline and loved me devotedly. Who took me for walks up mountains and on Easter egg hunts, and never let me give up. Thank you, Granddad, I know you are happy wherever you are. We are all looking after Grandma still! I love you, I miss you.

Grandma – for being the most senior lady I know to take the elderly on fun trips and the hard of hearing on regular outings. The lady who devoted her life to her kids, grandkids and husband. Who made my granddad a very happy man, cooking, cleaning and caring for him every day for sixty years! Who makes me want to follow in her footsteps and have the wonderful life that she and my granddad experienced. You are the most lovely lady in the world and I love you very much!

Aaron – I fell in love with you the day I met you and I couldn't think of my life with anyone else. Thank you for giving me the chance to fall in love, to know what it's like to feel lost without someone, to be another person's other half and to spend every living moment sharing everything with someone. For making me laugh when I'm close to tears. For head-locking me when you mean to cuddle me. For not kissing me in front of people, but giving the best kisses. For giving me butterflies every time I know I'm going to see you – even now. I love you. I'm in love with you. I can't wait to live my life with you and grow old with you. Grandma and grandpa Barham.

Lee Lee – for doing everything for my sister and my mum. For caring about others' comforts over your own. For fixing the garden and loft house, even though it makes my boyfriend look as lazy as he is. I love you x

My family – to anyone I haven't mentioned, all of my family have influenced my life so greatly and I wouldn't be 1 per cent of the person that I am today without any of you. I love you all so much and wish that one day I can do the same back to you all. Marilyn, Robert, Sonny, Anna, Elliot,

Daniel, Alison, Steve, Joanne, Robin, Elias, Donna, Michael, John, Wendy, Heather, Jim, Nick, Jen, Mary, Dave, Vicky, Chloe and Emily.

Ree and Stu – Mum and Dad No. 2 – for the minute I stormed into your lives and turned your world into an unorganized mess looking after me. For taking me everywhere, dealing with my monthlies, paying my parking tickets, washing my drawers, making my bed and cooking my dinner! But most of all for making me laugh every time I step through the door and sit down.

Dyl and Bas – for always having us round to lunch and for making my Malibu and Coke a glass of Malibu! For texting me every time you think of me and Zachary, and always trying to see us and make us happy!

Friends

Dayna Lauren, Danni and James – for being the friends who have stuck by me from the very beginning. The friends who when I haven't rung, they call. When I haven't visited, they visit and when I need them, they are there. The best friends. I love you all with every inch of me!

Dicki – the person unmentioned in this book, but who is a massive part of my life – for being the boy who has never stopped dipping in and out of my world and making it the funniest and happiest times!

Tubs, Hank, Hurricane Rae, Krust, Jorden, Jade, Debbie and Mole – the new friends who feel like they've been there for ever and treat me like I've known them all my life! Love them to pieces and can't wait to spend the rest of my life with them all. Roll on BBQ season!!

Ben – my first ever manager in the whole world! For being the man who had 100 per cent belief in me. The man who pushed me up when everyone else pushed me down and who convinced others to believe in me – thank you for everything.

Modest – for being a part of the path that led me to where I am now. For that I am very grateful.

Tour Managers Jerome, Lance and Tobias – for driving me around while I drove you all mad!! For eating M&S when all you wanted was Burger King! For including my family and friends in everything we did.

Rebecca – who had to suffer all the late nights and long hours working on this book! Not only that, she had to turn my verbal diarrhoea into 100,000 words!! and had to meet me at the most annoying and inappropriate times, no doubt finding it very difficult to arrange even those meetings! What a masterpiece you have created, thank you so much, you are a great writer and I am so privileged to have worked with you!

Everyone at the wonderful Penguin for giving me the opportunity to write this book. It means so much to me. You have been a part of ensuring I will never, ever forget these most special and important memories now that they are not only catalogued in my brain, which isn't always reliable, but thanks to you in hard copy as well, which will stay on the Solomon shelf for ever and ever! I am so grateful, thank you! What an amazing journey this has been for me – I've enjoyed every step of it.

Photo Credits

ALICE MONTGOMERY

KATY PERRY: THE UNAUTHORIZED BIOGRAPHY

The remarkable true story of pop sensation Katy Perry

Sassy, cheeky, classy, sexy . . . Katy Perry isn't your average girl next door. She's not even your average multi-platinum, award-winning pop star.

Ever since charming (and shocking) the world with 'I Kissed a Girl', she's been making headlines. From reaching No. 1 in charts worldwide to selling out concerts everywhere, Katy's amazing success has made her a superstar.

But how did a choir girl, brought up in a deeply religious community and allowed to listen only to church music, make it?

Following her dream meant honing her musical gifts and required a lot of willpower. Not even during the years of obscurity, releasing record after record, did Katy once stop believing. And here she is now, the brightest star in the sky, married to one of the most talked-about men in the world – Russell Brand.

This is the intimate story behind the most exciting and unpredictable pop star around.

He just wanted a decent book to read ...

Not too much to ask, is it? It was in 1935 when Allen Lane, Managing Director of Bodley Head Publishers, stood on a platform at Exeter railway station looking for something good to read on his journey back to London. His choice was limited to popular magazines and poor-quality paperbacks – the same choice faced every day by the vast majority of readers, few of whom could afford hardbacks. Lane's disappointment and subsequent anger at the range of books generally available led him to found a company – and change the world.

'We believed in the existence in this country of a vast reading public for intelligent books at a low price, and staked everything on it'
Sir Allen Lane, 1902–1970, founder of Penguin Books

The quality paperback had arrived – and not just in bookshops. Lane was adamant that his Penguins should appear in chain stores and tobacconists, and should cost no more than a packet of cigarettes.

Reading habits (and cigarette prices) have changed since 1935, but Penguin still believes in publishing the best books for everybody to enjoy. We still believe that good design costs no more than bad design, and we still believe that quality books published passionately and responsibly make the world a better place.

So wherever you see the little bird – whether it's on a piece of prize-winning literary fiction or a celebrity autobiography, political tour de force or historical masterpiece, a serial-killer thriller, reference book, world classic or a piece of pure escapism – you can bet that it represents the very best that the genre has to offer.

Whatever you like to read – trust Penguin.